BRKEN STRINGS

ERIC WALTERS AND **KATHY KACER**

PUFFIN CANADA

an imprint of Penguin Random House Canada Young Readers,
a division of Penguin Random House of Canada Limited

First published in hardcover by Puffin Canada, 2019
Published in this edition, 2020

4 5 6 7 8 9 10

Cover illustrations © 2019 by Celia Krampien

Manufactured in the USA

Library and Archives Canada Cataloguing in Publication

Title: Broken strings / Eric Walters, Kathy Kacer.
Names: Walters, Eric, 1957- author. | Kacer, Kathy, 1954- author.
Description: Previously published: Toronto, Ontario: Puffin Canada,
an imprint of Penguin Random House Canada Young Readers,
a Penguin Random House Company, 2019.
Identifiers: Canadiana 20190237147 | ISBN 9780735266261 (softcover)
Classification: LCC PS8595.A598 B76 2020 | DDC jC813/.54—dc23

Library of Congress Control Number: 2018955366

www.penguinrandomhouse.ca

Penguin
Random House
PUFFIN CANADA

To my writing partner, Kathy.
Your understanding, passion, perspective, and in-depth
background knowledge made this such a moving writing process.
—Eric

For Vanessa and Jeremy—my newest "children."
—Kathy

CHAPTER ONE

The bell sounded. People jumped to their feet and gathered their things.

"And don't forget there's a unit test on Friday!" Mr. Herman, our math teacher, called out over the noise.

A collective groan rose up from the class. Some people started to argue for a postponement till Monday to give them more time to study. On any other day I would have stuck around and joined in the argument. But not today. Today I needed to get out of the classroom as fast as I could. I had something more important to think about than a math test. I threw my books into my bag and joined the crowd funneling out of the room. I'd gone only a few steps when I almost bumped into Natasha, my best friend. She flashed me a big smile. Smiling was the last thing on my mind.

"Are you ready, Shirli?" Natasha asked.

"No!"

"We don't have to go," she said. "We could go to the mall, get a soda instead, maybe buy something."

"And just not look at the cast list?" I asked.

"It'll still be there tomorrow."

"Tash, I've waited all week. Do you really think I can wait another day?"

She flashed that smile again. "Patience is a virtue."

"This coming from *you*, the least patient person I know?" I asked.

"Okay, you're right, and I was just joking. Let's go and look."

The hallway was packed, and it felt as if we were salmon fighting our way upstream. We were the largest junior high in New Jersey, but the building didn't seem big enough to hold all 1,600 of us who called this place our home away from home. We squirmed and shuffled our way forward.

"You know you have nothing to worry about," Natasha said.

"Thanks. Neither do you."

"Oh, I'm not worried, Shirli. You know that."

Natasha and I had been friends, and pretty much inseparable, since third grade—like two peas in a pod, or peanut butter and jam. But there was a big difference between us. Natasha had never been in a school show before. In fact, she had only tried out this time because I'd practically dragged her to the auditions. It really didn't matter to her whether she got a part or not. The problem was that for me it mattered way too much.

"Ms. Ramsey really likes you," she pointed out. I knew she was trying to reassure me.

"She likes everybody," I said.

"It's more than that. I think she sees herself when she looks at you."

I laughed. "Like she's looking in some sort of fun-house mirror?"

Ms. Ramsey was our drama teacher. She was in her early thirties but looked a lot younger. She was blond and slim and moved in this slinky, smooth way like someone who'd had years of dance training. We couldn't have been more different in appearance, but I guess I had the same way of moving, thanks to my own dance classes.

"I didn't mean the way you two look," Natasha continued. "Ms. Ramsey is *so* beautiful."

"Gee, thanks."

"Come on, you know what I mean. You're really pretty, but not like her. You look more like me!"

Well, true, we did look a lot alike, even though my family was Eastern European and Jewish, and Natasha's was Portuguese and Catholic. But where the heck was this going?

"I mean she sees you as being talented like her."

"Thanks, Tash." Now *that* was a compliment.

Before becoming a drama teacher, Ms. Ramsey had been in some Off-Broadway productions. She had great stories to tell, like the time she auditioned for Harold Prince, one of the greatest Broadway directors of all time. Or the time she met Kristin Chenoweth in an audition and got to ask her what it felt like to win a Tony Award for her role in *You're a Good Man, Charlie Brown.* Ms. Ramsey tossed those stories out like pieces of confetti and I grabbed each one of them. She could act, she could dance, and she could sing—a real triple threat. It was great to have her here teaching us. And awful at the same time. If somebody with that much talent couldn't make it as a professional actor and ended up teaching junior high school drama, what chance did anybody else have? What chance did I have? Especially if I didn't get the part today.

My dream was to perform in front of thousands of people. Something always happened to me when I stepped in front of an audience. Sure, I was nervous. Every performer I'd ever talked to got butterflies—some worse than others. But for me, the nerves would fade and a rush of excitement would take over—like being at a fireworks display, or being a *part* of the fireworks. The first time I felt that, I knew I wanted to be a performer. My father always joked that I could dance and sing before I could walk or talk. I had been taking dance classes, singing lessons, and piano lessons for as long I could remember. And for the past two years I'd added acting lessons as well.

My parents had been so encouraging, not just paying

for everything and driving me to lessons and competitions and recitals and plays, but always being there. They are the best. They really are. Still, I was pretty sure that they would have been happier if I'd been leaning toward something a little more traditional in terms of career. My brother Adam, who's eight years older than me, was following in my mom's footsteps and was in pre-med at Rider University. My father was an accountant. He'd taken over his father's—my Zayde's—business in Manhattan. But my father was also the musical one in the family. He said he'd always wanted to learn an instrument, but my grandfather had said no. Dad claimed he was the only Jewish kid on the planet whose parents hadn't put him into violin or piano lessons. And he didn't have a bad voice—well, he didn't have a bad *untrained* voice. I guess I got the musical bug from him.

We turned down the hall toward the drama department. The cast list was supposed to be posted on the wall outside the auditorium. Up ahead I saw a crowd gathered around the bulletin board. I came to a dead stop, my heart pounding out of control.

"Okay, Shirli, take a deep breath and relax," Natasha said.

"Easy for you to say!"

We joined the crowd at the back. So many people had tried out. Some schools were football schools. Some were basketball schools. Ours was a musical school. Of course, we had all those sports as well, but we were known as the junior high that put on big musicals. We had a great reputation, and that was one of the reasons why Ms. Ramsey had come to teach here.

Last year we had put on *A Chorus Line*. Of course, I didn't get one of the leads, but I did end up with a featured spot, which was pretty amazing for a student in seventh grade. And I'd also ended up being the understudy for two of the supporting roles. I didn't actually get the chance to play either part during the run, but people who heard me sing in rehearsals said I was better than the people who did perform. This year's production was going to be *Fiddler on the Roof*. And the part I wanted was Hodel, one of the daughters. Not only did she sing "Matchmaker, Matchmaker" in the sisters' trio, but she had the most beautiful, haunting solo in the whole production as far as I was concerned—a song called "Far From the Home I Love." Yup, Hodel was the part I was holding my breath for.

As we shuffled forward I watched the people in front. Some would look at the list and come away looking pretty upset, while others jumped up and down and shrieked. With each joyful scream I knew a part was gone. And with each disappointed face I knew another person had been eliminated from the competition for the remaining roles. Was it wrong that I was secretly happy to see those faces? Not that anybody could tell what I was thinking or feeling.

We got closer to the front, closer to the list. I started to think that I understood what it would be like to walk along the corridor on death row, moving toward my execution. Okay, a little dramatic, but I was *more* than a little dramatic.

Mohammed let out a yell—"I got a part!"—and pumped his fist in the air. I couldn't help but smile. Mohammed and I had acted together before, and he was talented. I wasn't surprised at all. He worked his way back through the crowd as people slapped him on the back and offered their congratulations.

"What part?" I asked as he came up to us.

"Perchik. I'm playing Perchik, the scholar!" he said excitedly, running a hand through his jet-black hair.

"You'll do a great job."

"Thanks, thanks so much, Shirli."

If I got the part of Hodel, then he would be playing my stage husband. It wasn't like there was any big romance between the two characters, just some hand-holding and staring into each other's eyes. I could do that. I liked Mohammed. He was funny, and pretty smart.

We were getting closer to the front, and I realized that I was now shoulder to shoulder with Mindi McConnell. We gave each other a perfunctory nod and a slight, polite smile. Mindi was a year older than me, but we were in the same dance company and we took private lessons from the same vocal coach. She used to be nice to me, but that was before we started competing for the same dance parts, and my applause at recitals began to rival hers.

At our last recital she had sung a Destiny's Child song. *Why does everybody think they can do Beyoncé?* Well, really, she did a pretty good job. Me, I went old school and sang an Aretha Franklin classic, and the audience went wild. I even got a standing ovation. That was when Mindi pretty much stopped talking to me completely.

We both knew it was either going to be me or her to snag the part of Hodel. She was a better dancer, but I was a better singer—I'd proven that. The big advantage she had was that she was in ninth grade and I was in eighth. Our school had a tradition of giving the leading roles to kids in ninth grade.

The crowd was moving forward again and suddenly we were right in front of the list. I felt sweat running down my sides and my hands were getting clammy. Tash was wrong. I did have a lot to worry about. Oh, why had Ms. Ramsey chosen *Fiddler on the Roof* when there were so many other incredible musicals with so many more good parts to choose from? I knew I shouldn't complain. At least we were getting to stage a show. In the first months following 9/11 some people said we shouldn't have a production at all this year. I wasn't sure if they thought it was disrespectful or because they didn't think large groups of kids should be together in the same place—like we made too good a target.

It had been almost five months since the attack now, since the towers had fallen. In some ways it seemed like yesterday. In others, like it was forever ago, or, in a way, as if it had never happened at all. Then you'd turn on the TV and see people still cleaning up at Ground Zero—cranes loading dump trucks taking away concrete and tangled metal beams . . . and other things.

Most of the time I didn't really think about it much, but there was still an uneasiness in people. It hung in the air like the black smoke that had risen from the site. People wondered if things would ever be the same again. I guess that's what putting on the show was really about for us—trying to make things the same as they were before. In the end, our school had decided that the show would help us heal from the sadness of that terrible time.

Someone flipped the pages of the list and—

"I'm in the ensemble!" Natasha cried out, and then she added a delighted little shriek.

"Congratulations!" I was happy for her. I just wanted her to get to the sheet that showed the rest of the roles—including the one I was after.

Natasha lifted up the page and now the featured player roles came into view. First the lesser-known male roles, and then two female parts that, technically, I could have gotten—Hodel's youngest sisters. I let out the breath that I was holding, grateful and relieved not to see my name beside either role.

Somebody turned another page and more roles appeared, bigger ones, including Tzeitel and Chava—the two other sisters. My name was absent again. Those had been my safety spots—they also got to sing "Matchmaker"—but they had gone to other people.

That left only three major female roles. *Come on*, I prayed. *Somebody turn the page!* I could feel my heart pounding, and I started winding my long, curly hair around my fingers, a nervous habit.

And then I heard another shriek. I knew *that* voice. It was Mindi. She was jumping up and down like she had just won a Tony Award instead of some part in a junior high school musical. Her friends crowded around her and hugged her and added to the shrieks. That was when I saw her name beside the role—beside *my* role. Mindi had been given the part of Hodel—the daughter with the very best solo.

I felt numb. I wasn't the lead. I wasn't one of the lesser sister roles. I wasn't in the ensemble. I was nothing. How could that possibly be?

"Shirli, you're in! You got a lead!" Natasha screamed and threw her arms around me.

Had I read it wrong? I peered at the list again, and finally saw my name, Shirli Berman, come into focus.

"You're Golde!" Natasha yelled. "You got a lead role!"

Golde! Golde was the mother, the wife of the male lead, Tevye—yes, technically she was also a lead. But while she sang in a couple of duets, she had no solo and no real standout moment on stage. *I'm playing Mindi's mother. I'm playing* everybody's *mother. I'm playing an old Jewish woman who has no solo.*

Natasha was still squealing and jumping up and down. But I wasn't nearly as happy for me as she was.

CHAPTER TWO

My mother's car was in our driveway. I hadn't expected that. In fact, I never knew when she was going to be home. Mom was an obstetrician, and she worked the most unpredictable hours. As she always said, "I've never delivered a baby that was wearing a watch."

She was sitting at the kitchen counter sipping coffee when I came in. Most days, she practically inhaled caffeine. It was her way of compensating for the interrupted sleep that came with the job.

"You're a bit late getting home," she said.

"Just a bit."

"I was starting to get worried."

"There was nothing to worry about," I said.

"I know, but worrying is what I do. You know that."

That was partly because she was a mother, and partly because she was a doctor. But her worrying had gotten worse since 9/11. Everybody seemed more worried.

I took a seat across from her.

"So?" my mother asked.

"So what?"

"It was today, wasn't it? Wasn't it today that they were posting the cast for the play?"

"Oh, yeah, that's right. I guess I forgot," I said.

My mother stared at me for a minute, and then started to slowly clap. "I'm glad those acting lessons are paying off. You almost convinced me!"

I made a slight bow.

"So, what part did you get?"

"I got a lead."

"Congratulations!" She reached out and took my hands in hers. "So, shall I start calling you Hodel?"

I shook my head. "I got the part of Golde."

"Golde?" There was a half-second delay. "That's wonderful!" she exclaimed. "That's even better."

"I don't know if it's better, but it is different." All the way home I'd been practicing hiding my disappointment, so she wouldn't feel disappointed for me.

"As I recall, she's in a lot more scenes."

"But she doesn't have many songs."

"That just means you get to show off your acting chops more than your singing."

"I guess so."

"And in many ways *Fiddler* is really more a play than a musical."

That was such a good line, even if I wasn't sure it was true.

Mom stood up and moved over to the fridge. She rummaged inside and pulled out a jar of peanut butter, turning to hold it up to me. I nodded and she grabbed a box of crackers and a couple of plates and knives, putting them on the table. We munched in silence for a little while.

"Rehearsals start in a couple of days," I said. "I just wish I could talk to Bubbie and tell her about it." My Bubbie was my grandmother—my father's mother— and she'd recently passed away. Sometimes I still had trouble believing she was gone. "It would have been great to get her help to understand the character I'm playing."

My mother laughed. "She would have had a fit if you'd asked her. She wasn't *that* old! *Fiddler* is set well before her time."

"I know that. I just meant her being a Jewish mother and all."

"Last time I checked I'm also a Jewish mother, but I wasn't there either! It was your Zayde's mother who would have known all about it. She lived through the pogroms, when Jews were massacred by the Tsarist Russians."

Mom offered me another cracker, but I shook my head. Then I took our plates and knives to the sink and put the peanut butter back in the fridge.

"I wish I could have met her," I said. "I didn't know about that family history."

"She wasn't there for the first pogroms, of course," Mom continued. "Those go way back to the 1820s. But there was another wave of violence that started in 1905."

"That's when *Fiddler* is set," I said. "But I thought Dad's family was from Poland."

"The family fled Russia and ended up in Poland. Your Zayde was the baby of the family. I think his mother was in her mid-thirties when she had him. He was born in 1930, so she was probably born around 1894 or '95—she would have been ten or eleven when those pogroms took place."

"Do you think Zayde would talk to me about what he knows?" I asked. "Maybe his mother told him stories."

She shrugged. "Sometimes he talks; sometimes he doesn't. The memories are hard, especially since your Bubbie passed away."

The death of my grandmother had been hard on all of us. It wasn't just that *we* missed her, but we knew how much *he* missed her. We could see the pain in his eyes, and the way his body had become stooped and slow, like his breath was being sucked out of him. I think if he'd had his way he would have died instead of Bubbie, or along with her. It had been almost six months. For us the pain was fading. For him it was just as strong.

"All you can do is ask him," my mother replied. "Aren't you supposed to get him some groceries tomorrow?"

"Tomorrow or the next day."

Once a week, I'd stop into the little grocery store near his house and get him a few things. It was a store we'd shopped in our whole lives. The owner, Mr. Merkin, let my father run a tab, so all I had to do was pick up the groceries, and he paid later. Grocery shopping was one of the things that my Bubbie always did. I don't know if my Zayde had ever gone shopping in his whole life. I actually liked doing it, and really, it was less about getting the groceries and more about visiting him, helping him feel less alone.

"Go today. He'll be happy to see someone," she said. "Besides, you probably need props for the play."

"We do! Ms. Ramsey mentioned that during the try-outs."

"You know, his attic is filled with old things that might work."

"Really?"

"Everything he or your Bubbie ever owned is stuffed in that attic. I'm sure he'd let you borrow things if you asked. You know he'd do just about anything for you."

❧

I pulled the collar of my coat up as I turned onto the path to Zayde's house. The wind was pretty fierce, and snow was blowing up from the garden and into my face. Underneath the snow were the sleeping flowers and shrubs that my grandparents had loved and tended with such care. I could never walk that path without being flooded with memories.

When I was little, my Bubbie and Zayde used to babysit me at their home once or twice a week. We'd have Bubbie's special chicken noodle soup, talk, or watch TV. Sometimes they'd take me out to the mall for an outing. The mall had an indoor amusement park, and I got to ride the merry-go-round and the Ferris wheel. I loved it. Later, when I started school, their house was where I often came at the end of the day. My parents worked such crazy hours that I could never rely on them being home. And Adam had a busy life and couldn't—or often wouldn't—babysit his little sister. So, I came here, did my homework, and hung out with Bubbie and Zayde.

Before I even got to the back door I could hear the TV blaring. Zayde was a little hard of hearing, but he also just loved to have the TV on loud. I had my own key so I let myself in through the kitchen. I could imagine Bubbie standing at the sink, washing dishes, and then turning around to greet me, drying her hands on her apron and giving me a big hug and . . . she wasn't there, but the dishes were done and drying on the rack. Everything was tidy, but not as clean as when Bubbie was alive. I know some people think of their grandmothers when they smell gingerbread or chocolate chip cookies, but I thought about Bubbie every time I smelled Pine-Sol or Mr. Clean.

My parents had been bugging Zayde to have a cleaning woman come in, but he wouldn't hear of it. "I don't want a stranger in my house," he said. Zayde tried his best to keep the house tidy and care for the yard. When Adam was at home he would help out, and my father dropped by whenever it snowed to lend a hand. Doing the grocery shopping was my way of chipping in.

There was talk about Zayde coming to live with us, but he insisted that he didn't want to be "a burden." Besides, he liked living here. He told me he couldn't leave because he'd have to leave behind his memories of Bubbie, and that was really all he still had.

I put the bags down on the table. The grocery list was the same every week: some dark rye bread, cold cuts, a package of oatmeal, a pint of coffee cream, seven cans of tomato soup, some crackers, a box of chocolate chip cookies, a bottle of apple juice, two chocolate bars, and three or four bananas. And even though I knew the list by heart, Zayde still went over it with me as if it were the first time I'd ever heard it. He was very particular, especially about the bananas. There couldn't be too many, and they couldn't be too ripe or too big.

Zayde was watching TV in the living room. I couldn't see it, but I could hear that he was watching wrestling. My Zayde loved wrestling.

I walked in and gave him a kiss on the forehead, then used the remote to turn down the volume. I knew better than to turn it off. He was wearing a shirt and tie and a suit jacket. He always dressed in a suit, even to sit in his own house. If he'd been going out, there would have been a hat on his head and his shoes would have been perfectly shined.

"Shirli, it is so good to see you!" he chirped.

"It's good to see you, too, Zayde."

"Did you bring me my groceries?"

"They're in the kitchen," I said.

"Did you bring the oatmeal? I'm almost out of oatmeal."

"I brought the oatmeal."

"And the bread, did you bring the bread?"

"I brought the bread. Dark rye, the type you like."

"Excellent. And what about the—?"

"Zayde, I brought you everything I always bring you. The bread, the cold cuts, the cookies, and a bunch of *thirty* bananas."

He chuckled. It was our standard joke. "Not forty?"

"No, this week it was only thirty. Next week it will be forty."

"I hope they're not too big," he said.

"They're the perfect size and perfect ripeness."

"It's just that I can't eat too much and I don't want food to go to—"

"To waste. I know. One half banana each day is what you want, and that's what I brought you." He would slice them and put them on top of his oatmeal.

He smiled. "You're such a good girl."

"I try."

"Sit and watch wrestling with me."

"I'll sit, but do we have to watch wrestling?" I asked.

"Come, and I will explain it to you." He pointed to a seat on the couch next to his chair. There wasn't much choice. I sat down.

"So, you really don't like wrestling?" he asked.

I smiled. This was a conversation we'd also had many times—sort of like his grocery list. What was there to like about a bunch of half-naked men running around in a cage and pummeling each other?

"Not really."

"Strange. How can you not like wrestling?"

"It's, well . . . it's just that it's fake."

"What are you talking about? It's real! You see that man there? He's one of my favorites."

I looked at the set and saw two large men grappling in the ring.

"That's Stone Cold Steve Austin," he said. "He was the wrestler of the year in 1998 and '99. He was robbed when he didn't win in 2000, but I hope 2002 will be his year again."

I knew enough to know that he was the wrestler with the shaved head. As I watched, he flipped the other guy over the ropes and right out of the ring!

"These guys are very skilled," Zayde continued. "They know exactly what they're doing."

Zayde was getting excited now. His hands were twitching and his face was animated. "They know when to hold back. And when to push more—they are *real* athletes."

Zayde spoke with a kind of soft European accent that made him sound like Arnold Schwarzenegger, except that Arnold was from Austria and Zayde was from Poland. But some things were the same. Every *w* sounded like a *v*. And saying *th* for Zayde was impossible. It sounded more like a soft *z*. So when Zayde said the word *athlete*, it sounded like he was saying *azzz-lete*. He caught me trying to stifle a grin.

"When you're able to speak five languages as I can, *zzzen* you can laugh at me."

"Sorry, Zayde." I knew he wasn't angry. This was just another of our games.

"Wrestling is like ballet and gymnastics and acting all rolled into one. Now that's something you should understand." Zayde sat back in his armchair and folded his arms across his chest.

"I guess that's another type of triple threat," I said. By now I'd had enough of discussing the merits of wrestling, and I had a question of my own. "Zayde, do you think I could look in your attic?"

"You want to go up into the attic?"

"I'm just looking for some stuff that Mom said you might have up there."

"What is it you're looking for?"

"We're doing a play and we need props," I explained.

"Is your play about an old Jewish man living in New Jersey?"

"Not New Jersey, but there is an old Jewish man. We're putting on *Fiddler on the Roof*. Do you know it?"

"Know it? Of course I know it. Did you know that your Bubbie once saw *Fiddler on the Roof* on Broadway, starring Mr. Zero Mostel?"

"Wow! I didn't know that."

"He was the first Tevye—the original star of the show."

"And did she like it?"

"Like it? She *loved* it. She went on and on about it. She even tried to get me to go and see it with her."

"And you didn't go?"

He shook his head. "You know that sort of thing never interested me."

I sighed. I did know that. Bubbie had gone to almost all of my recitals, but Zayde had never been to one.

"So, since Bubbie told you about it, Zayde, you know this show is about what happened to Jews in Russia at the turn of the century."

"I know what it's about. That's what confuses me. Hundreds of thousands of Jews were persecuted and killed. That's nothing to sing about. What's next, a musical about the Holocaust?"

That caught me by surprise. I knew Zayde had been in a concentration camp, but the Holocaust was something he never talked about. Once in a blue moon, if he rolled up his shirt sleeves, you could catch a glimpse of the line of blue numbers that had been tattooed onto his left forearm. When I was still little I asked my father about those numbers—even then I had a feeling I shouldn't ask Zayde directly—and he explained what they meant. Of course, you couldn't grow up in a Jewish home and not know something about the Holocaust. Besides, we'd learned about it at school, and I'd read some books, and we marked Holocaust Remembrance Day every year. But somehow that number on Zayde's arm was what made it all seem real. Too real. Sometimes I wondered if that was why he always wore long-sleeved shirts buttoned at the wrist.

"It's okay, Shirli," he said. "You go up to the attic, look, and after wrestling is done we can have tea. Would that be good?"

"That would be perfect."

I got up and gave him another kiss on the top of his head, smoothing down the fluffy tuft of hair that always managed to stand straight up like it had a mind of its own.

"You be careful on those rickety stairs," he said.

"I will."

"It's been years and years since I've even been up there. If you find a couple of gold bars you be sure to share them with me," he said.

"Fifty-fifty."

Before leaving the living room, I turned the sound way back up on the TV. He gave me a little thumbs-up and another smile and I left him and the wrestlers behind, with the noise from the match following me out of the room.

I climbed up the stairs and hesitated at my grandparents' bedroom door. Bubbie had spent the last few months of her life there, and I hadn't been in their room since she died. I peeked in, somehow expecting her to still be there. But nothing, not even the smell of Pine-Sol or Mr. Clean.

The attic was accessible only from their bedroom, with a set of pull-down stairs. I went in and grabbed a flashlight that I knew Zayde always kept by his bed, flicked it on to make sure it worked, and stepped into the walk-in closet. One side was filled with my Zayde's things: white shirts, dark suits, and a row of almost identical shoes on the floor, all polished and waiting for him to slip them on. These were the components of his "uniform," the clothing he had worn to work every day. He said that an accountant had to always look like an accountant.

On the other side was my Bubbie's entire wardrobe, still there waiting for her, as if she'd never died. My parents had offered to help Zayde clean everything out but he'd refused. I guess I understood. Getting rid of Bubbie's things would probably feel to Zayde like he was getting rid of her memory once and for all. And that was way too difficult for him to do.

I reached up and grabbed the cord that pulled down the little set of stairs. They were stiff and stuck, and I had to pull hard until they popped open, releasing a spray of dust as they descended and hit the floor.

I looked up into the darkness. I'd only been up there a few times, and always with somebody else—usually my Bubbie or my father. Maybe this wasn't such a good idea, I thought. Maybe I should wait until my grandfather was done watching wrestling and he could come up with me. No, actually, Zayde trying to climb these steep old steps was an even worse idea. But he would have tried if I'd asked. He hardly ever said no to me—or to anybody. That was part of who he was.

Slowly, one shaky step at a time, I started up, led by the beam of the flashlight. When I was almost at the top I stopped and lifted up the light, letting it play around the dark space. There were boxes and big, bulky shapes that looked like old furniture, covered with plastic or sheets. There were a couple of old trunks, and some framed paintings leaning against the wall. The attic was big and crowded and kind of spooky-looking . . . *Stop that!* I told myself. There was nothing to be scared of . . . unless the murderer was hiding under one of those sheets, or behind one of the trunks! Okay, enough! I was willing to be dramatic, but stupid wasn't in my repertoire.

Up I went until my head and shoulders were through the trapdoor to the attic and I was able to climb in and get to my feet. Down below—way down below—I could still hear the wrestling match going on. That was reassuring and disturbing all at once. With the TV that loud my Zayde would never be able to hear me scream! Swinging the flashlight around, I spotted a string hanging down from a bare lightbulb in the ceiling. I grabbed at the string, missed it the first time, grabbed it a second time, pulled, and the attic filled with muted, dusty light. Now I was finally able to look around and see more clearly what was what.

Even with the light on, the whole attic still felt kind of creepy and unwelcoming. *How did Zayde even get all this stuff up here?* I wondered. I couldn't imagine lugging cases and paintings and tables up those rickety steps, although judging by the thick layer of dust most of it had been up here since he was much, much younger. The bulb above my head was swinging gently from side to side, lighting up first one half and then the other half of the attic. One side seemed to disappear into a dark corner where the roof sloped at a steep angle. Even when I aimed the flashlight in that direction, it was impossible to make out anything except some shadowy objects. The other side opened up into a larger space that was crammed with boxes and covered furniture. Back and forth the lightbulb swung, inviting me to pick a direction. Dark corner?

Open space? I was no fool, I was going to stick with the open space.

"Okay, if you were props, where would you be hiding?" Talking out loud seemed to help. The sound filled the space and made me feel less alone.

I lifted up a striped bedsheet, yellowed with age, and found two small tables and a couple of my Bubbie's antique wooden chairs underneath. They would be perfect for Tevye's house—in good condition, but old enough to look like they could have come from the early 1900s. It was a good start. There were two suitcases on the right that looked pretty new. Those must have been the ones that Bubbie and Zayde used when they made their last trip, that cruise to Greece, just after Bubbie was diagnosed with cancer. She had always wanted to see the Greek islands. It was bittersweet for both of them, knowing it would probably be their last chance to travel together. Still, she had come home so happy to have finally seen that part of the world. When she took to her bed shortly after that, she told me she had no regrets.

Okay, I needed to stop thinking about that and focus on finding some props. The table and chairs were great, but I was hoping to find some clothing. The new suitcases probably didn't contain any old clothes so I knew I didn't need to open them. But just behind them, I spied a big old trunk, the kind held together with thick leather straps and rusty buckles. It was about four feet wide and three feet high, and it looked like something Tevye might have brought to America from the "old country." Perfect! Now *that* was bound to have some treasures inside.

I had to push aside some heavy cases, and I heaved a big dresser out of the way—and that's when a giant spider crawled out from underneath it and scurried over my foot and into a corner.

"*Eeeeeek!*"

I dropped the sheet I was holding. I hated spiders, probably more than bees or even snakes. Well, snakes were pretty bad too. But this spider looked absolutely prehistoric! I realized the attic was probably crawling with spiders. I grabbed at my hair and started winding it around my fingers, trying to calm myself. Now, when I looked around, I could feel a million creepy little eyes staring at me from behind every object.

But I was on a mission—I had to pull myself together. I swallowed my fear, let go of my hair, willed myself to stop shaking, and shoved the dresser fully out of the way, exposing the old trunk.

The buckles that held it together looked as if they hadn't been touched in decades. They were stiff and rusty, and it took all of my strength to twist and bend and unbuckle until they finally gave way and dropped to the side. I pushed open the lid. It took a minute or so to recognize the smell that wafted out from inside. And then I remembered. Mothballs. They were small white balls of chemical pesticide that were used to keep mold and moths—the ones that would eat through clothing—away. They looked like round mints, the kind my parents kept in the candy bowl. Bubbie used to put them in with her sweaters and other woolens when she was packing them away for the summer. Then one day, when I was really little, I found some while I was playing in her bedroom. I was just about to pop one into my mouth when my grandmother discovered me and probably saved my life! The mothballs had a strong smell, kind of like gasoline and bleach and nail polish remover mixed together.

There was a flat tray inside the trunk at the top, which I lifted out and set aside. And underneath was a treasure trove—exactly what I had hoped to find. Old skirts that fell to below my knee, flowery blouses with poofy sleeves and big collars, a dozen or more aprons—Bubbie loved to cook. There were even some old high-heeled shoes and a couple of hats, the kind you had to hold in place on the top of your head with a long, fancy hat pin. I wasn't sure how much of this stuff would fit the period of *Fiddler on the Roof*, but I made a big pile to show Ms. Ramsey. She could decide.

The top half of the trunk contained Bubbie's old clothes, and underneath them were Zayde's. There were old pleated trousers and a couple of faded brown jackets and some knitted sweaters. And thanks to the mothballs they were pretty intact. There were even shoes and boots that were in remarkably good condition. I knew

Zayde was a packrat and hated to get rid of anything, but this trunk was making him look like a hoarder. There was enough here to provide wardrobe for practically the whole cast of our show. Ms. Ramsey was going to be thrilled!

My pile was growing so high I knew that I would have to call in reinforcements to get all the stuff down the stairs. Maybe my father would come over later to help me carry out the clothes, along with the table and chairs. By now I had pretty much forgotten about gigantic spiders and murderers. I was completely focused on finding as much stuff for the show as I possibly could.

Under Zayde's old clothes there was one more tray. I lifted it out, but there was no more clothing to be found. The bottom of the trunk was filled with papers and files and what looked like old legal documents. Interesting, maybe, but nothing that was going to help with our show.

And then, just as I was about to close the lid of the trunk, something caught my eye. Among the documents was a big sheet of paper—no, not paper, more like a poster of some kind, with tall black words printed on top. I pushed aside the other stuff and pulled it out, holding it up to the dim light to try and make out what it said. No luck. The writing was in a language I couldn't read. Maybe Polish, I thought. Or probably Yiddish, which was the language that many elderly Jews from Eastern Europe spoke. It was what Bubbie and Zayde had spoken at home. I hadn't heard Zayde speak Yiddish since Bubbie died. Yup, this had to be Yiddish. Maybe we could use the poster in *Fiddler* as well, I thought. There was a tavern scene in the show, and maybe this could be hung on a wall.

Then I realized there was one word I did understand—*Berman*—our family name. And below that name was a faded black-and-white photograph of four men and a woman. Were these people distant relatives of mine?

Each person in the photo was holding a musical instrument—a violin, a clarinet, tambourine, accordion, and double bass. The men—actually, two or three of them were just boys—were wearing dark jackets like the ones I had found in the trunk, and they had caps on their heads. One face jumped out from the others, the youngest one in the picture, and I gasped when I realized that it was Zayde. I'd never seen a picture of him when he was young, but that face, that expression, those eyes . . . there was no mistaking him. He looked just like a combination of my father and Adam. He held a violin under his chin and a bow up to the strings. But that made no sense. Zayde couldn't play the violin—he didn't even play the radio! There wasn't even a radio in the house. He never listened to music, not even in the car.

And who were those other people with him in the picture? Were they family members? I studied the older man to Zayde's left—his father, perhaps? And on his right, could that be a brother? Suddenly I felt as if I was looking at a part of my own family tree. I knew I had to show it to Zayde and ask him to tell me all about it. I grabbed the poster. I'd leave the clothing until later, but this was coming with me.

As I stood up, one more thing caught my eye. It was a case of some kind, not very big, and it was sitting in the dark on the floor behind the old trunk. I pulled the flashlight from my pocket and shone the light toward it. I knew instantly what it was—a violin case. I picked it up and carried it over to the table so that I could have a good look. The case was old and battered around the edges. And, like everything else, it was covered in a thick layer of dust. I turned it over and noticed a couple of initials on the back: *T.B.* Those were Zayde's initials! Tobias Berman. Was this Zayde's violin? My head was spinning.

I flipped open the latches and opened the case. And there, nestled in a deep-blue silky lining, was an old violin. It was a bit beaten up and weathered, and a couple of strings were broken. But the wood, which was a dark, rich chestnut color, shone as if someone had polished it that very day. There were four small Stars of David carved in the corners of the front of the frame.

I looked at the photo on the poster and compared it with the violin in front of me. "It's the same one," I whispered. The mystery of where this had come from and its relationship to my grandfather was getting bigger and deeper by the minute.

CHAPTER THREE

I'm not sure how I made it down the rickety stairs and back into my grandparents' bedroom. My mind was only on trying to figure out how I was going to talk to my Zayde about the poster and the violin, both of which were safely tucked underneath one arm.

The TV was still on downstairs, but when I listened more closely I realized that it wasn't the sound of wrestling that blared from below. It was something else— maybe a documentary, or some newscast. That just confirmed for me that Zayde had probably fallen asleep. And sure enough, when I crept back into the living room, there he was, head back against the headrest of his armchair, eyes closed, mouth slightly open and slack. He was snoring softly, and his glasses had tilted so that one lens was up on his forehead and the other on his cheek. I glanced at the now familiar scene on the TV. There was a reporter standing in front of the wreckage of the Twin Towers, with a machine lifting pieces of concrete into a dump truck in the background. He was interviewing a man in a white construction hat. I didn't want to hear what he had to say.

I took the remote from the table at Zayde's side and turned the TV off. I hesitated just a second before leaning over my grandfather and whispering softly, "Zayde, wake up."

"Huh? What?" He startled and raised his head, quickly reaching up to readjust his glasses. "Shirli. What happened? What time is it?"

"It's about 6:30." I knew I needed to get home for supper.

"I fell asleep. Just closed my eyes for a second and I was out like a light."

"Sorry to wake you up."

"No, no, I didn't mean to doze off." He squinted at the TV. "Wrestling is over?"

I nodded. "I think it's been over for a while."

"And did you find anything worthwhile upstairs?"

And with that simple question, everything changed between my grandfather and me. I was just about to tell him about the clothing and furniture I had discovered. I was going to ease him into the conversation, and then gently turn it toward a discussion about his younger days. But that plan was suddenly derailed when Zayde took one look at the poster and violin still snugly tucked under my arm. His mouth fell open and his face went the color of chalk.

"What are you doing with that? Where did you find those things?" His voice was hoarse and trembling.

"In the attic. You told me I could go there to look . . . remember?"

"Yes, yes . . . I just didn't know those were there . . . were *still* there." His whole body started to tremble, and he suddenly seemed so frail and old.

"Zayde, are you all right?" I knelt down in front of him and reached out to touch him, terrified that he was going to have a heart attack or a stroke. He shook my hand away.

"Those are my private things. You shouldn't have them."

His voice had gone from hoarse to harsh. I'd never heard him sound so angry with me. I was his cherished granddaughter—the one he'd do anything for. And now I was really scared, not only about Zayde's well-being but about having dug into something that was none of my business.

"I'm . . . I'm sorry. I didn't mean to do anything wrong. I just found this stuff up in the attic. You said I could go up there. I'm really sorry." My voice trailed off into a whisper.

Zayde looked away. "Those weren't supposed to be there. They were to be gone, given away or thrown out. Your Bubbie promised me she'd get rid of them."

"The poster was in a big trunk under some clothes. I'm sorry," I said again.

"These are not yours to touch. Please just leave these things here."

He wasn't sounding as angry anymore, just weak and a bit sad.

"But I don't understand, Zayde. Why . . . ?"

"I said please leave them."

That was the end of the conversation, and I knew it. I carefully placed the poster and violin on the sofa and turned back to my grandfather. "Is there anything I can get you, Zayde? Some tea maybe?"

"No, I'm fine, just fine. Sorry I yelled. It's just . . ."

"No, I get it. I shouldn't have touched your stuff. I hate it when Mom comes into my room and moves my things around. Or when Adam takes stuff that isn't his." I was babbling now, trying to lighten the mood, but failing miserably. Zayde just sat there and said nothing. At least he'd stopped shaking.

"Okay, well, I guess I should get going. You're sure I can't get you anything?"

No response.

I headed for the door, but just before leaving, I turned around once more. "I'm really sorry, Zayde. I found some great old clothes and hats in the top of that trunk, stuff that would be perfect for our show. And I guess I got so excited that I just kept digging to the bottom. That's when I found the poster." I needed to know that everything was okay between my grandfather and me. I wouldn't be able to live with myself if he stayed angry.

Finally, he raised his head and looked at me. "I understand, Shirli. And don't worry. Everything will be fine. You're welcome to take the clothes for your show," he added. "You'll come back for them. We'll have tea together another day."

That was the olive branch. And it was good enough for now. I nodded, turned, and left the house.

CHAPTER FOUR

The next morning, I arrived at school really early. I was all by myself as I ran up the steps to the front door, nobody to be seen except for the security guard posted there—a precaution that had been put in place following 9/11. I was betting Ms. Ramsey would already be in her office, though, and it turned out I was right. The door was slightly open and there was a soft glow coming from inside.

Gently I tapped on the door.

"Come in."

I pushed the door all the way open and stepped in.

"Hello, and congratulations!" Ms. Ramsey sang out. She jumped out of her chair and threw her arms around me, giving me a big hug. "Have a seat, make yourself comfortable," she said.

I sank into a soft, comfy chair. In her office, Ms. Ramsey had repainted the school's industrial yellow walls with a soft pastel green, making a gentle backdrop for her posters and art. The overhead fluorescent lights had been turned off in favor of soft mood lighting from a couple of table lamps. She'd made a school office into a personal style statement. Only Ms. Ramsey could have pulled that off.

She had the same sense of style when it came to her fashion choices. Today she was wearing a flowery top and a long black skirt slit up the side. She always dressed "just right," although I got the feeling she could have worn a potato sack and made it work. Some people always looked like they were trying too hard, but not Ms. Ramsey.

"I wanted you to know that I think I found some props and costumes for the play," I said. I stopped myself before adding "and a violin and a poster." My mind was still in overdrive from those discoveries and the mystery of my grandfather's past. I really did need to talk to somebody, but I hadn't even told my parents what had happened—I didn't really know how to tell them.

"That's terrific! Thank you for already going above and beyond," Ms. Ramsey replied. She paused and looked at me thoughtfully. "But that's not why you're here this early, is it?"

I shook my head. Ms. Ramsey knew me so well. I needed to get some other things off my chest.

"You're here to talk to me because you're disappointed in the role you got."

"Yes . . . I mean, no . . . I'm just confused."

"Because you wanted to be Hodel."

"She has the best solo."

"You do realize that you get to sing 'Do You Love Me?' with Ben, right?"

"Ben . . . Ben Morgan?"

"He got the part of Tevye, so he's going to be your stage husband."

"I didn't know that." I hadn't even bothered to look at who got the male lead—the *real* lead in the play.

"You know Ben, don't you?"

"Sort of." Everybody knew Ben. He was the captain of the football team, the team that had just won the district championship. He was just about the most popular guy in school.

"I thought that might have made it a little easier. I gather there are a lot of girls who have a crush on him."

She stared straight at me when she said that. I didn't know what to say, but I knew my mouth was hanging open and I was turning red.

Ms. Ramsey chuckled. "I think a lot of girls would love to be playing opposite him."

Ben was smart—and a year older than me. He had been going out with Emma Price for the past year, but they had recently broken up, which technically made him available—but not for me. He ran in a different crowd, an older, more popular crowd.

"Look, I know that Golde isn't the role you wanted," Ms. Ramsey continued, "but it's the second most important role in the whole play, after Tevye."

"I guess so."

"Shirli, I see *Fiddler* as a play, really."

Wait, had she been talking to my mother?

"But it has songs, so it's a musical, right?" I said.

"Or you could say it's a play that has music."

I lowered my head and began to pick at a loose thread that dangled from the corner of the chair. I was really grateful to be in the show, but how could I make Ms. Ramsey understand how much I didn't want my part—despite the fact that I would be playing opposite Ben Morgan?

"The magic of this play is in the acting," Ms. Ramsey continued, "in the emotions, and that's why I need you to play Golde."

"Couldn't you have needed me to play Hodel instead?"

"Hodel doesn't have the same impact on the whole story. Yes, her solo is quite lovely."

Understatement!

"But here's what I also want you to do. I want you to understudy Hodel and Chava. You'll have to learn all their lines and songs. Can you handle that?"

I looked up quickly. This sounded interesting. "Of course. But how could I play Golde and one of the daughters as well?"

"Quick costume changes. There are a number of scenes that aren't shared by Golde and her daughters. We'll just hope it isn't necessary."

It was probably wrong to wish that Mindi was going to fall down a well or get attacked by wolves, but still, that thought was in my head.

"It also seemed right that Mindi get that big song. After all, it's her last year at this school."

"Does that mean I'll get the best part next year when I'm in ninth grade?" I blurted that out, and then realized what I'd said and how it must have sounded. "Sorry."

Ms. Ramsey paused and then got up and closed the door. "I think we need to have some privacy."

I sat up straighter in my chair, wondering what was coming. When Ms. Ramsey returned to her seat, she was smiling.

"I can't promise anything for sure right now," she began, "but I've got something big in mind for you next year."

I could hardly believe what she was telling me.

"As I said, it's not 100 percent certain, and you absolutely cannot tell anybody else. Not even your parents, do you understand?"

"I won't. I promise."

"It's just that next year, with Mindi gone, you'll be head and shoulders above everybody else, and I'm going to need someone with serious vocal chops."

"What show are we going to do?" I asked.

"I'm not completely committed yet, but it will be a *major* production. I was thinking about going big with something like *Funny Girl.*"

"I'd be Fanny Brice?" I gasped.

"You have the range to be Fanny."

That was maybe the nicest thing anybody had ever said to me.

"But it's not necessarily going to be *Funny Girl,*" she continued. "It could be *West Side Story* or *The Sound of Music* or—"

"I'd be Maria . . . or Maria?"

She laughed. "But it could also be *Grease* or *The Wizard of Oz* or even *Carousel.*"

My head was spinning. There were memorable female leads in all of those shows.

"After everything that's happened in the world, I had thought of switching this year's production to something more upbeat—something that would help people feel happy again. But *Fiddler* has such an emotional score and a powerful message. I think everyone will connect with it," she added.

There was no need to say any more about "what happened in the world," because it was hanging in the air like a bad dream, even five months later. Two kids at our school had lost parents in 9/11. And even if you hadn't lost anybody, everybody knew somebody who had been killed. I guess that just made mathematical sense. Over 2,600 lives were lost when the Twin Towers collapsed—2,600 people with wives and husbands, sons and daughters, nieces and nephews, neighbors and friends. Like a stone dropped in a pond, its ripples radiated out almost endlessly.

As long as I lived, I would never forget the day it happened. I was in school, at the start of science class, when we were suddenly aware of activity in the hallway—people running back and forth, the sound of sobbing and cries of disbelief. Our teacher left the class to see what was going on. That was when the principal came on the P.A. to tell us that there had been "an accident"—a plane had crashed into one of the towers of the World Trade Center.

Some of the teachers tried to carry on as normal—after all, at first we really did believe that it was just an accident. But before long the whole school had gathered in the cafeteria, where the television coverage was being projected onto a big screen. There was a strange feeling in the room. It was still an excited vibe, and some people were just treating it like an excuse to get out of class. But that all changed when the second plane hit the South Tower. I couldn't believe what I was seeing, no matter how many times they replayed it. None of us were laughing or goofing around anymore, we were just quiet, worried, scared. They were closing the school, they said, and calling our parents to come and get us.

I gathered my stuff and went outside. Mom was

already there waiting for me. Lots of other parents and grandparents were there; they had all left their workplaces to come pick up their kids even before they were called. Adam's university was in New Jersey, so we knew he was okay. It took a while to get through to Dad in his office in uptown Manhattan. He assured us he was fine, though pretty shaken up by what had happened, and it would probably take him a long time to get home. That's when Mom decided that we would drive down to the Hudson River. There were so many people there, lining the riverside, looking across the water to Manhattan. We stood there together in silent disbelief. It was like a dream . . . no, a nightmare. By the time we'd arrived the South Tower had already collapsed. *How was that possible?* And then the North Tower dissolved before our eyes. It just sort of crumbled. We all gasped and screamed. Even though we knew we were safe, so far away across the river, it felt as if that giant, spectacular tower had fallen right onto us.

"So, for this year I need you to be Golde," Ms. Ramsey was saying.

I snapped back from my memories. "Yes, of course. I'll be the best Golde anybody has ever been in a school production."

"I know you will be."

"Ms. Ramsey? You know I'm Jewish, right?" I blurted out.

She looked a bit puzzled. "Well yes, but—"

"So I might be able to get information about the time period that will help with my character. My father's grandmother lived in Russia way back then."

Ms. Ramsey nodded. "That's perfect. I knew I could count on you to embrace this part."

She could. I was going to be the best Golde I could be. After all, what teenage girl didn't want to appear on stage in front of her entire school dressed as a frumpy, middle-aged Jewish mother living in poverty and oppression?

It would have been so nice to be Hodel . . . but it was time to let that go. Next year . . . well, I was going to be Maria from *West Side Story*, or Sandy from *Grease*, or maybe Dorothy from *The Wizard of Oz*. This year I could be Golde.

CHAPTER FIVE

By the time classes started that morning, the news about who had landed which part in the show had spread through the halls of our school. And for the rest of that day, I was stopped by kids I knew—and even some I didn't—all offering their congratulations. I had to admit, it was a nice feeling, and I actually started to feel better and better about being cast as Golde.

But that night, after I got home, finished my homework, and went to bed, the memory of Zayde's reaction to my discovery in his attic came crashing down on me.

I had decided not to say anything to my parents about it—at least for now. I couldn't stop thinking that I had screwed up big time, and I didn't really want them to be mad at me for upsetting my grandfather. All I knew was that some dark secret from Zayde's past was tied up with that poster and violin. I had to get to the bottom of it, but I had no idea how.

And now, after talking with Ms. Ramsey, I had another secret, the one about next year's production. No wonder I couldn't sleep! My brain was working on too many things at once and my thoughts kept spinning around and around. *Too many secrets!* That's what I was thinking as I staggered down to breakfast the next morning feeling like a zombie. I walked into the kitchen and slumped down at the table.

I've never been much of a talker in the morning, so that was nothing new. My mom just shoved a glass of orange juice under my nose and backed away. She must have figured that I was nervous about the first rehearsal for *Fiddler* before classes. And I was! There was a lot of pressure on me—I had to learn my part and the parts I was understudying. I had to prove to Ms. Ramsey that I could be a team player and do my best with the role I was given. Plus, I had to convince her that I was indeed worthy of a big lead the following year. But I felt like I was a bit of a mess. It was like that nightmare I used to get about walking on stage for the first performance of a show only to realize that I had forgotten all of my lines. In my dream, my mouth would open and shut, and nothing would come out of it. I hadn't had that nightmare since last year's show, but the memory of it came rushing back to me now. I had barely even started to learn my lines for this show and I was already nervous about forgetting them. On top of all that, I was anxious about how I was going to pull off the role of

Golde—it was unlike anything I'd ever tried before—and doubly anxious about performing with Ben Morgan. I definitely had to put this stuff about Zayde on the back burner and get my head into the show.

My father drove me to school that morning. As he drove away he yelled out the window, "Break a leg!"

When I walked into rehearsal, Natasha took one look at me and made a beeline across the room. "You look awful," she said.

"Thanks."

"No, I mean, you look *really* awful."

"I heard you the first time."

That's when she narrowed her eyes in that *you-can't-fool-me* kind of way and said, "What happened?"

I only had a few minutes. Our accompanist, Mr. Nevarez, had already taken his place at the piano and was warming up. He was a former teacher, and Ms. Ramsey had pulled him out of retirement to come and play for us. Ms. Ramsey was about to come in and start the rehearsal, and then it would be all business—no time to chitchat about personal stuff. As easygoing as she was outside of the classroom, when it came to rehearsal time, she was all about focus. "Discipline is the bridge between goals and accomplishments," she was fond of saying. Well, she didn't actually make that line up. It was from some motivational speaker she was always quoting.

I'd already told Natasha about the props and costumes I'd found in Zayde's attic. But now I told her the strange story about the violin and the poster and his reaction. She nodded and gasped in all the right places.

"It was like he'd seen a ghost, Tash. I'd never seen him like that before."

"Did he say why?"

"No, that's the point. He just got really angry and then really quiet."

"I can handle the angry part," Natasha said. "But when somebody gets quiet, that's the part I hate."

"That's because you're hardly ever quiet," I pointed out.

"Takes one to know one." She paused. "I just wonder what it could be. Hey, maybe your grandfather was involved in some kind of crime and you stumbled on the evidence!"

"Whoa, back off, Sherlock!" I exclaimed. "You've been watching too many movies. This is my grandfather we're talking about. He's the kindest, sweetest man in the whole world. Besides, he was just a boy in the poster. No, I'm sure this has something to do with his life during the war. I just don't know what."

"What are you going to do?"

I exhaled a big long breath. "I'm guess I'm going to have to talk to him again. I'm just not sure how."

Right then, Ms. Ramsey entered the rehearsal hall. When she began to clap her hands to call us to attention, there was instant silence. Most of us had been in shows before and we knew what was expected.

"Thank you for quieting down so quickly," she began. And then she started to talk about the background to *Fiddler*.

It was set, she explained, in a little village, or shtetl, called Anatevka in Russia in the early 1900s. She told us that the ruler of Russia at that time was Tsar Nicholas II, who continued a long tradition of brutally anti-Semitic policies and practices instituted in the past by Russia's leaders. "The kind of men who inspired this hatred of Jews that led to decades of violence against them," she said.

"Those were the pogroms," I whispered to Natasha. She nodded.

"And in the midst of all this," Ms. Ramsey continued, "there was a poor Jewish milkman named Tevye, his wife, Golde, and their five daughters, all just trying to go about their simple lives."

She smiled at me and at Ben when she named our characters. I looked over at him, feeling my face warm up instantly. Then I checked myself. There was no way I could let Ben see my attraction to him—not that he would notice me even if he tripped over me. We were just doing a show together, that was all. But I had to admit that he did look awfully cute that morning. He was wearing a checkered shirt with long sleeves folded up to his elbows, jeans, and white running shoes. He had spiky short hair that made you wonder if he'd rolled out of bed that way or if he'd spent hours in front of the bathroom mirror.

Ben turned and glanced at me. At first I thought he might have caught me staring at him—like I was some kind of weird stalker! But then he smiled briefly and looked back at Ms. Ramsey. He had the darkest eyes, and they seemed to look right through me.

Natasha dug her elbow into my side. She'd seen, and she knew what was going on in my head!

Ms. Ramsey was naming all of the other characters in the story, pointing out their importance. When she got to the part of Hodel, I thought Mindi's face was going to split in two, she was grinning so hard.

"We are going to bring all of those characters to life. And we are going to re-create that small Russian village right here on the stage of our school. I'm excited to start."

That brought a flutter of enthusiastic clapping from the whole cast. Ms. Ramsey held up her hand and quieted us again.

"Now, normally at this time I would sit us all down and just read the script from start to finish. But I thought I'd do something different this morning. I want to dive right into the meat of this play and begin by exploring the relationship between Tevye and his wife. It's really at the heart of this piece."

Uh-oh, where was this going?

"And I want to begin with some singing instead of reading. I'd like Ben and Shirli to come up here. We're going to go to act 2, scene 1. I'm going to have the two of you sing 'Do You Love Me?' The rest of you take a seat."

I think Natasha must have shoved me to the front of the rehearsal hall, because honestly, I didn't remember getting there. I couldn't believe that Ms. Ramsey was starting the whole process off with this moment in the play and this song between me and Ben! I couldn't help but wonder whether she was doing this for the sake of the play or to make me happier about playing Golde.

Ms. Ramsey placed two chairs side by side. "The two of you can sit here. Just pretend you are on a wooden bench outside Tevye's home. Open your scripts to page 117."

I sat down and glanced over at Ben. He seemed just as nervous as I was. I hadn't expected that. Ben always looked so cool. But right now, as he flipped through the script, his leg was bouncing up and down as if there were a motor attached to it. The guy was human after all!

"Now, at this point in the play, all of Tevye's daughters have rejected the notion of arranged marriages in favor of 'love matches' and finding their husbands on their own," Ms. Ramsey explained. "The daughters are going against a tradition that has been part of this community and culture for years. This song sums up the realization in Tevye's mind that things are changing. Even though his own marriage was arranged years earlier, he wants to know if Golde really loves him."

With that she cued Mr. Nevarez at the piano, who put down the crossword puzzle book he had been working on. Ben turned to me and asked, "Do you love me?"

I opened my mouth to reply, and then froze right there on the spot. It was like the ice age had descended on me. My face went rigid, my mind stopped working, and the rest of my body felt as if it were encased in mud. This was my nightmare come to life! I forgot everything—the lyrics, the melody, the lines, you name it. I don't know how long I sat like that. Ben was staring at me as if I had turned into some kind of sideshow freak. I glanced out at the rest of the cast. Natasha was leaning forward, almost willing me to do or say something. Mohammed was off to one side and gave me a weak thumbs-up. But it was the look on Mindi's face that finally snapped me out of my trance. She looked smug, almost as though she knew I was going to fail at this. And that's when I pulled myself together. I was an actress, I reminded myself. And I loved performing. I had been given this part because of my ability to act. So, acting was what I was going to do. And I was intent on impressing everyone in the room with my skill. I took a deep breath.

"Sorry, Ms. Ramsey," I said. "I'm just getting my head around this part. Golde is strong and independent, right? She runs the home and does a million things. She has no time to sit with Tevye and chat about things like love."

"Good, good," said Ms. Ramsey, nodding enthusiastically. The oversized earrings she was wearing bobbed along with her. "It's really important to think of the character's motivation." She said this as much to the whole cast as to me. "Yes, Golde is a pretty hard nut on the outside. But don't forget that deep down she really does love Tevye. And she'll admit that by the end of the song."

I gulped and looked at Ben. "Okay, can we take it again from the top?" This time I was the one who cued Mr. Nevarez. And when Ben started the song, I joined right in.

And that's when the joy of performing took over. I was on a stage, with an audience in front of me—well, technically only my cast mates, but an audience is an audience. And I wasn't going to let them or myself down. I responded to every line that Ben gave me, trying to sing in perfect harmony even when his voice was slightly off-key, and acting like there was no tomorrow. When we finished, the whole cast burst into spontaneous applause.

Ben was grinning at me. "You were awesome!" It was as though he'd noticed me for the first time.

"Thanks!" I beamed. "And you sound amazing!"

Did he actually blush when I said that?

When Ms. Ramsey came over, she leaned down and whispered in my ear, "I knew I made the right choice giving you this part. Well done!"

CHAPTER SIX

A couple of days passed before I was able to talk my father into coming with me to Zayde's to collect the props and costumes from the attic. We'd had only one rehearsal since the first one—a long after-school session of learning the music for the show. Ms. Ramsey had decided that we needed to know all the songs before we could really begin to stage the whole thing.

I climbed into the car beside my father and he started up the engine.

"Thanks for coming with me," I said.

"My pleasure. You really couldn't move all that stuff without some help."

Of course, my father knew that I also wanted him with me for emotional support. I'd finally told my parents everything about the poster and the violin and Zayde's reaction. They'd tried to help me understand it all, but I think they were as surprised—no, shocked—as I was. And it was all just as mysterious to my father as it was to me.

We backed out of the driveway.

"Are you nervous?" he asked. "About going to see your Zayde?"

I nodded. "A little."

"Just a little? You're really twirling your hair."

I hadn't noticed. I unwound my finger. "Okay, a lot."

"That's understandable."

I had expected him to say something like, "You have nothing to be nervous about," so I was surprised by his reply.

"It's good we're going today," he added. "The longer you wait, the harder it gets."

We stopped at a set of lights—the only lights in the short drive between our house and Zayde's. I was kind of hoping the light would stay red for about an hour, so I could have more time to think about what I was going to say. But that would have also left me more time to worry about how Zayde would react. If I could have gone back in time and stopped myself from snooping down to the bottom layer of that trunk I would have, in a heartbeat. But all I could do now was try to fix the rift that had opened between us. That was all I wanted . . . well, that, and to find out more.

"You know that Zayde never speaks about his past," my father said. It was like he was reading my mind.

"Obviously he survived the war and the Holocaust, but I've never known how, or even where."

"It's still hard for me to believe that you didn't know anything about Zayde and his family being musicians."

My father shook his head. "I stopped trying to get him to open up to me years ago. It's all been a big mystery."

"But now maybe we'll have some mysteries solved," I said.

"Well, I guess we know now where your musical ability came from," he said.

"And why you love music so much, too. I guess it's in our blood because it's in Zayde's blood."

"And his parents', as well. It all makes sense."

I looked at my father and realized that I wasn't the only one who was anxious. Dad had a worried look on his face, the kind he had whenever he couldn't direct what was happening. My father was a bit of a control freak: he loved being in charge, loved organizing things, and hated uncertainty. He was like that with everything, which was probably a good character trait for an accountant. He was the one who organized all of our family holidays, right down to the minor details. If anything went wrong—a delayed flight, a lost bag, a room that wasn't ready for us—he would freak out. Mom was the one who had to talk him off the ledge in those moments.

He pulled the car up to the curb in front of Zayde's house.

"Look, Shirli," he said, turning in his seat to be sure he had my full attention. "I know you want to understand what went on in Zayde's past, and I know you want to set things right between the two of you, but please don't push him too hard. He's just started to come around since Bubbie's death. And I don't want anything to upset that apple cart."

"I got it, Dad. And trust me, I don't want to upset him either."

"So, we'll get your stuff out of the attic, and if Zayde isn't in the mood to talk, we'll just leave, okay?"

For now, it was better to just nod my head and leave it at that.

It was dark inside Zayde's house when we entered. And it was quiet. The TV wasn't even on, and though I didn't want to imagine the worst, I could feel my heart rate start to speed up just a bit.

"Zayde?" I called out. No answer. "Zayde, are you here?" This time I turned up the volume. And that's when I heard his soft reply.

"I'm in the kitchen."

It was a good thing it was dark in the hallway or my dad would have seen the look on my face—a combination of anxiety and relief. I wondered if the darkness hid the same expression on his face. We took off our coats and made our way to the back of the house. And there was Zayde, sitting at the kitchen table, sipping on a glass of hot tea with lemon. The steam was rising in wispy coils that floated past his face.

"It's so quiet in here," I began. "No wrestling on tonight?"

"I'm not sure. I just needed some time to sit and think."

That's when my dad stepped in to the conversation. "You okay, Dad?"

"Fine. I'm fine."

"You taking your medication? Your vitamins? You getting out for a walk?"

Zayde stared at my father. "You're sounding more like my doctor every day."

Dad laughed nervously. "Just checking to make sure you're taking care of yourself."

"I'm taking my pills, I'm eating well, and I'm feeling fine."

Dad was looking more uncomfortable by the minute. "Okay...well...how about if I go up to the attic and get those things you were talking about, Shirli." He turned to look at me. "Are you coming with me?"

That wasn't what I had in mind. "You know what, Dad? I think I'm going to stay here and keep Zayde company. The clothes are in a pile beside the big trunk. Shout if you need my help, okay?"

Dad hesitated a second, and then nodded. But just before he headed off, he turned and gave me one more look, the kind of stare that I took as a reminder not to push my grandfather too hard.

I took a seat at the table across from Zayde. I was the one who finally broke the silence.

"We started rehearsals for *Fiddler*. And you won't believe it but the first song my teacher made us sing was 'Do You Love Me?'—my duet with Tevye."

Zayde lifted his eyes and I could see a spark of interest. "I know that song. Your Bubbie loved it . . . she said it was a real love song, but with so much humor."

"I was nervous at first, but it went really well. And the guy who is playing Tevye can really sing!"

"I'm glad," Zayde replied. His face relaxed, and in that moment, I knew we were back on the same page. "You're going to be wonderful. I have no doubt of that."

"Thanks. I wasn't sure I wanted this part to begin with. But now I think I understand why my teacher chose me for it. Do you think you might come on opening night?"

He reached out and put his hand on my arm. "You know it's hard for me to go to things. I don't want to make promises I might not be able to keep."

"It would mean so much," I said.

He smiled, and I was so thrilled to see it that I smiled back twice as broadly.

"I'll have to see," he said at last.

If there was a moment to try and turn the conversation toward Zayde's childhood, this was it. Dad was still in the attic, and I had just a few minutes. I wasn't going to waste them. I gulped and took the plunge.

"Zayde, I don't want to make you angry, but I can't stop thinking about the poster and the violin. Could I ask you a question?"

I thought I saw him stiffen, and I held my breath, afraid that he would pull away again. But instead he sat back in his chair and gazed at me. "I've thought so much about what happened when you found . . . those things. I didn't mean to get angry with you. You know I love you very much." His voice caught at that point and he hesitated.

My heart swelled. "And you're the best grandfather anyone could ask for."

Zayde smiled. "Now you're just trying to flatter me." Then he looked serious again and said, "I don't talk much about my life, but I think I owe you an explanation."

This was the moment I was waiting for. But so many questions were running through my mind, I barely knew where to begin. Zayde must have understood my hesitation.

"Okay, let me help you out. Yes, that was of course me in the poster you found. And yes, I played the violin in a klezmer band. Do you know what klezmer music is?"

I shook my head.

"It is the traditional Yiddish music of our communities in Poland and across Eastern Europe—the most beautiful folk songs you've ever heard. I was pretty good on the violin, even as a young boy. But my father, now *he* was the real musician in the family."

"Was that the man in the photo standing beside you?"

"Yes. He played the clarinet. He could make that instrument sound as if it was laughing one minute and crying the next. He could almost make it talk. My one brother, Aaron, played the accordion. The other one, Leo, played the upright double bass. And my mother? She played the tambourine. They were all there in that picture too."

My relatives—a great-grandfather, great-grandmother, and great-uncles. *What had happened to them?* I had an idea—a terrible idea that I didn't even want to think about.

"We were a musical family and we traveled from village to village, playing at weddings and concerts. We were as poor as dirt, even though we were in high demand. It was a difficult life on the road, and anti-Semitism was everywhere—even before the war. But we were together as a family. And I loved the stage. I loved the music. I loved the reaction of the audience. I loved it all."

Behind my grandfather, I caught a glimpse of my father standing just outside the kitchen. He was holding a pile of clothes from the attic and he had come to a complete stop, mesmerized by what he was hearing. I was so afraid that if he entered the kitchen, Zayde would stop talking. And he seemed to be on a roll now. I stared at my father, willing him to stay where he was.

"September 1, 1939. Now that's a date to remember. Do you know what happened then, Shirli?"

"Germany invaded Poland to start World War II."

"That's right. Why am I not surprised? You are a very bright young lady. The war began. Before that, Jews had been treated like outcasts, untouchables—like we had some kind of disease."

I knew about the laws that took rights and freedoms away from Jews. No jobs, no homes, no education, and so many more restrictions.

"But if I thought life was difficult before, I realized that it was a piece of cake compared to what happened after the invasion. I have no idea how we managed to survive over the next few years. All around us, our Jewish friends and relatives were being arrested and sent to ghettos and concentration camps. We never heard from them again."

"Were you also arrested?" I barely managed to squeak out this question.

Zayde shook his head. "Not at first. Since we were a traveling group we were harder to pin a target on. But eventually we had to become like phantoms, creeping about so we wouldn't be seen. We slept wherever we could find a safe place—a barn one night, a meadow the next. We ate berries from bushes and dug up potatoes from the farmers' fields. Finally, we made our way to the forest and set up a kind of camp out there."

My father's face in the doorway of the kitchen had become quite pale. But he didn't move a muscle, frozen in one spot, still clutching the clothes from the attic.

"We had our instruments with us. That must sound ridiculous to you, doesn't it? When you are running for your life, as we were, you would think it would be more important to carry food, or clothing. But no. And, believe it or not, it was those musical instruments that brought us great comfort. In the pitch-black forest night, we would pull them out of their cases and play softly together. You'd think that we'd be worried about being heard. But somehow it was more important to us to play—to remind ourselves of the lives we had once had, and to dream that one day everything would be restored to us."

Zayde paused and squeezed his eyes shut, as if there was some memory lurking back there that he was struggling with. I held my breath, wondering what was coming next.

"We were starving. We were dirty. We were cold and wet so much of the time. But as the days, weeks, and months marched on, we began to think that we were going to make it—that we would be the lucky ones to get through this madness together and safe. That was not to be. One morning, as we slept, Nazi soldiers entered the forest and surrounded us."

By now the hairs on my arms were standing straight up. I couldn't begin to imagine what it must have been like for my grandfather, then just a boy, to have gone through that—one minute thinking he was safe, and the next believing his life might be over.

"They pointed their guns in our faces and ordered us to march forward. And that's when my father faced one of the soldiers and asked permission to play something before they took us away. Can you imagine my father having such nerve? Even the soldier was taken aback. I'm sure he'd never had a Jew ask such a thing before. He nodded, and my father pulled his clarinet from its case and began to play. It was such a beautiful melody, sad and uplifting at the same time, like he was playing for his life and the lives of all of us. Bit by bit, you saw the soldiers begin to drop their rifles lower and lower as my father played. And when he finished, the soldiers stood in silence. Seconds later, they raised their guns once more."

At this point, I couldn't stop myself. I grabbed my grandfather's arm. "Zayde, why haven't you told any of this before?" I cried. "You could have talked about it. I know about the Holocaust. I can handle hearing this stuff."

"It wasn't you I was worried about, Shirli. It was me," he replied, his voice breaking. "I never told anybody except your Bubbie. Even now, these memories are so painful, like a wound that hasn't healed."

I could see the sweat beginning to bead up on Zayde's forehead. And his hands were twitching and shaking so much I had to reach out and hold on to them.

That's when my father stepped into the kitchen. "Okay, that's enough, Shirli. You're upsetting your grandfather."

A veil descended over Zayde's eyes and he sat back in his chair. I knew he had withdrawn again. There would be no more conversation.

"Are you okay, Zayde?" I asked. It felt as if, lately, I had been asking that question an awful lot.

"What? Oh . . . I'm fine. Maybe just a little tired. I think I need to go lie down."

"Right," my dad said. "That's a good idea. You need to get some sleep. I'm just going to put these things for Shirli's school in the car. Shirli, you say good night to your grandfather."

With that, my father turned and fled from the house. It was as if he couldn't get out of there fast enough. At that moment, I wasn't sure who was having a harder time with this, Zayde or my dad.

Zayde rose heavily from the table and I walked over to give him a big hug. He held me in the tightest squeeze before finally releasing me.

"Thank you for telling me this," I began. "Would it be okay if I came back another time?"

He gave me a questioning look. "You know you are welcome here whenever you want."

"I mean, I want to come back and talk some more—when you're ready."

Zayde looked up and into my eyes. And then he nodded, ever so slowly, and said, "Yes, we will talk some more."

CHAPTER SEVEN

Natasha slumped into the chair across from mine at the cafeteria table. Over the noise of hundreds of people eating and talking and laughing I could still hear her deep sigh.

At first I ignored her. My head was still reeling after having heard Zayde's revelation a couple of nights earlier. And I was trying to figure out when I would go back to his house to ask more questions about his family—*my* family! My father said Zayde needed a break, a little time to recover, but I needed to hear what he could tell me . . . what *only he* could tell me. I was sure he was willing to talk more, even if it was difficult. And there was one other thing I was sure of—next time, I would definitely go to his place alone so Dad couldn't cut the conversation short.

Natasha let out another long, slow, agonized sigh.

"Natasha, what's wrong?" I knew she was expecting me to ask.

"Nothing . . . well, nothing except for the rehearsal this morning."

"It was a good rehearsal," I said.

"Yeah, because Ms. Ramsey didn't yell at *you*!"

"Don't be so dramatic."

"Look who's talking! Drama is practically your middle name," she said.

I didn't want to admit it because I was afraid it might make Tash feel more anxious, but she was right. Ms. Ramsey had been loud—very loud—yelling at Mohammed and Mindi when they'd forgotten lines. That put Mindi in such a foul mood that at one point she shoved past me when she was exiting the stage and didn't even stop to apologize.

But the ensemble, including Natasha, had gotten the worst of Ms. Ramsey's tirades. She threatened to fire them all when they kept messing up the harmonies on the opening number. I knew there was a lot riding on this show for our drama teacher. It was only her second production at our school—and the first she was officially in charge of—and we could tell she was feeling the pressure. But it didn't help to attack the cast. I had been one of the lucky ones, lucky enough to avoid the wrath of Ms. Ramsey.

"Maybe Ms. Ramsey didn't raise her voice with me because I didn't do anything wrong," I pointed out.

"Very sensitive, very supportive, very caring comment," Natasha said.

"Oh, come on, I was just kidding. Don't take it so personally. It wasn't just you she was angry at."

"And somehow that makes it better? Actually, maybe it is better. It's just that I didn't expect it would be this tough, that she'd be so demanding."

"You need a director who demands that you give it your best," I said. "Would you rather slack off and then be humiliated in front of an audience on opening night?"

"Isn't there a third choice?" she asked. "Maybe nobody yells at me, I'm naturally brilliant, and the audience just *adores* my performance."

"By opening night you *will* be brilliant. It'll get easier."

I didn't have the heart to tell her that it was probably going to get harder first. We were going to open on April 23—only a couple of months away. I knew that morning and afternoon rehearsals would turn into lunchtime rehearsals. And by the end, there would definitely be Saturdays and Sundays thrown in for good measure.

I looked around the cafeteria and spotted Ben on the other side walking toward us, tray in hand. All thoughts of the rehearsal schedule faded and I sat straight up in my chair, my heartbeat beginning to pick up its pace. He was walking straight toward us, straight toward our table. Everyone in the cafeteria was watching him, though he didn't seem to notice.

"I think he's coming to sit with us."

When Tash said that, I sat up even straighter. But . . . Ben suddenly veered off and joined a bunch of his friends at a table close by. One of those people was his old girlfriend, Emma. They looked good together, and they seemed to be comfortable—more like girlfriend and boyfriend than ex-girlfriend and ex-boyfriend. I slumped back down in my chair, hoping my face didn't betray the disappointment I was feeling.

I knew we were good together in rehearsal. Our voices blended well, and the energy between his character and mine was easy and natural. Even Ms. Ramsey said that we had great chemistry. But that was on stage. In between rehearsals, we rarely spoke. What else did I expect? We were in a play together and that was it. Still, it would have been nice if he'd come over.

"I'm going to get him," Tash suddenly said. She was reading my mind again. But this was crazy.

"What?"

"Aren't there things you need to talk about? Character? Motivation? All that theater stuff?"

"Tash, don't . . ."

But Tash was already up and heading over to Ben's table. I sank lower into my chair, wishing the ground could swallow me up. Then I watched through half-open eyelids as the two of them chatted for a few seconds. Finally, Ben stood, holding his tray, said goodbye to his friends, and followed Tash over to where I was sitting.

"Natasha thought it would be a good idea for you

and me to talk about the play, you know . . . maybe I should get to know my stage wife a little better. Can I sit down?"

I wasn't going to say no, but he didn't wait for an answer. He just took one of the empty seats. Tash was the one to break the awkward silence that followed.

"You have a great voice," she said. "I've been meaning to tell you that."

"Thanks, but I know it's not as good as Shirli's." When he said this, he turned to face me. "And it's not just your voice but the way you *own* the character. You just come to life when you're on stage."

I could feel my face burning. Without waiting for me to respond, he just opened his mouth and began to sing, "Do you love me?"

I almost choked on my sandwich. What had Natasha said to him?

"Do you love me?" He repeated the line, staring straight at me.

"Huh?"

"It's our duet, "Do You Love Me?""

What was I thinking? I shook my head and swallowed hard. "Do *I* love you?" I finally croaked back.

Ben didn't seem to notice my discomfort. He turned back to his lunch, shoving the last of a sandwich into his mouth.

"I guess you have a real advantage over me there, getting inside of the character and all," he said.

I thought I knew what he might be getting at. "You mean because I'm Jewish?" I asked.

He shook his head. "No, I mean because you're a good actor. I didn't know you were Jewish. My doctor's Jewish."

It was a classic old stereotype, but I let it go. I was still kind of melting over the fact that I was sitting in the cafeteria with Ben Morgan.

"I've been thinking that I might want to be a doctor," he continued.

"Did you know that Shirli's brother, Adam, is studying to be a doctor, and her mother is a doctor?" Natasha asked.

"No, I didn't know that," he replied.

That was when Natasha flashed me a little smile, and there was a twinkle in her eyes. Before I knew what was happening, she said, "I bet Shirli's mother would be happy to talk to you about what it's like to be a doctor."

I stared at Natasha, shaking my head ever so slightly.

"That would be great," Ben said.

"Maybe you could even go over to her place sometime," Natasha suggested.

"That would be even better!" Ben turned and looked right at me. "If that's okay . . . I didn't mean to sort of invite myself."

I gulped. "Sure. My mother is always happy to talk about life at the hospital. I'll warn her not to scare you off with her stories of med school and cadavers and crazy hours. Maybe we can even arrange it when my brother is home for the weekend from university, and you could talk to both of them."

"Awesome! And it would even help with the play. You know, Ms. Ramsey said we should be spending time together to get the feel of being a married couple."

"You can join us for lunch every day if you want." I blurted that out before I realized it might have sounded more desperate than inviting.

"Some days, for sure," he said.

He was probably just trying to be polite. I felt embarrassed and a little stupid. But Ben looked embarrassed too. He wasn't as smooth as he'd seemed from a distance. In fact, up close I could see he had a couple of zits that he was trying to cover up. Not as smooth and not as perfect.

"You know, during football season I eat lunch with nobody but my teammates."

"So, you're comparing Shirli and me to your football friends?" Natasha asked.

"Rehearsing this play reminds me a lot of football practices, actually," Ben said. "All of us working together the same way, with a coach who is sort of scary."

"You think Ms. Ramsey is sort of scary?" I asked.

"Oh, no, I take that back. She's *very* scary. I'm much more afraid of her than Coach Morrison."

"Really? He seems like one big, scary guy," I said.

"Yeah, but she's scary in a different way. He's like a big ol' grizzly bear. You know you should be afraid of him. She's so much more dangerous, all pretty and nice and then—*bang*—she pounces like a jaguar or something." He hesitated. "Please don't tell her I said that."

"We won't," I said, "but she would probably take it as a compliment."

"Let's not find out. She's sort of a combination of a coach and a Marine drill instructor . . . and believe me, I know about Marines because of my father."

"He's a Marine?" I asked.

"He's an investment broker now. He works on Wall Street."

"Wall Street? Was he there the day of . . . ?"

"He was right there. He saw the towers fall. He was covered in the dust," Ben said.

"Wow. It was bad enough from this side of the river, but to be right there . . ." My voice trailed off again.

"He doesn't really talk about it. You know, he's still a soldier. Like he's always saying, once a Marine, always a Marine. He's big into rules, regulations, order, organization, and being ready for everything. Marines are kind of like Boy Scouts except with guns," Ben said.

Tash and I laughed.

"Your parents must be proud of you for getting the lead role," I suggested.

"I'm not sure if proud is the right word. Maybe surprised, or confused . . . especially my father."

"I guess it's not quite the same thing as being the captain of the football team," I said.

"For sure. Quarterback, he understands; singing show tunes, he's not so sure about."

"In some ways, playing the lead role is like being the quarterback of the football team, isn't it?" Natasha said.

"Yeah, except playing Tevye is like being the quarterback, the middle linebacker, the punter, and the kick returner. That guy is hardly ever off the—"

The bell rang. It was always too loud and too long. Everyone around us was packing up and heading for the doors.

"I'll see you both at rehearsal," Ben said.

"Yeah, see you then," I said.

He got up and walked away, tray in hand.

"So, are you still feeling sorry about getting the role of Golde?" Natasha asked.

I smiled. "Feeling better about it all the time."

CHAPTER EIGHT

I stopped to get groceries for Zayde on the way over to his house after school.

"Hello!" I called as I walked into his kitchen.

There was no response and no noise, no TV blaring, nothing at all. I put the grocery bags down on the table, along with my school books. The books tumbled forward and a couple of them fell onto the floor. I'd grab them later—first I had to flex my fingers to get some feeling back. The temperature had dipped below freezing again—typical for early February. And though it was only a few blocks from the store to Zayde's house, the combination of the weight of the bags and the cold had made my fingers numb.

"Hello!" I yelled even louder, heading into the living room. "Zayde, it's me, Shirli!"

"I'm in here!" he called back, and I was instantly relieved. "The dining room!"

He was sitting at the dining room table, at his place

at the end, with a bowl of soup in front of him. He was, of course, wearing a jacket, but he had a white napkin tucked into the top of his shirt. I could see little red speckles of tomato soup splattered on it.

"I brought your groceries," I said as I kissed the top of his head.

"Did you get me forty bananas?" he asked.

"Sorry, only thirty. But from the looks of it, I was smart to buy you another box of crackers."

His tomato soup was almost a solid mass of crackers.

"You know how I like my soup."

"I do. Do you think you'll be able to get by for another week without the extra bananas?"

"I could try . . . or maybe you could come back sooner, if you wanted?" he said.

The truth was I had been feeling nervous about coming back to Zayde's. After I'd found his poster and violin, and then urged him to talk about his life in Poland, I wasn't sure if he'd even want me around! I was the one responsible for making him dredge up all those painful memories.

"Don't you usually eat in the kitchen?" I asked.

"Mostly . . ."

Then it hit me. This was where he and Bubbie usually ate.

"A little change is good sometimes," he said, catching my stare. "You're late tonight, aren't you?"

"Our rehearsal went a bit longer than usual."

In addition to being loud at rehearsal, Ms. Ramsey had also decided to keep us all late, going over and over the opening number until I couldn't bear to sing it one more time!

Zayde nodded. "The play, that's right. And how is it going?"

"Great, good, all right, I guess. By the way, those clothes I found in the attic were perfect."

"If they were perfect, they wouldn't have been in the attic gathering dust," he said. Then he sat back. "So, you wanted to talk to me about your role in the play. What did you want to know?"

That seemed like a pretty safe topic. "Well, the thing is, I'm playing a Jewish woman in Russia in the early 1900s."

"It sounds like the life my mother actually led."

"That's what I want to ask you about." It dawned on me then that maybe this wasn't such a safe topic after all. I hesitated, and then decided to dive right in. "Can you tell me about your mother?"

Zayde looked me right in the eye. "I can tell you about her. Maybe it would help us both if we looked at her picture."

"You have pictures of her?" I exclaimed.

"Pictures, no. Picture, yes. You saw it on that poster. Go and get it . . . it's in my room."

"Sure, of course," I said. And with that, I went down the hall and started up the stairs. They were steep and narrow. My father had talked to Zayde about getting one of those lifts to get him up and down the stairs. He'd even offered to pay for it, but Zayde refused to even discuss it.

The door to his bedroom was open and the poster was sitting on his dresser—along with the violin. It was still in its case, with the lid closed and latched. I was so tempted to open up the case and look at it again, but I stopped myself. I had the poster, and that was all I was asked to get.

When I walked back into the dining room, Zayde was just finishing up the last of his soup. I picked up the empty bowl and moved it aside before placing the poster on the table.

He let out a big sigh and then, with the index finger of his right hand, gently touched the picture. It was as though he was caressing the people in the images.

"Before you brought this down the other day, I thought I'd never see them again."

"You said you thought Bubbie had thrown the poster away. Why would she do that?"

"Because I asked her to. Twenty years ago."

"But why?"

"I didn't want to look at it. It brought back too many memories." He paused. "It still does."

I knew it! I didn't want to be the source of Zayde's pain. "I'm . . . I'm sorry," I stammered. "You don't have to do this if you don't want to . . . if you can't."

"I know. But I want to, I do. Let me tell you about this poster. I explained to you before that we were musicians. We performed at weddings and celebrations like all bands would. But we were klezmer musicians, and so we took pride in making the instruments sound like human voices, to show human emotions."

"You said your father could do that on the clarinet."

"He could make it laugh and cry. He was amazing."

"And could you do that on the violin?"

Zayde didn't react at first. And then a smile—a sad smile—came to his face. "I was good. As good as I needed to be to survive. But this isn't about the violin. You want to know about my mother, your great-grandmother."

I would have loved to know more about him playing the violin. But this would have to do—for now. I nodded. "Please."

"She was a good woman, a strong woman. You know how they say that a man is the head of the family?"

"Um . . . things have changed a lot since the feminist movement, Zayde," I pointed out, a bit nervously.

He chuckled. "Don't get me wrong. I did not say that the man *runs* the family. The man may be the head of the family, but the wife is the neck. The wife tells the head where to look, and without the neck the head just flops around and can't do anything. My mother ran our family, the way your Bubbie ran this house and your mother runs your home."

"I think my mother would agree with you about that!"

"My mother kept us going. There were bad times, and then there were terrible times. My father wanted to give up, but she wouldn't let him. She made him go on, made us all keep moving forward." He paused. "Until the end."

He let out a big sigh, and I could tell he was trying to fight back some tears. His hands, which always shook a little, seemed to be shaking even more.

"Can you tell me a story about her?"

Zayde paused again, took a deep breath, and began.

"Remember I told you that we were living in the forest—no, not really living. We were trying to survive in the forest. We all searched for things to eat—mushrooms, berries, plants. My mother would collect everything and then parcel some out to each of us. I never imagined that a few berries could taste so good.

"I assumed we were all eating the same amount, which was practically nothing, until one day I caught my mother taking her portion and dividing it up for me and my brothers. She never said a word. She just gave up her food for us. That was the kind of woman . . . the kind of mother that she was. She always acted very tough, but she was kind and had a really good heart."

"That's like Golde."

"Golde . . . ? Oh, yes, the character in the play. Do you think Golde would sacrifice for her children?" he asked.

"She'd give anything for her children."

"That was like your great-grandmother. She always made sure that what little she had was for the rest of us, for me and my brothers and my father."

"That's like Golde too. Just out of curiosity, was your parents' marriage an arranged marriage?"

"Most marriages were arranged in those times. Did you think they met on a website or something like that?"

I laughed.

"It was the way it was done back then. You married somebody from the village or the child of somebody your parents knew, or the rabbi knew."

"Did your parents love each other?"

"They grew to love each other. And then it was a deep love until the very end. She loved us all." He let out a sigh as his fingers traced the outline of his mother's picture. Then he looked up at me, his eyes moist. "Your Bubbie knew not to listen to me. She knew to keep this poster and not throw it out. And now it is yours."

"You're giving me the poster? But . . . it's your family."

"No, it is *our* family. These are my parents and brothers, but these are your great-grandparents and your great-uncles." He tapped his finger against the poster. "I shouldn't have asked your Bubbie to throw the poster away. It wasn't fair to them. They did not deserve that . . . none of it." Another sigh escaped his lips and his whole body seemed to shudder. "Your Bubbie understood even when I didn't."

"She was a good neck," I said.

"She was the best. And now, this poster is for you. You know, your great-grandmother would have been very proud of you."

"She would?"

"Because of the music you make, but also because you are so brave."

"I'm not brave."

"Aren't you? You spend your life getting up in front of an audience and letting them see into your soul. You don't think that is brave?"

I hadn't really thought of it like that. "I just love performing."

"And my mother was just the same. She came even more alive in front of an audience. Me? I would have been just as happy playing by myself on a log in the woods."

I thought back to the story he'd told us about his father playing that final time in the forest in front of the Nazis who had found them. Now *that* was brave.

"Thank you so much, Zayde. I'll take good care of it."

"I know you will. Now, you need to get home. You must be starving. We'll talk more another time. You go, go, get home . . . you call me when you get there so I know you're safe."

There was still a lot more to Zayde's story that I wanted to understand. But maybe this was best— letting it all unfold, like a novel, or a play, a chapter at a time, one scene at a time. I got up and he handed me the poster. Then I hugged him and he hugged me back. I knew it was time to go home—we both knew that—but neither of us seemed to want the hug to end.

CHAPTER NINE

It was almost time for me to leave for school but I couldn't tear myself away from the poster. Before going to bed the night before I had hung it above my dresser. And now I just stood there in my room, staring at it, staring at the members of my family.

I'd shown it to my dad the night before. Mom was out delivering a baby, so it was just my father and me. It felt right that it was just the two of us. He reacted the same way Zayde had—tracing the faces with his fingers. He had never seen pictures of his family before.

I also told him the things Zayde had told me, about how his family had lived in the forest, scavenging for food, and how Zayde's mother—his grandmother— had given her portions to her children. My dad lapped up every word, as though he had been thirsting for these stories for a long time.

"Shirli, hurry up or you're going to be late for rehearsal!" my mother yelled up the stairs.

"I'm coming, I'm coming!" I yelled back as I hopped around the room trying to put on a second sock. I got the sock on and grabbed my books from the dresser, and then I realized that my script wasn't there. I looked all around the room. Often I fell asleep with it in my hands—but that night I hadn't even looked at it. It wasn't there on the floor . . . wait . . . the floor. Some of my books had fallen off Zayde's kitchen table. In the excitement of getting the poster and the rush to get home I'd forgotten them, until now.

I hurried down the stairs. "Mom, can we stop by Zayde's this morning on the way to school?"

"It's not on the way, and I don't really have time. I have a C-section waiting for me."

"But I left my script there, and Ms. Ramsey will freak out if I don't have it with me."

"You could wait till your father drives to work and get a ride with him, but wouldn't it be worse to be late for rehearsal this morning?" she asked.

I had to think about that one. It was a hard choice.

"Besides, don't you have the part memorized by now?"

"Most of it." Actually, I had my part committed to memory, as well as the two roles I was understudying and most of the other parts as well.

"Then let's get going, chop chop!"

Ms. Ramsey would be mad if she found out I'd forgotten it. She'd be even madder if she discovered I'd lost it. No, it couldn't be lost. It had to be at my grand-father's house, and I'd get it right after school.

We scrambled into the car, squealed out of the driveway, and raced down the street. My mother always seemed to get away with driving too fast. She'd been pulled over by the police a number of times but she always told them she was an obstetrician on her way to deliver a baby. Sometimes it was true. Mom figured that the good deeds she performed outweighed the occasional white lie.

"I got in quite late last night," she said, "but your dad told me all about the poster this morning, and what your Zayde said. Your dad had trouble sleeping. He has so many questions."

"I know—me too."

"I was surprised your Zayde gave you the poster."

"So was I, especially after seeing his face when I found it."

"Many Holocaust survivors don't want to talk about what happened," she said. "Too many bad memories."

"But shouldn't the poster bring back some good memories, as well?"

"The bad usually overwhelms the good." She paused. "You know, you were lucky. You got to know your grandparents. Your father, of course, never did."

"But you knew yours, right?"

"They came out of Europe years before the war. And my parents were born here."

"Then they didn't go through the Holocaust."

"Every Jew everywhere lost family members. I guess we all went through the Holocaust, whether we were in Europe or not. Not that we can compare that to those who went to the concentration camps," she added quickly. "People are still living with those traumas. Your Zayde still feels it."

"What's really amazing for me is finding out that his whole family was so musical."

"Well, you certainly didn't get that talent from my side."

"But you play the piano," I pointed out.

"I hit the keys the way a trained bear dances. I have almost no sense of rhythm."

"But Dad can sing, kind of, so . . . I guess the musical talent in his family got passed down to him?"

"He is very musical. But he never had a chance. Your Zayde didn't want him singing in the house. Really, there was almost no music in their house at all."

"That's what I don't understand. If music was so much a part of Zayde's life, why couldn't he have music in his home?" I asked.

Mom sighed. "I don't understand it all either. All I know is that your Zayde is consumed with memories that he's hidden away all these years. And hardly anything brings back memories and emotions like music. You know that."

I thought about how much music meant to me, how

certain songs could move me to tears, or fill me with joy.

"Yeah," I said. "I guess I do."

∽

"Are you ready, Ben?"

"Yes, Ms. Ramsey."

"Quiet, everybody. Quiet."

The banging from the set-builders stopped. Everything stopped. And everybody watched as Ben walked out to center stage. I was sitting in the second row, Natasha beside me. I had dodged a bullet; Ms. Ramsey hadn't noticed that I didn't have my script. A couple of times I'd borrowed Natasha's and made sure Ms. Ramsey saw me holding it. I felt a little deceitful, but that was better than making her angry. I felt as though next year's lead role was half a promise and half a sword hanging over my head.

"So, how does it feel to be Ben Morgan's wife?" Tash whispered.

"*Stage* wife." I emphasized the word.

"It's cool that he'll have lunch with us sometimes now."

"It really is." It was funny how being around him seemed to make us so much cooler. "Do you think that maybe—?"

"Don't be ridiculous," Tash said, reading my mind as usual. "He's Ben Morgan. Just because he's available doesn't mean he's available for you . . . or me."

She was right. I knew she wasn't being cruel—it was just a fact.

Up on the stage Ben cleared his throat, and we all waited. This was one of the biggest scenes in the entire play, and Ben was up there all by himself. I held my breath . . . and then, trying his best to sound like an old Jewish man, he began to sing, "If I Were a Rich Man."

This was the part in the play where Tevye is trying to get home before the Sabbath begins. His horse has pulled up lame and he's dragging his cart behind him. He pauses on stage and speaks to God, dreaming about what it would be like to be wealthy. Ben moved around the stage, scattering make-believe chicken feed and pretending to use a pitchfork to put out hay for the livestock. He was flinging his arms up in the air the way Ms. Ramsey had demonstrated, as though he was pleading with God. He was really knocking it out of the park.

And then he sang out his last line: "*If I were a weee-althyyyy man!*"

There was a slight pause, and then everybody started cheering. Ben looked so happy—no, so relieved! He started to take a bow and—

"That was at best not completely terrible," Ms. Ramsey said. "You're an old Jewish man, not some teenage quarterback prancing around the stage."

"Quarterbacks hardly ever prance," Ben muttered quietly. Ms. Ramsey had turned to speak to Mr. Nevarez at the piano so she didn't hear him, thank goodness!

She turned back to face the stage. "And from the top," she said.

I don't know what I'd expected but Ben slowly nodded his head. "Yes, Ms. Ramsey. And this time, I promise, no prancing."

He turned directly to me, smiled, and winked. I was pretty sure that was Tevye to Golde and not meant to be Ben to Shirli. Tash was right—I couldn't let myself be stupid.

CHAPTER TEN

I'd left school as quickly as I could at the end of the day to get to Zayde's. The TV was on when I opened the back door.

"Zayde!" I called out.

"I'm in here. In the living room!" he yelled back.

I went over to the kitchen table and glanced underneath. There were no books, no script, just a few crumbs and some dust bunnies. That would never have been allowed when Bubbie was still alive. What was I thinking? That wasn't my worry. Where was my script?

When I got to the living room, I had my answer. It was in my Zayde's hands. He was reading it.

"I thought I might see you today," he said. "I was going to call you and tell you that you left this here, but I didn't want to disturb you in school. School is important."

"I'm just glad you found it. You're reading it?"

"There was nothing much on TV." He paused. "I think I understand why your Bubbie liked this play so much."

"You like it?"

"Very much. The writer of this play, he was Jewish?"

"I think everybody who helped create it was. The music is by Jerry Bock, and the lyrics are by Sheldon Harnick. The book—that means the dialogue and the stage directions and everything—is by Joseph Stein. And the whole thing is based on some stories by a Yiddish writer, Sholem Aleichem."

"I'm familiar with the stories," he muttered.

"I'm glad you liked the play," I said.

"Why wouldn't I like it? And this Golde, I can see why you'd want to know about my mother. There is much they have in common. They were both power-houses . . . but then so is my granddaughter."

"Thank you, Zayde . . . but don't you kind of have to say nice things like that because you're my grandfather?"

He chuckled. "There is always choice. I could choose to say nothing. I never lie, you know that."

That was true. My Zayde always said what was on his mind—good or bad. My father said that his father sometimes lacked a "filter."

"You are going to do wonderful. I know you will break an arm."

"Break an arm . . . wait . . . you mean break a leg!"

"I knew it was something like that, but neither makes much sense. Just as long as you don't break your voice, am I right?"

"Do you think that maybe you could come to the show?" I had asked before, but it was worth another shot.

He shrugged. "Who can predict the future?"

I had promised my parents that I'd be gentle with Zayde so I wasn't going to push. But then I turned my head and saw it—the violin. It was in the dining room, sitting on the buffet, out of its case, its broken strings spiking into the air and its bow at its side. There was something about the way it was catching and reflecting the light that made it seem to almost glow. And more than that, I felt as if it were looking right at me as I looked at it.

"Your violin," I said, my voice barely a whisper.

"Yes, yes, it has been sitting there staring at me all day."

It startled me that he was thinking the same thing I was thinking. "I just thought it would be in your bedroom, or back in the attic again."

"Those stairs to the attic are steep and I promised your father that I would not climb them anymore."

"I could take it up if you wanted."

"No, I don't think so. Even up there I would still know it was in the house." He hesitated and then looked at me. "I think I want to tell you more of my story. Do you want to hear it?"

I nodded. As much as I had come to find the script, I had also come hoping to hear more about Zayde's life.

He closed his eyes as though steeling himself to face the past. Finally, he opened them and began to talk.

"After the Nazis had surrounded us in the forest, they marched us away. We had no idea where we were going— where they would be taking us. All we knew was that we had to stay together. My mother—your Golde—it was as if she grew longer arms to wrap around all of us."

He paused. I could almost see her, my great-grandmother, casting her arms out like a giant fishing net to encircle her family.

"We ended up in a train station in Warsaw. I knew the city so well. We had played there as a family band many times. But nothing prepared me for the sight that greeted us on the platform. Hundreds, no, maybe thousands of Jews huddled in families like ours, waiting, just waiting. And the soldiers, they were everywhere, shouting, ordering us to move closer, then to stay put, then to move again. And just when I thought the platform could not hold one more person, the train slowly chugged into the station."

He paused again. His chin was trembling. I wanted to tell him he didn't have to go on, but before I could say a word, he began again.

"If I thought the platform was overcrowded, it was nothing compared to what it was like inside that train. You've been on a train, Shirli?"

I nodded. We had taken the train into New York many times.

"This one wasn't for people. It was for cows. An empty, smelly box. And the soldiers shoved and pushed and forced us inside until we were packed so tightly we could barely breathe. And somehow, my mother still managed to keep us together. And I held that violin in my arms. All the other instruments had been left behind or taken away, but somehow I'd managed to keep my violin. People were shouting at me that it was taking up too much space, but still I held on to it. I don't even know why it was so important for me to keep it. But I did. And I held it all the way until we arrived . . . we arrived at . . . we . . ."

He faltered. I leaned forward. Where had they arrived? Suddenly he pointed to the violin.

"You know, a violin is more than an instrument. It is a living thing, an animal. Each one has an individual voice. But this one—it's a wounded animal. With the broken strings it is incomplete, unable to speak."

That's when I knew I had to step in. "I'm glad you didn't get rid of it," I said.

"I guess your Bubbie knew better than me. What do you think I should do with it?"

"My brother played the violin."

"Your brother? He never played the violin—he tortured it!"

We both laughed—finally!

"We're lucky your brother is good with math and chemistry. He will be a fine doctor, but he never had music in his soul . . . please never tell him I said that."

"I won't."

We sat there together in silence, staring at the violin. It was so quiet that I could hear the clock on the wall ticking. I wanted to ask him one more question, and even though I worried I might be pushing him, I had to know.

"Zayde, were you a good violinist?"

He shook his head. "I was not good. I was *brilliant*."

I laughed, and he smiled.

"I just wish I could have been there." I cringed as the words came out of my mouth. "I mean, I wish I could have heard you play."

"I thank God every day that you were not there or your brother or your parents. That you were able to be free, to be safe." Then he shook his head. "But enough. No more for today. You came for your script." He handed it to me.

"Thank you, Zayde."

"Now, where are my manners? Here you are, my precious granddaughter, and I did not offer you something to drink. What sort of host am I? Would you like some apple juice?"

"I'd like that."

He got up from his chair. "Come to the kitchen and I will pour us both a glass." He took a few steps down the hall and then stopped. "Do you think you could do me a favor?"

"Anything."

"Do you think you could put the violin away for me?"

"Up in the attic?"

"No, no, just in the case. And then close the clasps. I could do it, but I think maybe it would be better if you did. Okay?"

"Of course."

He shuffled down the hall leaving me and the violin alone. I walked toward it slowly, cautiously, the way you would approach a wounded animal. *Where did you and my Zayde end up?* I wondered. *And how did you get here?* That was what I wanted to ask. But instead, I whispered, "It's all right. I'm not going to hurt you. I'm just going to put you in your bed."

The snapped strings splayed out like tentacles, and I was careful not to touch the shredded fibers as I gently picked it up. It was cool and smooth and somehow felt right in my hands.

My Zayde was right. This was more than an instrument. It was a time machine, a link to his past, and my history.

I placed it into the case, nestling it into the blue velvet, snuggling it down into the spot where it belonged.

"Good night," I said as I closed the case.

CHAPTER ELEVEN

B en was coming to our house for Friday night dinner. And I was freaking out! Actually, it was Natasha, *my dear friend*, who had orchestrated the whole thing—cornering me and Ben after rehearsal on Tuesday and then shoving her face right in front of his.

"So, remember when you said you wanted to find out more about a medical career?" she asked.

Ben nodded. My mouth went dry.

"I happen to know that Shirli's brother, Adam, is going to be home from university this weekend." And then she stared right at me with that look on her face that said, *Do it. Ask him. Or I'll do it for you.*

"Um, yeah," I blurted. "Do you want to come for dinner on Friday? We could use it as a chance to rehearse at my house." Could I have sounded any more pathetic or desperate? But to my surprise—no, to my *shock*—he said yes.

And now I was running around the house like an Energizer bunny, checking the table to make sure that it was set properly and that we had enough chairs. Zayde was coming, and of course Adam would be there. I had begged Natasha to come but she'd turned me down. "Hey, I did the hard part. I got you to set this up," she said. "Now the rest is up to you."

The rest? I didn't even know what that meant! Tash and I had both agreed that I didn't have a chance with Ben. Now she was hinting at something else. I couldn't even think about that. What I did know was that I had to prep my family for the conversation that might come up at the dinner table.

"Okay, here are the rules," I said, assembling my parents and Adam in the dining room. "Don't ask him if he's got a girlfriend. Don't ask about religion. I've already told you that he isn't Jewish. And please . . ." and I paused here to make sure they knew I was dead serious, "do not ask him what it's like to be my onstage husband!"

"Okay, so now I know the first three things I'm going to ask him. Thanks, Sis!" my brother said. Then he smiled. "Come on, Shirli, give me some credit. I've been in the hot seat in this family, and as much as I'd like to torture you in the same way, I will try to rise above it."

About six months earlier, Adam had brought home a girl he was dating and dinner had practically turned into a courtroom interrogation. My mother had even asked her if she ever wanted children! I thought Adam was going to die of embarrassment!

"Is there anything we *are* allowed to say?" my father asked.

I ignored the sarcasm in his voice. "Sure," I replied. "I told you he wants to be a doctor. So, stick to questions about medicine."

"Stop twirling your hair, Shirli," my mom commanded. Then she sighed and went off to the kitchen, muttering something about having to take orders from her daughter, and how she might as well just stay in the kitchen all evening.

By the time Ben arrived I was close to a meltdown, and just to make matters worse, he walked in the door with Zayde! I'd been hoping to get my grandfather on his own and give him the same instructions I'd given the rest of the family. But no such luck!

"I met this young man when the taxi dropped me off," Zayde said, removing his coat and handing it to me. "He helped me up the walkway. Such a nice boy. We introduced ourselves. His name is Ben Morgan."

"I know, Zayde. He's my friend."

"Friend?"

Oh no! Zayde was raising his eyebrows and winking at me like he had something stuck in his eye.

"Aren't you a little young to have a boyfriend?" he asked.

"He's not my *boyfriend*—he's a friend who is a boy," I sputtered. "We're in the play together, Zayde. Ben is playing Tevye."

Ben hadn't said a word yet. He was just standing in the doorway, looking kind of awkward, which I would have guessed was impossible for him. From the look on his face I wouldn't have been surprised if he had turned around and bolted out the door. If he did, I was running out with him. Why had I invited him for a proper family dinner instead of a casual snack?

"Did you say your last name was Morgan?" Zayde asked.

Ben nodded, and I gulped.

"The rabbi at our synagogue is Joseph Morgan. Used to be Morganstern in the old country. Do you know him?"

My face was burning. We hadn't even made it past the foyer and Zayde had already started with the embarrassing questions and forbidden topics. At this point I was silently thinking of ways to punish Natasha for setting this whole thing up. But before I could say a word, Ben replied.

"No, Mr. Berman, my family isn't Jewish."

There it was, right out in the open.

"Not Jewish? And you're playing an old Jewish milkman in this play? How do you do that?"

This time, I got there before Ben. "Zayde, it's called acting. Ben is a great actor. And a really good singer."

Now it was Ben's turn to blush. "Shirli's exaggerating," he said quickly. "But Tevye is a great part to play. And I'm learning a lot about Jewish history."

Zayde didn't look convinced. "Not Jewish, huh?"

"Okay, why don't we go to the table? Is that Mom calling us to eat? I'm sure she's calling us to eat." I grabbed Zayde by the arm and steered him into the dining room. Ben followed. I was in charge of the seating plan— another rule I had established well in advance—and I managed to put Zayde at one end of the table and Ben next to Adam at the other end. I figured it was better to keep them as far apart as possible.

My brother had promised he'd help me out. But just for good measure, I gave him one of those pleading stares, begging him to help keep the conversation in neutral territory. Adam grinned as though he was really enjoying the whole awkward situation, and then he turned his attention to Ben.

"So," he said, "I hear you're thinking about going to med school. Anything you want to ask me?"

I could have hugged my brother! For the next forty minutes or so, through the soup course, salad, and chicken with potatoes and vegetables, my family actually managed to keep the conversation focused on medicine. Adam talked about pre-med and all the courses he was taking to get himself ready to apply for med school, my mother talked about pursuing a specialty, and my dad talked about the long hours and the sacrifices a doctor has to make. Twice, my mother had to answer her pager and go to the kitchen to call the hospital. At one point, just before the main course, it looked as though she might have to go in for a delivery, but it turned out to be a false alarm.

Ben asked a million questions that my mom and Adam were only too happy to answer. There was more medical talk at the dinner table than I had ever heard, and that was just fine with me. I was feeling pretty good, actually starting to relax. There was only dessert to go, and then Ben and I could excuse ourselves and go rehearse.

Through all of this I still had one eye on Zayde, who had been very quiet.

"Are you okay?" I asked him after we had cleared the dinner plates.

He looked up at me. "Hmm?"

"Can you hear everything, Zayde? Do you want us to speak up?"

He shrugged. "What's to hear? I feel like I'm at a medical convention, not a family dinner."

"That's my fault, Mr. Berman." Ben spoke up from the other end of the table. "There was a lot I wanted to find out about a career in medicine."

"After all these questions, you could be a surgeon by now," Zayde said.

"But I'm also interested in finding out about your

background—maybe getting some information that could help me with my character in *Fiddler*?"

My whole body suddenly clenched. I had been so focused on making sure that my family didn't ask Ben any personal questions that I hadn't for one second thought that Ben might ask something personal of my grandfather. My parents, Adam, and I all froze, staring at Ben and at Zayde.

"Wait, is . . . is something wrong?" Ben stammered. "Did I say something I'm not supposed to?"

I leaned toward him and lowered my voice. "My grandfather is a little sensitive about his past."

That's when Zayde interrupted me. "You think if you whisper I can't hear you? I'm not deaf."

Under any other circumstance that would have been hilarious, because my Zayde was definitely hard of hearing and everyone, including him, knew it. But suddenly, it was as if he was tuned in to every word that was being spoken.

"I wasn't trying to hide anything from you, Zayde. I just didn't think you'd want to talk—"

"I can answer the question myself," Zayde said. And then he turned back to Ben. "So, Ben Morgan, you want to know about my background? Let me tell you about it. Do you know anything about the Holocaust?"

My stomach dropped.

"I know some things," Ben said. "I know there were concentration camps. And I know that Jews were tortured and killed in them."

Zayde nodded. "And do you know the name of the concentration camp that was one of the worst? Where over a million Jews were killed?"

Ben shook his head. I was still sitting in silent disbelief that the conversation had suddenly turned this way. I stared at Ben, and then at my grandfather.

"My family . . . we were sent on a transport to one of the concentration camps, the worst one. When the doors of the train opened, I asked a man where we were. 'Hell,' he replied. I soon discovered what Hell was called. Auschwitz," Zayde said. "My family and me. We were imprisoned in Auschwitz."

And then, slowly and deliberately, Zayde began to unbutton the cuff of his long-sleeved shirt. I couldn't believe what he was doing. He rolled the sleeve up, up, past his elbow, to reveal the line of blue numbers tattooed on his forearm. Seeing it coming didn't make it any less shocking. Then he extended his arm toward Ben.

"Have you ever seen one of these?" he asked.

"No, sir." Ben gulped and stared along with the rest of us.

"Our names were taken away. Our homes were gone. Our families were gone. And this is what we were given instead. This is how we were greeted in Auschwitz—with a tattoo carved into our arms."

With that, Zayde drew back his arm and rolled his shirt sleeve back down.

"This is always with me, Ben Morgan. Even when I cover it up. My past is never simply in my past."

CHAPTER TWELVE

"**I** hope your grandfather isn't mad at me."

Ben and I were in the downstairs rec room. After Ben's question had led to Zayde's revelation about having been imprisoned in Auschwitz, conversation at the table had—not surprisingly—kind of stalled out, and we'd managed to excuse ourselves from the table to go and rehearse. We hadn't even waited for dessert.

"Did you know that he was in that place?" Ben asked.

I shook my head. "That was the first time he's ever talked about where he was sent . . . at least to me. I guess my father knew." Although, judging from his surprised look, I wasn't really sure that was true. "I've seen the numbers on his arm before, but kind of accidentally, not because he showed me. It's always been this unspoken rule not to ask. But lately, my grandfather's been telling us about this stuff, and it's kind of a shock for everyone."

I'd have liked to confess to Ben that it was me asking Zayde questions that had caused all this emotional upheaval, but I was feeling too guilty to say it out loud. Somehow, my getting a part in *Fiddler* had opened doors I didn't even know existed.

"I had a great-uncle who was part of a unit that liberated one of the concentration camps," Ben said. "He never talked about what he saw when he went in. We all figured it must have been pretty awful. And then, just before he died, he started to tell us everything. I think he needed to unload it all, you know, like he needed to get it off his chest."

I nodded. "That's the way it's been with my grandfather, except that he talks, then he shuts down, then he talks again. I know there's so much more to his story. I just don't know when he's going to reveal it all."

"He seems like a pretty remarkable guy."

"He is. And there's a whole part of his life that has to do with music and this old violin that I found in his attic when I was looking for costumes for the play."

"Speaking of the play, we should probably get to work rehearsing."

Right! We were here to practice our parts. But it had become surprisingly comfortable—easy, even—to sit and talk with Ben. Maybe that was because our being more than just friends wasn't even in the world of extreme possibilities. The whole school had been in shock when he broke up with Emma. We all figured it was a forever deal—the golden couple that meets in junior high and goes on to get happily-ever-after married. If he was going to end up with somebody else, it would probably be another kid in ninth grade, maybe Mindi or somebody like her.

"So, do you want to run through some scenes?" Ben asked. "Maybe the dream sequence in the first act?"

There is a moment in the play when Tevye promises his daughter Tzeitel that she can marry the man she loves instead of the man who has been chosen for her. But then he has to find a way to tell Golde about this, because she still thinks that an arranged marriage is the way to go. So Tevye concocts a story about an elaborate dream he's had, in which he was visited by a ghost who told him to go with Tzeitel's choice. Golde is so superstitious that she falls for the whole scheme. It's a great scene, complete with screeching phantoms and a song that's a real show-stopper.

Ben and I rehearsed as much of the scene as we could in the absence of the full ensemble. We both knew our lines and it went really smoothly. We were completely in sync with one another. Ben was starting to put away his script when he suddenly looked up at me.

"I know you're understudying Hodel. Why don't you sing her solo? I'd love to hear you do it."

"You mean now . . . right now?" I stammered. "Here?"

"Sure. Unless you don't know it yet."

Hodel's song comes at a point in the play when her love has been imprisoned in Siberia. She is leaving her home, her parents, and her siblings to go and be close to him. She's at the train station, saying goodbye to her father, Tevye, not knowing when or if she'll ever see him again. I knew the song. I had sung it dozens of times—rehearsed it in my room and in the bathroom and just about everywhere else, including my dreams. But I had never yet sung it in front of anyone.

"So, will you do it?"

I gulped. "Sure. Okay. Just don't laugh or anything."

Ben frowned. "Why would I laugh? You have the best voice of anyone I know."

If I hadn't turned to put my script away, Ben would have seen my face go beet-red. By the time I turned back to him, I had composed myself. He sat down on the couch and I stood in front of him.

"Whenever you're ready," Ben said.

I took a deep breath, closed my eyes, and began to sing the heartbreaking words of a girl who is making the hardest decision of her life, and hoping her father can understand why she has to leave her home—and everything and everyone she has ever known—to be with the one she loves.

I sang through the whole song, putting as much feeling and emotion into it as I could. And a strange thing happened. As much as I had started out wanting to impress Ben, as the song went on I actually almost forgot he was in the room. The joy of performing simply washed over me, and everything else disappeared. I *became* Hodel, devastated to be leaving her father, but firm in her desire to be with her true love, no matter what.

When I was finished, I just stood there, eyes still closed. And then, slowly, I opened them and looked at Ben. But, to my surprise, he wasn't looking back at me. His eyes were focused over my shoulder and behind me. I turned to follow his gaze and there was Zayde standing in the doorway of the rec room, his mouth open, his eyes glued on me.

"Zayde! How long—?" I didn't have a chance to finish the question.

"I had no idea," he said, breathless, as if someone had punched him in the stomach, knocking the wind out of him. "All these years . . . I had no idea."

"Zayde, do you need to sit down?" He ignored the question.

"Your voice. It's like . . . it's like an angel. I never knew. How could I not know this?"

I shrugged. "Bubbie heard me sing. I used to perform for her when you were out of the house. And she came to my recitals." And with those words I felt such an ache, such a sense of loss that she wasn't still here. "But I understand that it's been hard for you," I added.

Zayde shook his head. "I've missed so much. I think your grandmother had hoped I would come out to one of your performances. But I never did. I couldn't."

"That's okay, Zayde. Really it is. I'm glad you heard me now. And you liked it?"

"Liked it?" His eyes were lit up in a way that I had never seen. "I loved it!"

Just then I heard someone cough and clear their throat behind me. *Ben!* I had forgotten all about him. I whirled around just as he was rising from the couch.

"I should probably get going," he said.

"No, you don't have to go."

"I've got an essay due Monday that I haven't even started." He paused. "You were great, Shirli. Like your grandfather said—the voice of an angel."

I didn't say a word, but I thought my heart was going to explode out of my chest.

"It was very nice to meet you, Mr. Berman." Ben extended a hand to my grandfather, who grasped it and shook it slowly, up and down.

"Nice to meet you too, Ben Morgan." Zayde squinted at Ben. "Do you sing as well as my granddaughter?"

"I try. But I don't think anyone comes close."

The pounding in my chest was moving up to my ears.

"Hmm." Zayde looked thoughtful. "One day, I may just have to listen in on you as well."

CHAPTER THIRTEEN

Deliberately, slowly, I walked toward the dressing room as Mindi stood on stage and began to sing *my* song. I didn't need to watch her, but there was nowhere to go where I wouldn't have to hear her. It was kind of painful for me. I had to admit she was pretty good, but I knew I could sing it better than her. Even Ben had said that I had the best voice of anyone he knew. As she began to sing, I began to quietly hum along.

My head was still spinning from our Friday night dinner—Ben being there, Zayde's revelation about Auschwitz, and then him hearing me sing and telling me I had the voice of an angel. Maybe, just maybe, I could convince him to come and see the show. It was still too soon to pose the question again. But after Friday night, I felt as if we had crossed a hurdle. When the time was right—whenever that might be—I'd ask again.

I closed the door behind me. The dressing room was empty, and I was grateful for that. I didn't want to hear anybody complimenting her "wonderful voice" or saying what a great singer she was. She was good, and her performance made the play better overall. I wish I could have just been happy for that.

My phone chimed in my pocket. The cellphone had been a gift from my parents after 9/11. They wanted to know where I was all the time, and how to reach me in case of an emergency. Many of my friends had been given one, too, around that time. It wasn't just my parents who were worried. Sometimes it seemed as though everybody was worried.

I pulled the phone from my pocket, surprised because I almost always remembered to silence the ringer. If Ms. Ramsey had heard it, she would have had a fit.

"Hello?"

"Hello?" The speaker had a thick accent that I didn't recognize. "I need . . . speak . . . somebody." Even worse, the reception was bad, and I was only picking up every second word.

"Hello . . . hear me?" he said.

"Not very well. Who is this?"

He mentioned a name but I couldn't quite make it out. "Look, I can't really hear you. I don't know if you can hear me. I think you might have a wrong number."

More static and then: "... my store ... at my store ... please come."

Not a wrong number. It was some sort of tele-marketer. I was about to hang up when there was another burst of static and then one word: "Zayde."

I yanked the phone back up to my ear. "Did you say Zayde?" I exclaimed.

More static, then a couple more words. "At my store ... Zayde."

"My Zayde is at your store?"

More static.

"Wait, wait, please. I have to get outside so I can hear you!"

I pushed open the door just as Mindi was reaching for the high notes. She tended to over-sing everything. The girl didn't know subtle.

The fastest way out was through a door that opened to the football field behind the school. "I'm coming. I'm coming," I yelled into the phone. Then I stepped through the door. "I'm here. Can you hear me?"

The line was dead; the call had dropped. I looked at my phone in disbelief. Whoever it was they were gone. It certainly wasn't my Zayde, but was it something to do with him? Or had I just misheard through all the static and broken words?

The number was there on my phone. I was just about to call it back when the phone rang again in my hands. I pushed *accept* and it came to life.

"Hello, hello, I'm here, I'm here!" I practically yelled.

"This is Shirli?"

"Yes, this is Shirli. You called me. You mentioned my Zayde."

"Yes, yes."

"Is he all right?" I felt panicky.

"Yes, he is fine . . . mostly good and fine."

"Mostly?"

"He fell down and needs assistance. I am observing him."

"Is this a hospital? Are you calling from a hospital?"

"This is a store. Amir's grocery store. I am Amir. He fell on the sidewalk in front of my store. I went out to gather him from the pavement."

"And he's okay?" I gasped.

"Do you wish to speak to him?" Amir asked.

"Yes, yes, please!"

There was silence, and then I heard muffled voices, and then, my grandfather came on the line.

"Hello, hello, is this my Shirli?"

"Zayde, what happened? Are you okay?"

"I'm fine."

"He said you fell."

"A little trip over my big feet. It's nothing. My friend Amir is simply being too cautious. I told him I could walk home."

"Home from where? Where are you?"

"Amir's store. It's on Jefferson Street."

"Jefferson . . . you're downtown?"

"It's the only place I could get what I needed. Amir does not want me to leave on my own. He's worried."

"I'm worried too. Should I call Mom or Dad?"

"They are both so busy, you know how hard it is to get in touch with them. I was wondering . . . would you come and get me . . . take a taxi maybe?"

I'd never taken a cab on my own before. But I answered without hesitation. "Yes, of course. Tell me where you are, the address."

"I'm not sure exactly. I'll pass the phone back to Amir."

~

I tried to pick out the numbers on the buildings from the back seat of the cab. I was getting pretty close now.

The whole thing felt like an anxious blur—the phone call, telling Ms. Ramsey I had to leave early because of a family emergency, calling a cab, and then waiting for what felt like an eternity until it arrived. The driver was trying to make small talk, and the ride through rush-hour traffic seemed to be taking forever. The address I'd been given was close to forty blocks away. How had Zayde got here to begin with? Had he walked?

I pointed at the sign—AMIR'S GROCETERIA— before the driver picked out the address. He pulled into an open space in front of the store. Then, I got out of the cab so quickly I almost forgot to pay! Thankfully, the driver was a sympathetic guy and patiently waited for me to fumble with some bills.

A bell above the door announced my entrance.

"Amir . . . Zayde?" I called out.

"Here, back here!"

I rounded a big display of potato chips and there was my grandfather. He was sitting on a chair. His pants were ripped at the knees and he was holding a bag of ice to the side of his head. I could see traces of dried blood on his face.

"Zayde!" I ran over and threw my arms around him.

"It's all right, it's all right. I'm fine."

"He's doing much better." A short man with brown skin was standing next to him. The man appeared to be younger than Zayde but older than my parents.

"This is my good friend, my new friend, Amir."

"I'm pleased to meet you," I said.

"And I, you," he answered.

Amir was dressed in narrow-legged trousers and a long white shirt that fell below his knees. He took my hand and shook it vigorously.

"I'm so sorry to have put everybody to such trouble," my grandfather said.

"It was not trouble. It was a pleasure to meet such a fine gentleman," Amir said.

"The pleasure was mine. You know, Shirli, we were telling stories about coming to America. Fifty years apart, but some things haven't changed."

"Human nature remains a constant," Amir said.

"Amir tells me he is from India. And back there, he was a lawyer," my grandfather said.

"You would not suspect from my present surroundings. From the courthouse to the snack aisle. But at least here there is freedom and opportunity for my children."

"Yes, freedom is a good thing," my grandfather replied. "But now, it's time for me to go."

Zayde made a move to get up and Amir was instantly at his side.

"So, how much do I owe you for the ice?" Zayde asked.

"You would owe me nothing, even if you had the money."

"Then the next time, I will treat you to coffee, understood?" my grandfather said.

"Yes, of course. It would not be for me to argue with you. It would be my pleasure and my honor to share a coffee, sir."

"Now, before I leave, I need to use your facilities one more time," Zayde said.

He tottered down the aisle toward the back of the store, leaving Amir and me alone.

"What was my grandfather buying in your store?" I asked.

"He was not going *to* my store, but *by* my store."

"Oh, I see. Do you know where he was going?"

He shook his head. "I only saw him through the window as he tripped on the pavement. I went outside to offer my assistance."

"Thank you for doing that."

"It was just courtesy. Then I realized that he had far to go, and at night after dark in this neighborhood is not the best time. He told me that he spent all his money and could not afford a cab."

"But he always has money." That was confusing.

"I would have lent him the fare, but still I felt he should not go unescorted. He bumped his head. That is when I insisted that I call somebody he knew. I would have driven him myself but there is no other person to run the store. I'm working alone this evening."

"I'm just glad you called."

"Speaking of which, would you like me to call a taxi?"

"Yes, please," I answered.

⁊

Twenty minutes later we were in a cab, and Zayde was waving to Amir, who stood in the doorway of his shop waving back.

"That Amir is a fine fellow."

"He seems very nice."

"Did you notice how his store had a fresh coat of paint?" Zayde asked. "Some fools spray-painted all over the side of the building. Do you know what they wrote?"

Before I could even think to answer he continued.

"They wrote 'Terrorists' and 'Taliban.'"

"That's awful."

"It's disgusting," he said, spitting the words out. "Amir is Hindu. But even if he were a Muslim, that does not make him a terrorist. Those people with the spray cans, *they* are the terrorists. It makes you think of Nazi Germany. Amir said that since 9/11 things have been different."

"They've been different for everybody," I said.

"More different and difficult for some people, I think," Zayde said.

"I'm just glad he was there to help you. I'm glad you're all right," I said.

"A little bump on the noggin is not going to hurt me."

"Zayde, where were you going?"

"I had an errand to run. I needed those ten extra bananas."

"That's not funny. Whatever it was, you could have asked me to do it, or Dad or Mom."

"It was something you couldn't get. None of you could. It needed to be me."

"What was it?" I asked.

"Isn't an old man entitled to a secret?"

I didn't know how to answer that. My grandfather seemed to have no end of secrets. And now he was presenting me with another.

"Well, why didn't you have money for a cab?"

"I had money when I left home. I just didn't have enough on me. I spent it all on my purchase. I had no idea how much they would cost. So, I thought I would just walk home. I like to walk."

"And you're not going to tell me what you bought?"

"Not now. Maybe I'll show you, but not now, not yet."

"Okay, if you didn't want to talk to me, then why did you have Amir call me instead of Mom or Dad?"

"I could only remember your number."

"Then I have to get the cab driver to take us to the hospital to have your head checked," I said.

"What?"

"You remember every number you've ever heard." Zayde could forget a name a second after he heard it. But numbers? After years of being an accountant, numbers had become his life.

"Okay, maybe I remembered their telephone numbers, but I didn't want them to come and pick me up. You know how busy they are."

"I don't think that's the reason," I said. "Was it because you thought they'd be angry?"

"I thought they'd be worried. And that is why I'm going to ask a favor of you."

"You don't want me to tell them, right?"

"Such a smart girl. I was hoping it could just be our little secret."

More secrets! When was it going to end?

"Well?" he asked.

"Okay, here's the deal," I replied. "I won't tell Mom and Dad about this if you tell me why you were out. What do you think about that?"

"That sounds like blackmail," he said.

"How about we just say we have an agreement?"

"Then we have an agreement. But I don't want to *tell* you my secret, I want to *show* you. Tomorrow. Is tomorrow good?"

"Tomorrow is good." It was looking like the best deal I was going to get.

CHAPTER FOURTEEN

I don't know how I made it through my classes the next day. My brain was so focused on Zayde's latest secret that it was nearly impossible to concentrate on anything else. Teacher after teacher trained their death stares on me when I failed to answer a question. Even Natasha, who knew me better than anyone, couldn't figure out what was wrong.

"Okay, spill it," she said, cornering me in the cafeteria. "You look like you're on another planet."

I quickly filled her in on Zayde's last escapade, culminating with his promise to *show* me what he had gone all the way downtown to buy.

"Any guesses about what it might be?"

"Not a clue," I replied. "But I'm going over to his place as soon as I can to find out."

First, though, there was an after-school rehearsal to get through. No, not just get through. I had to be fully focused, or Ms. Ramsey was going to get on my case. Today I'd need my acting skills to make the rest of the cast believe I was Golde . . . *and* to make Ms. Ramsey believe that the play had my full and undivided attention!

Everything started well. Everyone in the cast was pretty well prepared. We still had a couple of months before our opening, but most of us were "off book" so we knew our lines and didn't need to hold our scripts. Ms. Ramsey was smiling and complimenting us on how well we were doing.

"At this rate, we'll be able to block the whole show by the end of next week."

Blocking meant coming up with a plan for where we'd stand and walk for every single moment we were onstage. It was basically like setting the choreography for the entire show.

"And once the blocking is set, we can just run the show every rehearsal until opening." Ms. Ramsey was beaming.

But that was before everything began to go horribly wrong. I think it must have started when Ms. Ramsey said, "Let's take it from the top."

The opening sequence of the show revolved around a song called "Tradition." Each of the villagers—referred to in the script as the Mamas, the Papas, the Sons, and the Daughters—sang about who they were and the important role they played in the community. The entire cast was on stage, and the blocking that Ms. Ramsey was talking about was critically important, because each group took a turn at the front of the stage and then moved off to make room for the next group.

It all started pretty smoothly. Ben—as Tevye—was introducing the town of Anatevka where the play was set, and the Papas were about to sing their opening. But a moment later there was chaos onstage. The Papas collided with the Mamas, who bumped into the Sons and then the Daughters. And before long, everyone was mixed up with everyone else and no one knew where to go or what to do. Meanwhile, the Rabbi, played by this guy named Michael, was supposed to be nodding his head back and forth as if he were deep in prayer. But something had gotten into him and his prayer had turned into a convulsion. It looked as if he had a Hula-Hoop around his middle and he was desperately trying to keep it up! Mindi started to have a laughing fit that was bubbling over to others in the cast. I thought Ms. Ramsey was going to have a stroke.

"Stop, stop, stop!" she shouted, each command louder than the one before. "What is *wrong* with you people? Why can you not follow a simple stage direction?"

Her face was red and her eyes were practically bulging out of her head. She had yelled at us in rehearsals before, but this felt like a full-blown meltdown. The compliments from earlier in the rehearsal disappeared, and the good feeling about how the play was progressing went with it. The room fell still.

"I didn't think we were that bad," I muttered under my breath to Natasha, who was standing close to me.

"Do you have something to say, Ms. Berman?"

I didn't think anyone but Tash had heard me, least of all Ms. Ramsey. But it was as if she had suddenly developed super-sensitive hearing.

"Sorry, Ms. Ramsey," I said.

"No, please. If you have something to say, then say it to everyone. I know you know how to project."

The room went even quieter than before. Everyone was staring at me, and then at Ms. Ramsey, as though we were squaring off in one of those wrestling matches that Zayde watched on TV.

Zayde! I had no time for a fight with Ms. Ramsey. I needed to get through the rehearsal and then get over to his house. Besides, fighting with Ms. Ramsey might compromise my chance of getting that juicy lead role next year, and I certainly didn't want to risk that. But it seemed as if I had waded into something, and instead of stopping myself I decided to dive.

"I was just saying that I thought we were doing well, Ms. Ramsey," I said, trying to be respectful and honest.

"You think that last run-through was good?" Ms. Ramsey wasn't backing down. Her eyes were pretty steely and her jaw was set.

My hands were winding my hair up and down like a yo-yo. I gulped and glanced over at Natasha. She edged slightly away from me, and the expression on her face seemed to say, *You're on your own.* But then I looked over at Ben. At first I thought he was going to abandon me too. But he fixed me with a look of admiration and nodded his head. That was the encouragement I needed. I took a deep breath.

"Everyone is working really hard, Ms. Ramsey," I said. "We all want the show to be good. We want your constructive criticism, but it doesn't help when you yell."

And that's when I saw her flinch. Her face went pale and she looked away. When she turned back to me, her expression had softened.

"I'm . . . I'm sorry, Ms. Berman . . . Shirli," she began. "You're right. Yelling doesn't do anyone any good."

Wait! What? Was Ms. Ramsey actually apologizing?

"You are all really quite wonderful." She was addressing the whole cast now. "And if I become impatient, it's only because I feel as if I'm under a lot of pressure with this production. I had hoped that there would be more staff support coming forward, but Ms. Lofsky, who had originally offered, has extended her leave of absence, and Mr. Martello, who had tentatively agreed to work with the set designers, felt he needed to fully commit to the school trip to Greece."

I'd been surprised from the beginning that so few of the school staff were involved. I'd heard rumors that Ms. Lofsky was going to come back and join us, but apparently now it was just going to be Ms. Ramsey and our accompanist, the ever-silent Mr. Nevarez.

She went on, "I understand their reasons, but there are really no other teachers who can assist me. I'm kind of left carrying the ball all by myself here."

The pressure that Ms. Ramsey was feeling had to be enormous. I wondered if she could handle it alone.

"But that's no excuse for me to lose my temper," she added. "And the next time I do, and there will probably be a next time"—and then she looked at me—"I want you to call me on it again. Do we have a deal?"

It felt as if all the tension in the room evaporated. Everyone on stage began to nod their heads.

I stared straight at Ms. Ramsey and said, "Deal!"

CHAPTER FIFTEEN

I bolted out of there the minute rehearsal was finally over. I didn't even stop to say goodbye to Natasha— I just pantomimed that I'd call her later. But when I reached the door and heard Ben call my name, I couldn't help it, I paused and waited for him to catch up. We hadn't talked much lately, and after rehearsals we'd been taking off in opposite directions. I had to wonder: was it possible he was avoiding me? Or maybe I was avoiding him.

"You were great back there," he said.

"Thanks." I glanced at the door, anxious to get out of the building and reluctant to leave all at the same time. I had to admit that my heart rate picked up whenever Ben stood close to me, the way he did now—his eyes staring right into mine. "I don't know what got into me. I'm usually not that bold."

"You had the guts to stand up to Ms. Ramsey. No one else did."

I hoped Ben wouldn't notice the line of sweat that had suddenly beaded up across my forehead. *Is it hot in here?*

"Ms. Ramsey is a great director and a really good teacher," I said. "She just needed to blow off some steam, I guess."

"So," he continued, "if the acting thing doesn't work out for you, you could be a lawyer, or a diplomat."

I reached to wipe my forehead with my sleeve. "Nah, I think I'll just stick with acting."

Then the two of us just stood there staring at each other, until Ben finally broke the awkward silence.

"I had a great time at your house the other night."

"You . . . you did?" I stammered. "I mean, yeah, it was good. I'm glad we got to rehearse together away from all of this."

"We should do it again."

I couldn't believe I was hearing this. Was Ben actually inviting himself over to my house again? Or was he just being polite? Wait until Tash heard this!

"Sure," I said eagerly—maybe a little too eagerly. And then there was silence again. "Look, Ben," I finally said, "I'm sorry, but I've got to get out of here. I'm supposed to be at my grandfather's."

"Can you please say hi to him from me?"

"Oh, for sure," I replied.

"You don't want to keep him waiting. I think he might be even tougher than Ms. Ramsey!"

At that, I finally laughed out loud. I opened the door and stepped out into the cold evening air, and I called back over my shoulder, "But he's really a teddy bear on the inside."

∽

I unlocked the back door to Zayde's house and walked in, brushing the snow off my jacket and taking off my boots. My stomach was churning. Ben wanted to come back to my house. Wow. I knew it didn't really mean anything, but . . . a girl could dream, couldn't she? And then there was Zayde's secret.

I hated surprises. The one surprise birthday party that I'd had—Natasha had organized it for me in sixth grade—had turned out to be a bust, because I got to her house early and ruined everything. Then Natasha got upset, which upset me. The whole thing was a disaster. It was so thoughtful of her and I really loved her for it, but I made her promise *never* to do it again. So the fact that Zayde had another secret—something he had to show me—was tying my stomach in knots.

I heard music coming from the living room. At first, I thought it was the TV. Was Zayde listening to some sort of concert, or was it just a commercial? I knew it wasn't the radio because he didn't have one, and while Bubbie had owned an old record player, she had used it only when Zayde was out of the house, and it had disappeared shortly after her death. We all assumed he'd tossed it out.

I made my way through the kitchen and down the hall past the dining room, moved by the sound of long, soulful notes from a violin, strung together to create a melody that was both sad and uplifting. It had to be on the TV, but there was something vaguely familiar about the tune—something I had heard perhaps as a child, buried in my memory. I didn't know what it was, but I was drawn to the song like a moth to light. The notes floated through the air, briefly suspended, like the snowflakes that were falling outside.

I turned the corner, entering the living room, and that's when I saw him. Zayde was standing in front of the fireplace, his back turned to me. The old violin that I had found in the attic was tucked under his chin. His right hand held the bow, which he drew across strings that had miraculously been repaired. Zayde was playing his violin!

He hadn't heard me yet and I didn't want him to. I just wanted to stand there and listen to him play. He swayed slightly from side to side, in time with the tune he was playing. His fingers on the neck of the violin seemed to skip over the strings as if they had lost all the stiffness that he often complained about. In fact, his whole body seemed lighter—younger—as if he had returned to a time in his childhood. I was frozen on the spot, captivated by the wonder of this sight, and by the music that was coming from my grandfather and his instrument. Finally, he finished playing and lowered the violin to his side.

"Zayde," I whispered.

He turned around to face me, his eyes glistening. "I've been practicing a little today. I didn't know if I'd remember how to play."

"I had no idea you could play like that—so amazing!" It was exactly like the moment when Zayde had heard me sing, except now we had switched places. "Is this your surprise?"

He nodded. "I found a place downtown that specializes in old violins. This one needed special strings, none of that synthetic phony stuff, real gut, and that was the only place that sold them."

"That's where you went the other day."

"Yes. I didn't know the strings would cost so much." He smiled sadly. "In the old country, they cost next to nothing. Now they've become as valuable as antiques. My father would have been in shock."

"And that's why you didn't have enough money to take a cab home." The pieces were all coming together now.

He nodded again. "That's why I had to walk, and that's when I met my new friend, that nice Mr. Amir, who helped me out when I fell in front of his store."

"Zayde, where did you learn to play like that?"

"From my father. I told you we were a musical family."

"Did you learn to read music?"

"Does a bird know how to read music?" he asked. "No, it just learns how to sing from its parents. That was me with my violin."

I paused. This whole moment was still so overwhelming. And then I remembered something else.

"Zayde, that song you were playing. There was something about it that was so familiar."

He smiled again. "It was your Bubbie's favorite. I would catch her humming it to you when you were young. She would stop when I walked into the room. But I knew the tune—one of the old folk songs my family played."

Yes, that was it! My grandmother had rocked me to sleep with that song. I hadn't heard it in years. But somehow my brain had held on to that musical memory. "I used to love it when she sang it to me."

"And she loved singing it."

I could feel my pulse racing, and my brain along with it. "This is fantastic, Zayde," I exclaimed. "It's like you've rediscovered something. My singing. Your violin playing. Maybe we could even rehearse together! You could play and I could sing and . . ."

I stopped when I noticed that my grandfather had turned away from me and was slowly replacing the violin in its case, which was sitting on the couch. He paused for a moment, letting his hands brush over the wooden frame as if he were caressing a child. Finally, he clipped the bow in its place in the lid of the case and closed it, clicking the latches down with a firm snap. Then he straightened.

"No, my sweet Shirli," he said. "I wanted you to see this and to thank you again for the chance to hear you sing the other night. But now, I need to put this away again. The playing . . . it was . . . it was too much for me."

"But Zayde, you have this gift," I began.

"Please don't ask me again, Shirli." Zayde looked down at the violin case. "I think this needs to go back in the attic. I thought I was ready, but I'm not."

I was at a loss for words. Why had Zayde shown me this, opened the door a crack into this world of possibilities, only to slam it shut again? It wasn't fair, and I wanted to tell him that. But then, I stopped. I couldn't imagine what it was that my grandfather was dealing with—what volcano of painful memories was bubbling up inside of him. I had to respect that. *You can't throw a kid into the deep end of a swimming pool and not worry that he might drown*, I reasoned. I had to let Zayde wade into his past at his own pace.

"Do you know why I needed to get the strings on my own?" Zayde asked.

I shook my head.

"I was afraid."

"Afraid of what?"

"Afraid that I would get to the store but wouldn't be able to go inside, or that I'd buy the strings, but instead of putting them on I'd just put them away. Or even if I put them on that it would be too emotional, too troubling, to ever actually play. And I didn't want anyone to see me if I couldn't go through with it all."

"But you did it. You did it all."

"I've done all that I can do."

I knew I couldn't push him any further. We both needed a way out.

"Do you want some tea, Zayde?" I finally asked.

"That would be nice. Did you bring me groceries today? I'm running out of bananas."

"I could come back with some tomorrow. Would forty be good?"

We left the living room and the violin behind and walked toward the kitchen. I felt as if I was losing Zayde once more. He was drifting back into that dark, painful place where the memories gnawed at him like a vulture on a carcass.

Had I lost him for good this time?

CHAPTER SIXTEEN

Rehearsals continued at a frantic pace over the next couple of weeks, interspersed with homework. I'd given up all my other extracurricular activities, but it still felt as if there was no break between day and night. Everything just blended into one continuous loop. Our opening in April, only six weeks away, was the reward we all had our eyes on.

One afternoon, I stood at the back of the auditorium looking down at the stage. Up close, it was obvious where there were faults and pieces of the set that didn't exactly fit together. However, from this distance, things looked remarkably real. Well, as real as a village sitting on a stage could look. Pretty much everything had been put together by the set crew—and they were still building. Any time we weren't actually using the stage, the noise of hammers and power tools punctuated the air and echoed around the auditorium. There was a barn, stage right, and the house, stage left, and at center stage there was a cart and a pile of hay. The hay had come from the farm where Mindi stabled her horse. Oh, that was another thing about Mindi. The girl had a horse. Of course, she was the sort who *would* have a horse.

Adding to the noise, the strings and the brass from the school orchestra were in the pit practicing the score. From the bits I could hear they apparently needed even more practice than we did. Strangely, the sounds of the hammers and power tools sometimes seemed like part of the music. I was pretty sure that the people wielding the hammers were deliberately adding a rhythm section.

The sets were supposed to have been finished by now. I think we had Mr. Martello's absence to blame for that. So now everything else was falling behind. Since we couldn't use the stage while set construction was happening, Ms. Ramsey had taken the ensemble into the drama room to work with them, leaving the leads to go over our parts and wait for her return. The fact that we were working alone was another sign that Ms. Ramsey badly needed help.

I'd mentioned all of this to my parents. In addition to blaming the problem on cutbacks and lack of funding for the arts, they talked about how "politics" was everywhere. They meant that since Ms. Ramsey was young and newer to the school there might be people who weren't happy about her suddenly being put in charge of the big school production, and so they wouldn't want to support her. That all made sense, until I started to think it through. I mean, who else was there who *could* have stepped up to help out at a time like this? To add to that, Mrs. Reynolds was the new head of the music department and she was still working hard to get a handle on her program.

Ben sat in an audience seat bent over his script. Every once in a while he raised his head and closed his eyes, and I could see his lips move as if he was reciting lines. A bit of his hair that usually spiked on top had fallen down over his forehead. I couldn't take my eyes off him.

At one point, Mindi walked past him, paused for a full minute, and then kept on going. Ben didn't seem to notice, but I did—I silently counted the seconds before she moved on. After Ben and Emma had broken up, and it became clear that they weren't going to be getting back together, other people started to see possibilities. One of those people was Mindi. Practically the whole school was watching her try to get close to Ben, so far with no success. By now, I thought I knew Ben well enough to know he wasn't interested. But that didn't mean she was going to give up trying.

I stood up and walked in Ben's direction, stopping in front of his seat. "Ben, do you think we could work on a scene together?" He looked up, startled, as if I'd pulled him out of a trance. "Oh, sorry," I added quickly. "Would you rather work on your own?"

At that, he jumped to his feet. "No, of course not. Let's go somewhere we can have more privacy."

He shuffled sideways along the row of seats, and together we moved toward a far corner, away from the stage, the set-builders, and the musicians.

"Hey, how's your grandfather?" he asked. "Last time we talked, you were in a big hurry to go see him. Do you visit him a lot?"

"Yeah, I try. I buy his groceries and we joke around. It's kind of our thing. I bring him bananas and we watch TV!"

And then, I started to tell Ben about my last visit with Zayde, about his violin, and how he'd gone to a special store to get the old strings replaced. I told him about listening to Zayde play for the very first time, and how incredible that moment had been. I didn't tell him about Zayde's fall—I knew Zayde would be embarrassed if others knew. But I told him just about everything else.

I'm not sure why I blurted all of this to Ben. I hadn't even told my parents about Zayde and the violin, because then I would have had to tell them about him getting the strings, and about him falling down and my having to go to the rescue and how we were keeping that secret. And yet, here I was, spilling it all to Ben. And he was staring back at me and hanging on to every word, and nodding and looking like he really cared— like he wanted to hear me talk.

"And you never heard him play before?" he asked when I finally stopped.

I shook my head. "No, it wasn't until a few weeks ago that anybody even knew that he *could* play the violin. It's all part of the past that he is just starting to talk about. Nobody knows about any of this, so please don't say a word."

He looked thoughtful. "I really like your grandfather."

"I think he liked you, too."

"I was wondering, do you think I could sit down with him again to talk, to ask him questions?"

At that, I hesitated. Not that I didn't want Ben to see my grandfather again. It was just that I still worried about how Zayde was dealing with dredging up his past.

Ben sensed my uncertainty. "Only if you think it'd be okay."

"I guess. We could go over together. I mean, I . . . I think I should go with you." I felt myself blushing.

"Oh, for sure, it would definitely be better if you were there. Could you ask him if it would be all right?"

"Sure. I'll ask him."

"I just think there's a lot more I could learn from him. And I don't just mean about playing Tevye. That tattoo on his arm was . . . well, it really bothered me."

"It bothers everybody." I was grateful that Ben brought it up. "I was so surprised when he showed it to you. He never does that," I said.

"Is it a good thing or a bad thing that he did?"

"A good thing, I think. At least, I hope. I guess we'll find out when I ask if you can come over." Then I thought through what I'd just said. "But really it's all pretty raw for him. I mean, if he says no, it's just because . . . you know, just, don't take it personally."

"I understand."

At that moment Ms. Ramsey marched into the auditorium with the ensemble in tow.

"All right, people! Everybody down front!"

People jumped to their feet and joined in the little parade.

"Here we go," Ben said as he stood up. He offered me a hand. "I guess we didn't have a chance to practice after all."

I took his hand, he pulled me to my feet, and we walked down the steps to join the others. But Ben kept holding my hand. I couldn't help noticing that people were watching us. I caught sight of Mindi, and I saw her stiffen as Ben and I joined the cast. Natasha flashed a big smile and gave me a little thumbs-up—I hoped Ben didn't see that.

Ms. Ramsey ordered the musicians and the set crew to stop what they were doing. The musicians stopped immediately, and a few hammer blows later it was completely quiet. When we got down to the stage, Ben let go of my hand. I was relieved . . . and a little disappointed.

My hand was a bit sweaty and I wiped it very discreetly on the leg of my pants.

"Okay, people, we're going to take it from the top. Scene 1. Everybody, places."

Ben let out a big sigh. "Wish me luck, Golde."

"You'll do fine, Tevye."

"I wish I could be so sure."

Ben headed in one direction while I headed in the other. The Papas would be coming in from stage left and the Mamas from stage right.

I'd only taken a few steps when Tash was at my side.

"You two looked pretty cozy," she said. "Were you rehearsing?"

"Actually, we were talking."

"Ooh, you don't say! Suddenly you two have a lot to talk about?" She opened her mouth to say something else but I warned her off with a death stare.

We settled into our places and Ms. Ramsey called for quiet. Everybody was smart enough—and fearful enough—to obey instantly. Ms. Ramsey had been yelling less since I'd confronted her. But less was still a relative term. The big difference was that now she'd apologize if she really went over the top.

Behind me were all the other Mamas and female villagers. Across the stage in the stage-left wing, visible to me but not to the audience, were all the Papas and male villagers. On the stage were only two people—Tevye, standing in front of his house—our house—and the fiddler sitting atop the roof.

Strange how the person the whole play was named after didn't even have a line of dialogue! All the Fiddler did was sit up on the roof and play his violin. In some productions of *Fiddler* the guy on the roof would be an actor simply pretending while a real violinist stood off-stage doing the actual playing. In our production, though, there was only one Fiddler, his name was Thomas, and he had the difficult task of balancing on the roof while playing his instrument. Ms. Ramsey thought it would add authenticity to the show.

"Okay, dim the lights and cue the music," she yelled.

The lights went down and in the background the "moon"—a spotlight—was turned on. Thomas started playing. Those first few notes sent a chill up my spine. And not the kind of chill you get when something moves you. This opening was meant to be soulful and emotional, but with every note Thomas played, I felt myself cringe.

"You'd better get better at that!" Ms. Ramsey yelled.

I felt sorry for him. It couldn't be easy to perch up there and play without hitting a few clangers.

The music continued. Thomas was hitting some good notes but more than his share of bad ones. I suddenly had an image of Zayde coming to the show and listening to Thomas scratch out this tune. What would Zayde, with his remarkable violin skills, think of that?

If he was going to come to a performance, I had to hope that Thomas improved.

The music faded. Ben climbed off the cart at center stage and started his monologue.

"A fiddler on the roof . . ."

I held my breath, waiting, hoping he'd get it all right. But I couldn't hold my breath too long. In a few more lines we'd all be rushing on to the stage from both sides, singing!

CHAPTER SEVENTEEN

"That was brutal—again!" Natasha said as we left the rehearsal and walked down the front steps of the school. "Remind me why I let you talk me into signing up for this torture?"

"Ms. Ramsey *did* say she wouldn't let us leave until we finally got it right. It's not her fault that some people couldn't remember their blocking."

"Don't make excuses for her. You just didn't mind that it was a long rehearsal because you were spending time with—"

"Stop right now," I hissed. "Somebody might hear you."

All around us other members of the cast and crew were huddled together against the cold on the steps in front of the school. It was already dark.

"Are you sure you don't need a ride with me and my mother?" Natasha asked as she waved to the driver of an idling car.

"Thanks, but my dad's coming to get me. You don't have to wait—oh, there he is!"

My father pulled up to the curb. And my mother was with him!

I said goodbye to Tash and a few other castmates. Ben was already gone, picked up by his dad.

"I wasn't expecting both of you," I said as I settled into the backseat of our car and we pulled away.

"Thought I'd just come along for the ride," my mother said.

"And the way your mother's schedule has been for the last few weeks, this is as close as we're ever going to get to a date," my father added.

"Does that make me the chaperone?"

"I think the correct term is 'fifth wheel,'" my mother said. "But hey, we're not the only ones who are busy, right? Even when your dad and I are home, we hardly ever see you!"

"So you're saying this actually counts as quality family time?" I said.

"You grab what you can grab," my father added.

"So, kiddo, how are things going?" my mother asked.

"It's pretty crazy, and it's only going to get worse as we get closer to opening night." It was still weeks away, but I knew we needed every second of that time.

"Judging from the late, long practice, things aren't going as smoothly as expected," my father said. "Are there problems?"

"Lots of problems."

"Anything we can help with?" he asked.

"Not unless you can help build the sets."

"The sets aren't finished yet?" my mother asked.

"No, and because of that, our practice time on stage is limited. It's hard to get the blocking right if you can't be up on stage. And on top of that, some of the cast still aren't off book."

"That's really not good," my mother said. "You know, if I could help, I would."

My father and I both started to laugh and then tried to stifle it.

"Okay, so I'm not so musical," she said.

"And you are incredibly busy," I added, to soften the blow.

"But your father is musical."

"And just as busy at work," I said.

He shrugged. "The new people I've brought in this year are doing a wonderful job. I have very capable staff."

"But it will still be all hands on deck as you get closer to tax season," my mother pointed out.

"Another problem we have is that our musicians are pretty mediocre," I added. "Even the violinist who's playing the Fiddler isn't very good. Zayde is *so* much better."

"Zayde is better?" my mother asked.

As soon as I'd said it, I knew I shouldn't have. But there was no way to take it back.

My father looked at me in the rearview mirror. "And how would you know that he's better?" he asked.

My brain began to spin. I could have just said that Zayde was a professional musician when he was young, so he was bound to be better. That would have been completely believable. I could have said that, but I didn't. I didn't like to lie, and besides, the secrecy was weighing heavily on me.

"I heard him play," I said.

"You heard Zayde play the violin?" my father asked. I saw my parents exchange a quick glance.

"He was playing that old violin from the attic one day when I came with the groceries. He didn't know I was there and I listened to him play, but he stopped the second he saw me."

"And you didn't tell us that because . . . ?" my mother asked.

"I'm not really sure." That sounded lame, but it was honest.

"And he was good?" my father asked.

"He was amazing. Just amazing."

"I can't even imagine how surprised you must have been," my father said.

"I was shocked."

"I wish I could have been there," my father said. "Do you think he'd play for me, for us?"

I could hear the longing creep into my father's voice. But I really didn't know how to respond. Would Zayde be angry that I'd told my parents? It wasn't like he'd told me not to, but in a way the whole thing—starting with Zayde's accident the day he went to buy the strings—was all like one big secret.

"Wait...the violin...you said it had broken strings," my mother said. "How could he play it like that?"

And here it was—the next part of my cover-up. I could have told my parents that I bought the strings for Zayde, or that he had another set in the attic, but that would have been a lie. Keeping a secret and telling a lie were different things, but how could I do one without doing the other?

"He went downtown and bought strings for the violin," I blurted.

"He went all the way downtown?"

"He had to. They're special strings and there was only one place that sold them."

"But why didn't he ask us to buy them for him?" my father demanded. The concern in his voice bordered on anger, or dismay. "I could have at least given him a lift."

"He told me he needed to do it on his own. He didn't want anyone to know he was fixing the violin because he wasn't sure if he'd be able to play it."

"You'd think it would be like riding a bicycle . . . it was such a big part of his early years."

"No, he wasn't worried about remembering *how* to play it. He was afraid he might not be able to *bring himself* to play. You know, emotionally."

My father nodded. "I guess that makes sense. It must have been so difficult for him."

There was only one more thing to say, and to say it was to break a trust with my Zayde. But to not say it was to break a trust with my parents. I was going to betray someone, no matter what I said or didn't say.

I took a deep breath. "He went downtown on his own. But I ended up going to get him . . . by cab."

There were a few seconds of silence. It was just the sound of the engine, the wind whispering by the windows, and the burring of the heater. There was a song playing on the radio but the volume was so low that I couldn't even make out the tune. I had the bizarre thought that I should ask my parents to turn up the volume so we could listen to the song and all just pretend I hadn't said anything.

Finally, my mother spoke. "You are going to explain what you mean, right?"

"I promised Zayde I wouldn't talk about it," I said.

"It sounds as if that promise has already been compromised. You need to tell us what happened," my father said.

"I know. I just don't know what to say or where to start."

"You start at the beginning and you say everything that needs to be said," my mother said.

I knew she was right. There was no point in even trying to tell just part of the truth when it was all so tied together.

It took the rest of the ride home and a lot of time after-
wards to explain it all. I kept trying to spin things a
little, to soften the worst parts, but it was impossible. I
wanted to leave out the part about him falling and rip-
ping his pants and bumping his head, but then why
would Amir have called me in the first place? I wanted
to leave out the part about him not having any money
because he'd spent it on the strings, but then why
wouldn't he have just taken a taxi? I was grateful, though,
that my parents let me tell the story without adding
more than an occasional "Oh!" or "How awful," or a
concerned look or thoughtful nodding of the head.

When I was done, I let out a deep sigh of relief. It
felt good to have it all out in the open.

"This must have been very distressing for you," my
mother said.

I hadn't expected that—instead of anger I was getting sympathy!

"And it wasn't fair of my father to make you keep it
all a secret," my dad said.

"It's just that he didn't want to worry you," I said.

"You know it's more than that," my father replied.

I nodded. "He doesn't want anybody to talk about
him needing to live somewhere else."

"I think that's exactly what I *do* need to talk to him
about. I'm going over there tonight and—"

"No, you can't do that!" I protested. My father raised his eyebrows at me. "He can't know that I told you what happened."

"You want us to pretend that the whole thing didn't happen?" he asked.

"Yes."

"I'm sorry, but I can't do that," my father said.

"Maybe Shirli's right," my mother said. "Maybe you should just ignore it."

I hadn't expected her to say that, and, judging from my father's expression, neither had he.

"Think about it. Even if you did talk to him, do you think you could convince him that he needs more help?" my mother asked.

"Well . . . probably not."

"And you certainly can't force him to move someplace against his will," she continued.

"I hope that day never comes."

"He's older and a bit slower, but he's as sharp as he is stubborn. If you tackle him on this issue right now, you have nothing to win and everything to lose."

My father looked puzzled.

"He'll feel that he can't trust Shirli," Mom continued, "which could make things even worse."

I hadn't even thought of that.

"He called Shirli instead of us because he trusted her. If he felt that he couldn't trust her either, who would he call if there was ever another incident?" she asked. My father didn't answer, which was, of course, an answer. "So, we all keep the secret. We know, but Zayde doesn't know that we know," my mother continued. "And maybe we all go over a little bit more often."

"I could do that," I agreed. "I could bring him groceries and then go back again every week just to visit." It was going to be hard to fit that in with all the rehearsals, but somehow I'd have to make it work.

"And we could have him over for supper twice a week. We'll all keep our eyes open," my mother added. "But he's your father, and we'll do whatever you think is best."

I thought about something my Zayde had said: "The man may be the head of the family, but the wife is the neck. The wife tells the head where to look." That was what my mother was doing right now.

"It's not like he's ever done anything like this before," Mom said.

"And he promised me he'd never do it again," I added. "He gave me his word."

"And you know that means everything coming from your father," my mother added.

"It's just that I don't like secrets," my father said. "But . . . perhaps it is best that we keep this among the three of us, for my father's sake."

And for my sake, I thought.

"I think that's the wisest thing to do," my mother agreed. "Besides, the way he's started to open up lately,

I wouldn't be so surprised if he eventually told us what happened himself. Maybe he'll even play his violin for us."

"Do you think so?" My father had a faraway look in his eyes, and I realized how badly he wanted a chance to hear Zayde play. And I hoped it would happen, too.

"Your father is certainly full of surprises these days," Mom said. "So who knows . . . who knows?"

CHAPTER EIGHTEEN

I was relieved to hear the TV blasting when Ben and I entered Zayde's house through the kitchen door. My grandfather had ignored the TV during my last visits, he was so preoccupied with the violin and reliving his story. To me, this was the sound of things getting back to normal.

"Is that wrestling?" Ben asked as we pulled off our boots and our jackets.

"Don't even ask. My grandfather's obsessed with it."

"No, this is great," Ben said. "I love wrestling!"

When we walked into the living room, there was my grandfather in his big armchair, his eyes glued to the television.

"Hi, Zayde." I raised my voice to be heard over the TV as I bent over to kiss his cheek.

"Shirli! I'm so glad you're here."

"You remember Ben, don't you?"

Ben shuffled forward, hands awkwardly stuffed into

the pockets of his jeans. He quickly removed them and extended one to my grandfather.

"Hello, Mr. Berman. Thanks so much for letting me come and visit."

"Ben Morgan, you didn't learn enough the last time we met?" Zayde asked, sighing heavily and looking tired.

"I learned a lot, sir, and that's why I want to learn more."

That was such a smart thing to say, but I couldn't tell from Zayde's reaction whether it worked. When I'd broached the subject of Ben coming over, he'd been less than enthusiastic.

"If you don't feel like talking, Zayde, Ben will understand."

It was as though Zayde hadn't even heard me. Instead he'd turned away to look out the window, and he seemed to be staring at the walkway and the bushes covered in snow. I wondered if he was imagining my grandmother when she used to tend to the garden every springtime. But then, he turned back to me, his eyes full of resolve.

"I told you he could come, and I always talk to my guests."

"I really appreciate that, sir," Ben said.

"So, Ben Morgan, welcome to my home. Sit. Sit. We'll have some juice in a few minutes. Shirli, you'll get us some apple juice, right?"

I sighed in relief, nodded, and turned toward the TV. The wrestler that Zayde had told me about a couple of weeks earlier—what was his name? Stone Cold something or other?—was back in the ring, pummeling some other poor guy who was pinned against the ropes. I was looking for the remote to turn down the volume when Ben piped up.

"Stone Cold is no Hulk Hogan, but somebody has to take care of the Undertaker."

What? Who was the Undertaker? What was Ben talking about?

"You know the Undertaker?" Zayde sat up in his chair and peered at Ben.

"He's just the biggest, baddest, meanest man to ever wrestle. He's pure evil."

Zayde looked even more curious. "So, you know something about wrestling?"

"Yes, sir. I've been watching the WWF for years, with my dad. The Undertaker is a legend, along with the Brothers of Destruction. He's won the World Heavyweight Championship three times."

They started discussing wrestling moves and the holds that each fighter specialized in, and it was as if they were speaking another language. I went to the kitchen to get some juice, and they were still going at it when I returned with a tray and three full glasses. Zayde looked more animated than I had seen him in a long time. He and Ben were debating the skills of people with names like Vader, X-Pac, and The Rock. It sounded like the cast of characters from a science fiction movie. But I could see that Zayde was impressed with Ben's knowledge. He was sitting on the edge of his armchair. His eyes were lit up and his hands were waving in every direction as he drove home the point that Vader was better than X-Pac who could last longer in any ring than Stone Cold.

I settled back on the couch and glanced into the dining room. The violin was still there, in its case, sitting on the buffet. I was glad to see that Zayde hadn't hidden it away after my last visit, when he had made it clear he didn't want to touch it again. Maybe he'd had a change of heart about that.

I noticed a few boxes sitting off to one side of the room. They were closed and taped, and something was written on top of them. From where I was sitting, I couldn't make out what it said, but I recognized my grandfather's shaky handwriting. I wondered what they were.

In the meantime, the conversation about wrestling seemed to be winding down.

"I also play football, sir," Ben was saying.

Zayde sat back in his chair and nodded approvingly. "Wrestling, football, *and* you sing."

"Well, my singing is probably the weakest."

"He's being modest, Zayde," I piped up.

"Like I said before, Shirli's the one with talent. I'm just along for the ride," Ben said.

Zayde looked thoughtful. "Well, perhaps you would like to humor an old man and show me how good you really are. Sing something with my granddaughter."

I couldn't believe what I was hearing. This was coming from my grandfather—the man who had shunned music my entire life! And now he was asking Ben and me to perform for him? I think my mouth must have dropped open, and I just stared at Zayde. But Ben clearly had an idea.

"Shirli told me you're an incredible violinist," he said.

I felt a shudder go up my spine. What was Ben doing?

"So, my granddaughter told you that she heard me play, did she?"

Was he going to be upset that I'd told somebody or, even worse, ask me who else I told?

"She says you can play brilliantly," Ben said.

"I can play," my grandfather responded, ever so slowly.

"So, I'm just wondering, if we sing a song from the show . . . would you consider playing something for us?"

And now it was like I was having a heart attack! This was not our deal! Ben was supposed to be asking Zayde questions that would help him understand his character in *Fiddler*. He was way out of line here, and I felt a sudden flash of anger. He had no right to talk about this—to ask Zayde to play. I'd told him about the violin in confidence. If Zayde exploded now, or shut down altogether, then I would never forgive Ben.

Zayde just stared at Ben, and then at me. I couldn't read his expression. Anger? Confusion? Hurt? But when he started to talk, there were none of those dark feelings in his voice.

"So, you think because you impressed me with your knowledge of wrestling that now you can talk me into doing something I've shared with my grand-daughter only?"

My grandfather was no fool.

"Zayde, you don't—"

He lifted his hand to cut me off.

Ben jumped in. "I'm not trying to trick you, sir, honestly. I didn't mean to be disrespectful. I really just want to hear you play."

My face was hot, and there was a pounding in my ears.

"Okay, Ben Morgan," Zayde finally said. "Sing for me, and if I like what I hear, then perhaps I'll play for you."

This was all getting more unbelievable by the minute!

I looked at Ben, he stared back at me, and then the two of us stood in front of Zayde and began to sing. We didn't even check with one another. We knew instinctively which song we would perform. It was "Sunrise, Sunset," a beautiful tune that Golde and Tevye sing at the wedding of their daughter, Tzeitel, to Motel the tailor, the man she has chosen to be her husband.

Our voices blended effortlessly. Our harmonies were pitch-perfect. We'd never been this good before in rehearsals. And as the last note trailed off, we stood there, looking at Zayde and waiting for his response.

A full minute passed before he spoke. It felt like the longest minute of my life. I just stood there, waiting, the clock on the wall loudly ticking out the seconds.

"You underestimate yourself, Ben Morgan. You have a fine voice indeed." Zayde's voice was thick with emotion.

I felt as though I could breathe again!

"Thank you, sir. Shirli makes me sound good."

Zayde tilted his head to one side and stared at both of us. "No, I think you make each other sound good. You're perfect together."

My face was practically on fire. I wanted the floor to swallow me up. But I also knew that my grandfather was right. We were *so* right together—and maybe Zayde just meant as singing partners, but I was letting myself believe that maybe it was more than that.

"So, what do you say, Mr. Berman?" Ben asked after another long minute had passed. "Will you play something for us?"

Zayde stared at the two of us, and then said, "Shirli, bring me my violin."

Still in a bit of a trance, I walked over to the buffet, picked up the violin case, and carried it over to Zayde. He stood up a bit shakily from his armchair, opened the clasps, and reached in to pull out the violin and the bow. Without saying a word, he placed the violin under his chin, raised the bow, and began to play. And the song that he played was the exact song that Ben and I had just sung—"Sunrise, Sunset." His eyes were closed, and he swayed slightly from side to side as he drew the bow across the strings. The fingers of his left hand danced along the neck of the violin as the sweet sound filled the living room. He didn't have any sheet music in front of him, and he played as if he had known this tune his whole life. I was breathless, practically shaking as the notes rose and fell. It was just like the last time I had heard him play, but even better, as if he had been practicing. Perhaps he had been.

I glanced over at Ben. His eyes were wide open and he was hanging on every note Zayde was playing.

Finally, the song ended, and Zayde lowered the violin. "So, what do you think?"

I was still at a loss for words.

"Thank you, sir," Ben said at last. "Shirli said you were really good, but I didn't think you'd be *this* good."

Zayde nodded, and then bent to place the violin back in its case.

For the next half hour or so, Ben and my grandfather just talked. Ben asked a bunch of questions about life in eastern Europe before the war, and about the pogroms. He wanted to know about the villages like Anatevka in *Fiddler*—my grandfather called them "shtetls"—and Zayde told him about the Jewish men of that time: the kinds of work they did, how religious they were, what motivated them, and what they believed about family and responsibility. Ben listened thoughtfully, and asked more questions, and Zayde answered every one of them. I didn't say much. I just sat back and watched the two of them and listened to their conversation.

I was still dumbstruck by everything that was unfolding in front of me: the way Zayde had played, the way Ben and I had sung, the easy conversation between these two. But it was even more than that. For the first time, I had to admit to myself that I liked Ben—liked him a *lot*. Any guy who could draw my grandfather out in the way that he had was someone worth going for. I'd been fighting the feeling, but I wasn't sure I could anymore. Not that there was anything that I was going to do about it—at least not right now. We had our show to get through, and I didn't want my feelings for Ben to complicate that. Besides, I might have been ready for a relationship with him, but I didn't want to be his rebound. It was enough to admit it to myself; I'd keep my feelings under wraps until the time was right. Funny, I noticed that I wasn't twisting my hair—which meant I obviously didn't even feel nervous! It just felt right.

Zayde closed the violin case, which signaled to me that it was probably time for Ben and me to get going.

I went over to my grandfather and threw my arms around him, squeezing tightly.

"You're incredible, Zayde," I whispered.

"There is still so much I have to tell you," he replied, his voice muffled by my hair. Then he pulled back. "Will you come again? To hear more of my story? I think I'm ready to tell it."

I nodded again, not trusting myself to speak.

"Thank you, sir," Ben said, coming to stand next to me. "You've helped me more than you know."

"It was a pleasure, Ben Morgan. You can come back any time you want."

Zayde smiled and winked at me and I thought I was going to die. But before he could say another word, I remembered something else.

"Zayde, what are those things over there?" I pointed to the sealed boxes on the other side of the room. And just when I thought there was nothing more my grandfather could do to surprise me, he did it again.

"I started to go through your Bubbie's things," he said. "I boxed up some clothes of hers and called a secondhand store to come and get them. I think I'm ready for that, as well."

CHAPTER NINETEEN

There was an air of semi-organized chaos about things. The musicians were practicing, the set-builders were hammering away, members of the ensemble were working on a song in the back of the auditorium, and Ben was up, center stage, with "our daughters" rehearsing a scene. The only thing missing was Ms. Ramsey. Practice was supposed to have started at 7:00 a.m., twenty minutes ago, and she wasn't here. She was usually such a stickler for being on time herself, and she was likely to bite your head off if you were even a minute late.

Mr. Nevarez sat at his piano. He was working on one of his crossword puzzles, as stone-silent as ever. Sometimes it seemed as though he was only vaguely aware that we existed, so there didn't seem to be any point in asking him questions about Ms. Ramsey's absence, or thinking that he might lead the rehearsal until she got here.

Finally, Ben stepped up to take charge. I guess that was the quarterback part of his personality coming out! He got people moving in the right direction. Mindi helped him, making sure that the actors were going over their lines in groups and generally making it feel as though the rehearsal had started, even though our director was absent. I had to give Mindi full marks for that, even if giving orders was something she seemed to like to do. Okay, I was being a bit mean. She was actually polite and even helpful to her "sisters" as they rehearsed a scene.

I looked at my watch again.

"She probably slept in," Natasha said.

"Probably."

"There's nothing to worry about."

"I know."

"But you're still worried," Natasha said.

"Unavoidable. You know me. Besides, we really can't afford to lose any more time."

"Yeah, but I'm sure Ms. Ramsey will just schedule an extra rehearsal to make up for it. Relax!"

I caught a glimpse of one of the doors at the back opening and I turned around, hoping to see Ms. Ramsey rushing down the aisle. Instead it was Mr. James, our principal. I knew he was always at school this early but he'd never been in to see us rehearse before. Maybe Ms. Ramsey had called him and asked him to step in and watch us until she arrived.

He came down the aisle slowly, nodding to people and exchanging a few words as he walked. That seemed friendly enough, but there was something about his expression that made me wonder. He seemed uneasy, which wasn't his usual vibe.

"Could I please have your attention?" he asked, climbing the steps onto the stage.

Those who were close enough got quiet, but the people working backstage and the musicians who were still tuning up didn't hear. He called out again, louder, and the noise finally settled down and stopped.

"Could everybody please come up here . . . come closer . . . I have to talk to you all."

Natasha and I exchanged a worried look. This couldn't be good. We got to our feet and moved toward the stage. I realized, judging from other people's expressions, that we weren't the only ones who were concerned.

"I want to start by telling all of you that Ms. Ramsey is going to be all right," he said.

"Something happened to Ms. Ramsey?" Mohammed asked.

"Yes, she was in a car accident late last night," Mr. James said.

Everyone started talking at once. Mr. James raised his hands to quiet us.

"But you said she's going to be okay?" Mindi asked.

"She was badly hurt," he said. "She suffered a broken arm, five fractured ribs, and a head injury, a concussion."

That brought a collective gasp from the group. I'd never known anyone who was in a car accident before. All I knew was what I'd seen on television, and it never looked good. This was Ms. Ramsey—someone I knew personally. I couldn't begin to imagine what she was going through. I shuddered and squeezed my eyes shut.

"I'll have more details to share later today, but right now, this morning's rehearsal is canceled."

"Sir, would it be possible for the designers to stay and continue to work on the sets?" Ben asked.

Mr. James shook his head. "I think it's best for everybody to just stop."

"But we really need to wrap up construction, and the crew can do that without Ms. Ramsey here." Ben was really pushing.

Mr. James let out a big sigh. "Ben . . . everybody . . . Ms. Ramsey's injuries are severe. As I said, she's going to be all right, she's going to recover, but that recovery is going to take time."

"How much time?" I asked.

Mr. James stared long and hard before replying. "It's still early, but we have to be prepared for the fact that Ms. Ramsey might not be returning to school before the end of the year, and certainly not for at least a month."

"But opening night is only five weeks away," Natasha said. This came out of her like a whisper.

"This is hard for me to say. I know you've all put in so much work . . ."

There was complete silence in the auditorium as we felt the implication of this sink in. And then Ben asked the question that each one of us was thinking.

"Are you saying the play is being canceled?"

Mr. James nodded his head ever so slightly. There were gasps, followed by more stunned silence.

"I'm so sorry, but without Ms. Ramsey there might not be a way to continue."

I couldn't believe my ears. This couldn't be possible.

"But what if we could find somebody else to be the director?" Mindi asked.

"There is nobody else. I can look . . . I can ask, but there was nobody else before the accident and there's nobody now. I'm so sorry," Mr. James said. "So sorry."

CHAPTER TWENTY

It was quiet when I entered Zayde's kitchen. But in the background, I could make out muted voices—two, one that was clearly my grandfather's. At least he was okay. The other voice was vaguely familiar but I couldn't quite place it.

I placed the groceries I was carrying on the counter, took off my coat, and walked toward the dining room, pausing in the doorway. Zayde was seated at the table, sipping tea. Across from him sat his new friend Amir. The two of them were engaged in an animated conversation and didn't notice me at first.

This was the first time I'd seen my grandfather since I'd been over with Ben three days earlier. And Zayde still didn't know that I had broken his trust by telling my parents all about his trip downtown to buy strings, and his fall in front of Amir's grocery store. I was still feeling a bit guilty about spilling our secret, even though I did it for all the right reasons.

And what did I have to take my mind off that queasy feeling? Oh yeah, the other huge problem in my life. Was the play seriously going to be canceled? That couldn't be real . . . Ms. Ramsey had to be fine. She'd walk back in tomorrow, her arm in a cast, a big bandage wrapped around her head, and the show would go on.

"Shirli?" Zayde lifted his head, spotting me in the doorway. "Why are you standing there? Come in."

That startled me out of my miserable thoughts.

"You remember my friend, Amir." I smiled and greeted Amir, who bowed slightly in my direction. "I wanted him to come over so that I could thank him properly for helping me out that day."

"Your grandfather kindly invited me to tea. We have been having a lively conversation."

"Did you know that Amir lost a nephew in 9/11? He was just a young man working for a financial company in the South Tower."

I couldn't imagine what to say to that.

Amir lowered his head. "A fine young man," he said. "So many great possibilities ahead of him. And all gone."

Zayde reached over and placed a hand on Amir's shoulder. "I am so sorry for your loss. There are no words to express the horror."

Amir lifted his head and looked at my grandfather. "It appears that we have both suffered many losses over the years."

"We seem to understand each other very well."

Amir nodded, and the two men sat in shared silence for a while, until Amir smiled and said, "And now it is time for me to leave."

"Oh, please don't rush out," I said.

"No, I must. My daughter is watching the store, but I don't like to leave her there alone for long periods. We have had some trouble in the past." He turned to Zayde. "Thank you, Tobias. It has been a most pleasant afternoon."

"We'll do it again, Amir, better sooner than later."

"Can we call a taxi for you?" I hadn't seen a car parked in the driveway and I knew how far we were from Amir's grocery store.

"No, it is only one bus ride from the corner. And I will enjoy the journey. But I thank you for the offer."

Amir bowed to me again, and walked to the front door with Zayde. He pulled on his coat, shook hands with my grandfather, and left.

"That Amir is a fine man," Zayde said as he returned to the dining room. "Who would have thought that we would become such fast friends?" He sighed and looked up at me.

"I brought your groceries," I said.

Zayde looked at his watch. "I am glad you brought groceries, but why are you here so early? Shouldn't you still be at rehearsal?"

I was going to tell him, but I didn't really know what words to use.

"You brought more than my groceries, my dear granddaughter. You brought troubles. What's wrong?"

I burst into tears.

✄

I took another sip from my glass of apple juice. Through the tears and gasps and questions and sips, I had told him all about the accident and the play being canceled.

"I'm so sorry," Zayde said.

"So am I."

"And there's nobody else who can take the place of your teacher?" he asked.

"It doesn't look like it, but Mr. James said he'd be willing to look at other options if something came up."

"So, there is some hope."

"Probably just false hope."

Telling Zayde about everything had made it seem more real. Ms. Ramsey wasn't coming back, in spite of my wishful fantasy. And Ben had spoken to the principal at lunch—he really liked Ben—but nothing had changed: there was still no staff member willing or able to come forward. No point hoping someone was going to turn up and ride to our rescue.

"All that work that you did, you and Ben Morgan and all the others," he said.

"I guess it was all for nothing."

"I would have liked to have seen you sing up on stage," he said.

"You were going to come to the show? You were going to come and see me perform?"

"I was thinking, perhaps, it was not impossible," he offered, and then he shrugged.

Somehow that made it even worse—and somehow a little bit better.

"You just have to believe that this will work itself out."

"How?" I asked.

It was his turn to shake his head. "I don't know. Sometimes bad things happen and we don't know why they happen."

"It's just that I can't think of *anything* worse than this," I said.

My Zayde looked astonished, almost stunned, and I realized what I'd said. I felt my face get hot.

"I know it's just a show," I said. "I know it doesn't compare to other things—things that have happened to Amir, and things that have happened to you and your family."

He reached across the table and put his hands over-top of my hands. "That happened to *our* family."

It *was* my family. Those people on the poster—his mother and father and brothers—were my family. Even further back, his grandmother and his mother, when she was a little girl, had lived through the Russian pogroms.

And here I was upset because a play about that part of history had been canceled. They had lived through it—or not lived at all. My Zayde's mother had fled the pogroms as a girl only to have to run for her life during the Holocaust. Where was the fairness in that? Where was the fairness in any of it?

"I am so grateful that for you the thing that is most distressing in your life is that the show will not happen. That is a blessing."

"I know . . . I know. I feel bad for being so upset about it."

"There's no need. I understand. We all live in our place and time. So today, in this time and place, I need to know: did you bring me forty bananas?"

In spite of everything, a small smile crept up to the corners of my mouth. "I didn't, but if you want I'll go and get you a million bananas."

"A million would be a waste. Let's not waste anything more. Forty is what I need."

"If I come back with more bananas, will you play the violin for me again?" I could see the case was nearby in its usual spot on the buffet. "Have you been practicing?"

"A little. Somehow it brings me comfort and distress all at once, to have it close. Does that make any sense?"

"I think it does. Would you play a little for me the next time I come?" I asked.

"If you come back with more bananas, and maybe sing for me, maybe I will play a little for you."

CHAPTER TWENTY-ONE

The five of us trudged up the steps of Morrison Memorial Hospital. I had told Natasha I was thinking of visiting Ms. Ramsey, but I was nervous—I wasn't sure what kind of condition I'd find her in—so Tash had agreed to come for moral support. Then Tash told Mohammed, who told Mindi, who mentioned it to Ben, and now we were all visiting together. I didn't even know if the hospital rules would allow that many of us in at the same time. I just needed to see my teacher and know that she was okay.

My father had offered to drive us, and Mindi's mother was going to pick us up at the end. During the drive we'd all been pretty quiet. The first few days after the accident had felt like a kind of limbo. We were all worried about our teacher, and not quite believing that the show was really over.

Mindi was carrying a big bouquet of flowers that she had been clutching the whole way to the hospital. Leave it to Mindi to think about that. She was so proper, so full of manners. Then again, I had to admit that it was a nice gesture—I wished I had thought of it!

"We'll just say they're from all of us," Mindi had said.

"Let us know what we owe you," I replied.

But Mindi shook her head. "Oh, don't even worry about it. It's no big deal. What's important is that they'll brighten Ms. Ramsey's day."

We entered the hospital lobby and approached the information desk, where a tired-looking guy not much older than any of us was sitting in front of a computer screen. We waited for what felt like an age before he finally looked up.

"We're here to see Ms. Ramsey," I began. "She was admitted two days ago after a car accident." Saying those words out loud was still so unreal.

"First name?" the guy said.

"I'm Shirli. Oh, wait, you didn't mean that, did you?" My face was getting hot. What was Ms. Ramsey's first name? Suddenly I just couldn't come up with it.

"Evelyn," Mindi said over my shoulder. "Her name is Evelyn Ramsey."

It figured that Mindi would know. The guy behind the desk studied his computer screen again.

"East wing, seventh floor, room 732." He glanced at the group of us, seemed about to say something, but then shrugged and pointed toward the elevator.

There was no one at the nurses' station when we emerged onto the seventh floor. The nurses must have been busy with patients. After first heading in the wrong direction, we finally stood in front of room 732. And that's when the panic hit me. What were we going to find behind that door? Would Ms. Ramsey be conscious? Able to talk? Able to recognize us? And would we recognize her? Mr. James had said that her injuries were severe. What did that mean? Without thinking, my hands found my hair and I began to wind it up and down, trying to calm myself.

"I get a little sick to my stomach in hospitals," Mohammed said suddenly.

"You're telling us this now?" Mindi exclaimed.

"I wanted to come. But maybe it was a mistake."

"Just take a couple of deep breaths and you'll be fine," Ben replied.

"And stay close to the door," Mindi added. "You can make a run for it, if you need to. But don't make a scene."

And then we all just stared at the door to Ms. Ramsey's room until Tash finally asked, "Are we just going to stand here, or are we going in?"

At that, Ben stepped forward and tapped lightly on the door. A moment later, a soft voice replied, "Come in."

Ms. Ramsey was lying on her hospital bed under a blue sheet and propped up with several pillows. One arm was bound in a thick white cast, and there were gauze bandages wrapped around her head. A bright-red cut descended from the outer corner of one eye to the bottom of her cheek. There was an IV line attached to her arm. Her face was ghostly white. Her eyes fluttered open as the five of us shuffled into the room and surrounded her bed.

"Oh, my goodness, I can't believe you came here." Her voice was weak—hard to believe it was the same voice that bellowed at us in rehearsals. From the distant look in her eyes I thought there had to be some pain medication dripping into her arm.

"We needed to see you," I blurted. "We wanted to make sure you're okay. Are you okay?" If I wasn't careful, I was going to start crying, and I didn't want to do that in front of Ms. Ramsey—or the group.

She nodded slowly and then winced. "I'm fine. Really, I am," she added as she glanced at our faces. "I know this doesn't look very good. But I'm so lucky. It could have been so much worse."

"Here, we brought you these." Mindi stepped forward to present the bouquet of flowers. "They're from all of us." And then she busied herself unwrapping them and placing them in an empty vase that she found on the windowsill. Finally, she stepped back and let Ms. Ramsey admire them.

"They're beautiful! You really didn't have to bring me anything."

Mindi beamed, and once again, I wished I'd been the one to think of a gift.

"Mr. James told us it was a pretty bad accident," Ben said.

"I just spun out on the highway—didn't realize I'd driven over a patch of black ice from that unexpected storm. And then I hit a guardrail, and I don't remember much after that. Luckily, there were no other cars around me. No one else was hurt." She stopped and took a labored breath, as if all her energy had been used up with that explanation. Then she smiled faintly at our stricken faces. "Really, I'm going to be okay. The doctors have told me so."

I exhaled. "Your arm . . ."

"Broken, along with a few other bones. It's the headache that's the worst part right now, though, even with the pain medication." And then she quickly added, "But everything will heal in due course."

I had to believe that what she was saying was true, even though it was hard to imagine when I looked at her. The gash on Ms. Ramsey's face stood out like an angry brushstroke on a painting. I felt a surge of guilt. My worry had been about the play being canceled, when I should have been thinking about my teacher and how much pain she must be in.

"So, do you have any idea when you'll be back at school?" This question came from Mohammed. Up until this point, he had hovered in the background, close to the door and partly hidden by Ben. Now, he stepped hesitantly forward.

Ms. Ramsey sighed. "I'm afraid I don't. And that's the part that I'm most upset about. I know Mr. James has explained all of this to you—I mean about the play."

"It's okay, Ms. Ramsey," Mindi began. "The most important thing is for you to get better."

Ms. Ramsey raised her hand—the one without the cast. "Let me finish. I wish there were a way for the show to go on. But with me here, and no one at school to step in . . ."

She didn't have to say any more.

"We understand," I said, gulping.

"Yeah," Ben added. "We've tried to think of someone who could take over from you—"

"Not that anyone could really *replace* you," Tash interrupted.

Ben frowned at her. "What I mean is, we've tried to find someone to step in, but it doesn't look as if anyone can do it."

"I'm so sorry," Ms. Ramsey said.

"We are too," I added. "But like Mindi said, the important thing is for you to heal and get out of here."

"There's always next year." Mohammed added this and then stopped. Mindi and Ben would both be gone next year, off to high school. This was going to be their last show at our school. I felt sorry for Ben. And, for the first time, I felt kind of sorry for Mindi, too.

"I wish there was something I could do . . ." Ms. Ramsey said. And then she closed her eyes and we all just stood there, not sure what to do next. We waited for her to say something else but she didn't, and her eyes remained closed.

I exchanged a glance with Ben and we both nodded toward the door. But before we could turn around, the door opened and a nurse entered the room. She stopped short, seeing all of us gathered around Ms. Ramsey.

"Did you not see the sign at the station? Two guests, max!"

"Sorry, we didn't," I said. "She's our teacher. We just wanted to see her."

That's when Ms. Ramsey resurfaced. "These are my students."

"They told me," the nurse replied. "It's nice that they came, but now it's time to go."

We said our goodbyes under the watchful eyes of the nurse, wished Ms. Ramsey a speedy recovery, and left her room.

As we were walking out the door of the hospital and down the steps to the street, Ben finally summed up what all of us were thinking.

"Well, I guess it's really over."

CHAPTER TWENTY-TWO

I went to see Zayde again a few days after our visit to Ms. Ramsey. When I got to his house, the first thing I noticed was that something was missing.

"Zayde! What happened to the boxes that were in your living room?"

"They're gone," he said.

"I can see that. But what did you do with them?"

"I found a store in the phone book called A Second Chance. It's a great name, no? A Second Chance." He repeated it while staring off into space. Then he looked back at me. "They give clothes to young women who have had hard times in their lives but are getting back on their feet. Your Bubbie would have liked that."

I wondered what young woman would want to wear my Bubbie's clothing, but I didn't say anything. I was sure they'd help somebody.

"How did it feel, letting go of her things?"

"Good," he said with no hesitation. "Sometimes letting go is the best thing you can do. It's taken me a long time to begin to understand that."

We were in the kitchen, and I was busy putting away Zayde's groceries and making tea for the two of us.

"I don't think I ever really thanked you for letting my friend Ben come over last week. He really loved talking to you." I placed a cup of tea in front of Zayde and sat down across from him.

He smiled up at me. "He's a nice boy, that Ben Morgan." I felt my face grow warm under Zayde's gaze. "And I think perhaps you would like him to be more than just a friend?"

I looked away.

"You know you can't fool your Zayde."

The warmth in my face became an instant heat wave. "It doesn't matter, Zayde. Ben doesn't see me that way."

"What, is he blind?"

"Zayde . . ." It was probably a rule that grandfathers had to think their granddaughters were pretty. "What I mean is, we have fun talking, and it was great rehearsing with him. But now that the play is off, I hardly see him."

That part was true. Since visiting Ms. Ramsey in the hospital, I had bumped into Ben only once in the hallway. And he had been walking side by side with Mindi, which made me stop in my tracks. I didn't know what to think. Maybe they had decided to start seeing each other. Or maybe they were just walking to class together. At any rate, the three of us stopped in the middle of the hall. I had a quick, awkward conversation with Ben while Mindi just stood there saying nothing and looking a bit smug—at least I thought that was how she looked. And then we moved on.

"I don't think anything was there for Ben," I told my grandfather.

"But something is there for you?"

I nodded. "But what's the point if I never see him?" I shook my head. "Anyway, you have to promise not to say anything if you ever meet him again—not that that's likely to happen. But promise me, Zayde."

"Me? I'm like a steel trap." He mimed locking his mouth with a key. "So, now *I'm* keeping a little secret for *you*."

I hoped my face didn't reveal the guilt I was feeling. I hadn't done a very good job of keeping his secrets.

"You and Ben Morgan sounded so beautiful when you were singing together."

"Thanks. I loved being able to perform for you."

Now Zayde leaned forward, staring intently. "Do you understand why listening to music has been so hard for me?"

I nodded. "I think so. I mean, I'm trying to understand it. I know that it reminds you of your family and what happened to them."

"Yes, but there's so much more, Shirli." He hesitated. "I said before that letting go is the best thing you can do. I think . . . I think maybe I need to let go of some things I've been carrying around for too long. I want to tell you more about what happened to me in the concentration camp—in Auschwitz. Do you want to hear it?"

I knew, as soon as those words were out of Zayde's mouth, that we were heading down a path from which there could be no turning back. Was I really ready to hear this part of Zayde's story? I nodded, and watched as he brought his hands together in front of his mouth as if in prayer. He closed his eyes, then opened them and looked at me.

"You don't have to tell me if it's too hard," I said.

"It's more than that. I feel as though I have to tell you. I *need* to tell you what happened . . . if that's all right?"

"Yes, Zayde. I want to hear."

He took a deep breath and then began to speak.

"I told you about getting off that train, yes?"

"That's where you stopped."

He nodded. "As soon as we got off the train in that terrible place, the guards had us line up in rows. We were marched in front of an officer who wore a cap on his head with a skull and crossbones on the front of it. I couldn't take my eyes off that crest. In German, they called it *Totenkopf,* death's head—such a fitting name. The officer looked us up and down and then waved his hand like this." Zayde moved his hand first to one side and then to the other. "He was ordering us to go either to the left or to the right. My mother was sent to the left. My father, brothers, and I went right. We didn't know it at the time, but going left meant going instantly to your death—the gas chamber." Zayde squeezed his eyes shut once more.

Of course, I knew what the gas chambers in Auschwitz and other death camps were. Over those years, millions of people were locked into concrete rooms and deadly gas was dropped in through openings in the ceiling. It was horrifying to imagine people dying like that.

When Zayde opened his eyes I could see that there were tears already gathering in the corners. He wiped them away before continuing.

"I was still carrying my violin—that same violin that is sitting in the dining room, holding it against my chest as if it were life itself. Another officer saw it and stopped me. He asked if I played, and I nodded. So, he told me that my 'job' was going to be playing in the orchestra. My father and brothers were sent on without me, I didn't know where. And I was very scared, but I was also just a little bit relieved—happy, even. I thought this must be a decent place if there was music here. But I quickly learned how wrong I was. The Auschwitz Orchestra. Do you have any idea what we did, Shirli?"

"No," I whispered.

"At first, we played to accompany the prisoners to and from work. The guards demanded we play music that would keep the prisoners marching." Zayde tapped on the table to simulate a drumbeat. "We had to play in a quick tempo like this, to keep everyone walking fast, even though I could see that most of these poor souls had barely enough strength to place one foot in front of the other. We played like this for weeks. I still didn't know where my father and brothers had been sent. I was in a barrack with the other musicians. My father and brothers would have been better than any of them, and I tried to explain that to the commander who ran the orchestra but he wouldn't listen to me.

"Every day, I hoped I would see my family members walk past me. Once I actually saw my oldest brother, Aaron. I barely recognized him. In a matter of weeks, he had become a living skeleton—so thin, so weak. I was able to catch his eye and I raised my eyebrows as if to ask about our father and our brother Leo. But Aaron just shook his head and marched on. I knew immediately that my father and my brother were gone, along with my mother."

The tears were now flowing freely down Zayde's face. I reached out and grabbed his arm. I didn't want my grandfather to suffer through the telling of this painful story. He had suffered enough by having to live through it.

He placed his hand over mine and continued. "Eventually, we were told that the orchestra had a new job. We were to play every day on that same ramp where my family and I had first arrived. We were meant to *welcome* the new arrivals to Auschwitz when, in fact, all we were doing was accompanying them to their death. Some of the Jews waved to us as they walked by. I could see the looks on their faces. They were thinking what I had thought when I was told to play in the orchestra. How bad could it be here if there was music? I had to close my eyes so I wouldn't see their faces. Seeing the children walk by was worse than anything else." Zayde's voice caught in his throat. "Beautiful little faces, unsuspecting. So many innocent lives . . ."

Zayde was sweating, and so was I. I tightened my grip on his arm.

"And I knew what they didn't know. Those sent to the left were already dead. I was watching the dead walking by, playing music for them."

I could feel my chest constrict; it was hard to get air. Zayde's expression was so full of pain, so full of suffering.

"Zayde," I began, "you really don't have to go on. We could stop, you could take a break and—"

He held his hand up to stop me. "If I don't finish now, I don't know if I'll ever be able to," he said. I continued to grip his arm, trying to pass some strength from my body into his. Finally, he began to talk once more.

"There was a man in the orchestra. His name was Josef and he played the clarinet, just like my father had. He became my friend, and we tried to help each other as much as possible—sharing a piece of bread or picking the lice off of each other's heads. It meant so much to have someone there to rely on. If one of us was down, the other could help. In this way we tried to keep our spirits up. Josef was there for me when I discovered that Aaron had been shot while he was on a work detail. I was all alone now, except for this one friend.

"Josef had come from a village close to mine. His wife and son were in hiding, he told me. He had one picture of them that he had managed to keep when he came into the camp. He had concealed it in the lining of his clarinet case. He would pull it out every night, show it to me, and pray that his family would remain safe. One day, we were on the ramp playing for the new group of Jews who were arriving on the train. Josef was next to me, as he always was. Suddenly he just stopped playing. When I looked over at him, he was staring at the train. His mouth was open and he had gone completely white. I thought he had become sick and I was about to say something. But then he cried out. And when I followed his gaze, I could see what he was staring at. His wife and son were getting off the train. I recognized them instantly from the photo. We watched as they were both waved to the left. Josef didn't say a word. But do you know what he did?"

I shook my head numbly.

"He put down his clarinet, placed it on the ground. And then he stepped out of the orchestra and walked across the ramp." Zayde looked deeply into my eyes. "Josef followed his wife and son to the gas chamber."

I lowered my head onto the kitchen table and wept. I cried for all my relatives who had been killed. I cried for this poor man, Josef, whom I didn't know but whose story had affected me so deeply. I cried for my grandfather who had lived through this hell and yet survived to be this loving, kind man.

Zayde didn't try to stop me. He just let me cry. Finally, I raised my head.

"There were so many times after that when I was tempted to do what Josef had done—to put down my instrument and walk to my death. But I didn't, though I don't know why. And somehow, I managed to survive until the end of the war when Auschwitz was liberated. I was alive, even though my family—*our* family—was gone. I had watched so many people go to the gas chamber. And it was all to the sound of my violin. That's what music meant to me by the end of the war— a soundtrack of death. Do you understand, Shirli? Do you understand now why it's been impossible for me to be anywhere near music all these years?"

I nodded, still unable to speak.

"I was broken, the way the strings of my violin were broken. And it's been that way up until now. I had forgotten that music could be joyful. You and Ben Morgan reminded me of that when you sang for me. And I'm grateful."

I continued to sit with Zayde at the kitchen table for a long time. The only sound was the steady ticking of the clock on the wall. Neither of us spoke; there was nothing more to say. I just needed to be close to him, and I sensed that he wanted me close by as well.

Finally, I knew it was time to go. As I was getting my coat on I told him about the visit to see Ms. Ramsey in the hospital.

"She's going to be okay, but she's not going to be back at school for a long time," I said.

"So it's over for good? The play?"

"It's over for good."

Zayde sighed. "Maybe next year."

It was such a long way away, and who knew what might happen between now and then?

"Sure," I replied. "Maybe next year." I hugged Zayde for a long time. "Are you going to be okay now?" I finally asked. "I mean, after everything you talked about?"

"I'm going to be fine," he said. "But listen to me, Shirli. I want to tell you one more thing."

What more?

"Don't give up on your friend Ben Morgan. You have to keep fighting for what you want. Promise me that."

I smiled and nodded. "I'll call you later tonight," I said before walking out the door.

CHAPTER TWENTY-THREE

I barely slept that night. My brain raced over the story Zayde had told me, again and again. I was reliving all the terrible moments, the sickening details, almost as if I had been there myself. When morning came, my head felt so thick and heavy I could barely lift it.

At breakfast I didn't say a word. Thankfully, my parents didn't ask me anything. I knew I couldn't tell them what Zayde had revealed to me. I would tell them things that affected Zayde's safety or his health, but nothing more. If he wanted to tell my parents about his life history— or didn't want to tell them—that was his decision.

It was a relief to get out of the house and get to school, where I knew my friends would distract me.

At lunch, Natasha reached over and took another couple of french fries from my plate and popped them into her mouth. She'd already eaten all of her fries and most of mine.

"I can't believe how much you can eat," I said.

"I can't believe the play is really over," she replied.

"Yeah, that one still doesn't seem real."

"But we have to look on the bright side, right?" she said.

"Are you kidding me?"

"No, really, think about it. We have more time free, there's less pressure, and now there's a zero percent possibility of me screwing up in front of hundreds of people."

"You were going to do fine. All of us were. It was really going to be something special."

"Are you talking about the play, now, or your relationship with Ben?"

"First off, it's my *friendship* with Ben. And we haven't talked in days."

"Oh, I can fix that," Natasha said. And before I could stop her, she jumped to her feet. "Ben!" she yelled.

I looked at where she was staring. Ben—along with a bunch of his football friends—was walking across the cafeteria. He waved and smiled. I gave a little wave back. He turned to his friends and said something. I imagined it was something like, "Can you believe they think we're still friends now that the play is over?"

He gave one of his friends a poke in the shoulder and then came walking in our direction.

"You're welcome," Tash said as she grabbed a couple more of my fries.

"Hey, Tash. And Golde, how are you handling our separation?"

"It's been tough, but Tash has been helping to get me through it," I said.

Ben put his tray on the table and sat down beside me. Tash reached over and took one of his fries.

He held out the plate to me. "Would you like a few?"

I took a couple. "I should fill up on yours since Tash has eaten most of mine. Thank you."

"You're welcome. So, seriously, how are you doing since rehearsals stopped? Are you experiencing some major withdrawal?"

I shrugged. "I'm okay, I guess. And you?"

"I've still got that stupid fiddler playing in my head all night long and keeping me awake."

"That would be annoying," I agreed.

"Do you think there's any chance your Zayde would come over and play me a lullaby, instead?" Ben asked.

"No fair!" Tash said. "I've been friends with Shirli longer than you, and I've never heard him play!"

"Ben's actually the only one he's played for, aside from me," I pointed out. "He hasn't even played for my parents."

"Really?" Ben asked. I nodded. "What I can't get over is how he just played without music or anything."

"He told me he just has to hear a song once and he can play it," I explained.

"He should really be playing for lots of people," Ben said.

"He did," I said. "I guess that's the problem."

"What? Does he get stage fright?" Ben asked.

I wanted to tell them but I didn't know if I should.

"Come on, Shirl, I get the feeling there's a story here. Tell us!" Tash said.

Would that be betraying him? It was all weighing so heavily on me, Zayde's story. I hadn't been able to think of anything else.

"Only if you want to," Ben said.

The decision not to tell my parents had been easy. But telling my friends? Tash was someone I had turned to with all of my worries. And Ben . . . well, he was someone I trusted.

"If you tell us, you know it won't go any further," Tash said.

"Yeah, what happens at this table stays at this table," Ben added.

"Seriously, you can't tell *anyone*," I said, suddenly lowering my voice. "Not my parents, and especially not my Zayde." I stared hard at Ben, since he had a slightly tarnished record where secrets were concerned.

"Promise," Tash said.

"Me too. You have my word."

I took a deep breath. I had to get this out. "You already know some of my grandfather's history."

"It's pretty terrible the things he went through," Tash said.

"It's hard to get your head around that much evil being in the world," Ben added.

"You know his family all died. *My* family died," I said.

They both nodded solemnly.

"After his family was captured, they were shipped to a concentration camp."

"Shipped? You make it sound like they were loaded onto a UPS truck," Tash said, and I could see from her expression that she instantly regretted it. "I'm sorry . . . I didn't mean to make a bad joke about something that terrible."

"I know you didn't. Sometimes making a joke is just a way of trying to make it less real." I reached over and gave her hand a gentle pat. "Zayde and his family were packed onto a train, in a cattle car with tons of other Jews, and sent to the camps—sent to Auschwitz."

"It's beyond what you think people could ever do to other people," Ben said.

"Yes, exactly." I nodded.

"I think I felt something like that on 9/11," Ben said. "Not on the same scale, of course."

The image of the towers falling filled my head. Would those images ever leave my mind? How could Zayde ever put the images he'd seen behind him?

"Auschwitz," Ben repeated. "It was the worst place, where the largest number of people were killed. I started doing some reading after talking to your grandfather. I needed to know more."

"It was the largest mass murder site in history," I said.

"But didn't everybody who went there die?" Tash asked.

"Over a million people," Ben said.

"But others were used as forced labor. They didn't die right away," I explained. "My Zayde was one of the lucky ones who lived. It was because of his violin."

"His violin saved him?" Ben asked.

"The one you saw, the one you heard him play. He brought it with him to the concentration camp. Because of his violin he became part of an orchestra." I felt my chest suddenly tighten—the same feeling I'd had when Zayde had told me all of this. I wasn't sure if I could go on. I also didn't know if I could stop. I took a deep breath.

"There was an orchestra in Auschwitz?" Tash asked.

And then I just told them the whole story— everything that Zayde had told me. I kept talking, the words kept spilling out. And finally I told them about Josef, who had simply put down his clarinet and walked to his death with his wife and son.

Natasha started to cry, and Ben looked close to tears. I realized that in trying to lighten the load of this story from my own shoulders I'd put some of the weight of it on them.

"I shouldn't have told you," I finally said.

"I'm glad you did," Ben said. "Your grandfather, your Zayde, is that why he didn't want to play music ever again, because it reminded him of all of that?"

"Yes, that's what he said. He felt that somehow his music was the soundtrack for all of that death."

"What he did . . . well . . . how could anybody be brave enough and strong enough to survive?"

"I don't think I could ever be that strong," I replied.

"And now he's brave enough to pick up that violin again," Ben said.

"And after so many years," Tash said. "Why now?"

"He told me that it was because of me and Ben," I said.

"Us?"

"He said when we sang it reminded him of the joy of music."

Ben's eyes were as wide as two saucers. "Shirli, thank you," he finally said. "Thank you for trusting us enough to tell us. And it all stays at this table, right, Natasha?"

She looked as though she wanted to speak, but no words came out. Finally, she just nodded.

"Would you ask your Zayde if I can go over and see him again?" Ben said.

"You know you can't let on that I told you any of this," I cautioned.

"Of course not. I just like talking to him."

The bell went. It was loud and long and jarring. All around us people started gathering up their things and heading toward classes. The three of us got up as well, but instead of leaving we just stood there. It was as if none of us wanted to be the first to go, or even knew how to leave.

"I can't afford to be late for my next class," Ben said, finally breaking the silence.

"Yeah, we'd better get moving," I said.

But we didn't. We all stood there.

Finally, Ben reached out and wrapped an arm around me and an arm around Tash. We stood there in a group hug as people all around us filed out.

CHAPTER TWENTY-FOUR

A couple of days later, the entire *Fiddler* cast and crew were called to a meeting in the auditorium. Everyone was shuffling in—the actors, the set people, the musicians. Even the ever-silent Mr. Nevarez was present, although instead of sitting at his piano he took a seat at the back of the auditorium. The only person missing was Ms. Ramsey, and I knew she wasn't coming.

It was comforting and disturbing to be all together again like that, sort of like a high school reunion for a class that graduated four days ago. Okay, *graduated* was wrong. We were a class that failed. We hadn't finished our big final assignment.

"How long are we going to have to wait?" Natasha asked.

Ben looked at his phone. "It's just 3:38 so he's only a few minutes late. I'm sure he'll be here soon."

He was our principal, Mr. James, who had called this meeting.

"I think the more important question is, why does he want to meet with us?" Mohammed said.

"I think it's to formally announce that the play has been canceled." Mindi had joined the conversation.

"I thought he basically did that when he told us about Ms. Ramsey," I said.

"No," Ben said. "He hasn't stopped looking for someone to save the day. He told me."

"And you think he found someone?" I asked.

Ben shook his head. "I don't think we should get our hopes up. But at least he's been trying. I know he's upset about this."

"Not as upset as we are," Mindi said. "Do you think there's any chance he'd let us run the play ourselves?"

"I already asked. He said we need to have a staff coordinator and adult supervision at all times," Ben answered.

"What about him?" I gestured toward Mr. Nevarez.

"Mr. James asked him if he would take over, but he said the only thing he could do was play the piano. Nothing more."

"Probably for the best," Mindi said. "I can't see him as a director."

"I just can't believe that not one teacher in the whole school would step up," Tash said.

"Well, to be fair, we need more than just any old teacher agreeing to come out and babysit us. There's a lot of skill and work involved. It almost wore out Ms. Ramsey.

I mean, it's not like the math teacher or the football coach could just jump in and do it," I said.

"Although it would be interesting to have Coach Morrison step in. I can hear him yelling, 'Those harmonies are pitchy! And you call those jazz squares? Everybody drop, and give me twenty push-ups!'" Tash kidded.

Suddenly the back door opened and Mr. James walked in. The conversations in the room died instantly. It was so silent that we could hear his footfalls as he walked down the aisle. I tried to read his expression to see if I could figure out the message in advance. He looked grim. But then again, he always looked grim.

He stopped at the front of the stage. "Sorry to keep you all waiting," he began. "I know you must be wondering why I called this meeting."

There was a nodding of heads and a mumbling of responses.

"I know how difficult this has been on all of you," he continued. "To work so hard on something you love and to have things put on hold must have been painful."

"Did he say 'put on hold'?" Natasha whispered to me. "Do you think that means something?"

I shook my head. That was just wishful thinking.

"I realize that what hurt the most was how close you were to having things ready to go," Mr. James continued. "From what Ben has told me in our discussions, you were probably 65 to 70 percent done."

"The sets are 95 percent finished," said Kevin, the head of the stage crew.

"Well, the closer you are to the finish line, the harder it is for everybody to have it canceled."

There was that word. That's what this was about. I just wanted him to say it—put us out of our misery. Give the bandage one good rip.

Mr. James looked down at his watch. Did he have some place he had to be? Or was he just stalling because he was nervous about breaking the bad news? Wasn't that a whole big part of his job description?

"The play's run was scheduled to be from April 23 through April 27," he said.

"If we delayed it to the end of May, would that allow Ms. Ramsey enough time to come back?" Ben asked.

"I'm afraid not," Mr. James said. "And pushing it further into May interferes with other school activities. Besides, Ms. Ramsey's injuries are severe enough that it has been determined she will be on medical leave until partway through the fall semester. Obviously, by then many of you will have already graduated."

He looked at his watch again and then glanced to the back door.

"As you all know," he continued, "our spring play has been one of the hallmark events of our school over the past twenty years. Some people have even come to this school just to be part of it."

I knew it was one of the reasons I had chosen to attend here.

"To try to fulfill our commitment, I spoke—more than once—to every teacher in the school. I'm afraid no one has both time available and the kind of skills that would qualify them to take on the responsibilities of a director," he said.

Okay, now he was getting down to it.

"And on that list of people who aren't qualified, my name is at the top . . . or you might say the bottom," he said. He looked at his watch again. "Which makes this perhaps my most surprising announcement ever. Please say hello to your new staff coordinator for the play . . . me."

"You?" I blurted this out loud and then clapped my hand over my mouth. But judging from the looks around the room, I wasn't alone in my shock.

"Does this mean the play is back on?" Ben asked.

"Yes, it does!"

There was a moment of stunned silence, and then the crowd erupted into cheers and hugs and chatter.

Mr. James allowed the celebration to go on for a few more seconds before raising his hands to quiet everybody down.

"But there will have to be some changes," he continued. "For one, the opening night has been pushed back. We'll start on April 30."

"That makes sense. It'll give us about four weeks,

and we're going to need the time," Mindi said, and there was a chorus of agreement and a nodding of heads.

"We'll still have five nights of performances with the final show on Saturday, May 4."

"That's five more than we would have had without your help. I think I speak for everyone here when I say, thank you so much!" Ben exclaimed.

"I have a question," Mindi said.

"I'm sure there are going to be many questions. Go ahead, Mindi."

"It's just, and I don't mean any offense, but how are you going to direct us when you don't have any experience?"

Mr. James paused and then shook his head. "Oh, I'm not going to direct you. I'm simply the staff liaison. It couldn't take place without a staff member being technically in charge. Your director is somebody from outside the school. His musical background is somewhat, well, different from the formal training of Ms. Ramsey."

I had a strange thought—had my father actually decided he was going to give it a try?

"I was hoping to be able to introduce him to you but apparently he's been delayed, and you might not meet him until practice tomorrow morning."

My eye caught some movement and I turned toward the door. A man wearing a suit and a hat walked in and—

"Shirli, isn't that your grandfather?" Ben asked.

He'd said it at the same instant my brain had clicked into it. My mind was instantly filled with worry. Had something happened to my parents? Had Zayde come to tell me that? Had he—?

"And with perfect timing," Mr. James said, "can we please have a round of applause for your new director!"

CHAPTER TWENTY-FIVE

There was a pounding in my ears, like a dizzying head rush. Had Mr. James really just said that Zayde was going to be the new director of *Fiddler*? My Zayde? The man who, for my entire life, had never listened to the radio or played a CD or even sat in a theater? The man who had just confessed to me the awful reason why music was so deeply painful to him? Was this the person who was suddenly going to step in and immerse himself in our musical production? I couldn't get my spinning head around it. The whole thing was bizarre and baffling and, well, just plain crazy. And what was more, I didn't like it one bit!

I reached out and grabbed the back of the seat in front of me, trying to steady myself. Meanwhile, all around the auditorium my castmates were staring in wonder and some confusion at the small, elderly man wearing a visitor's badge who was now walking down the aisle, a big grin creasing his face. He adjusted his tie and removed his fedora as he approached our group.

Mr. James cleared his throat. "I would like to introduce to you your new director, Mr. Tobias Berman."

The applause started slowly and hesitantly. It was certainly not an overwhelming ovation, but it was polite and respectful enough. The only person clapping really enthusiastically was Ben. He was whooping and cheering as if he had just won the football championship. Other castmates were staring at him, murmuring, clearly confused by his reaction.

At first I could hardly make out what anyone was whispering. All I could hear was the sound of blood rushing in my ears. My face was burning.

Zayde had reached the front of the auditorium and was shaking hands with Mr. James. "The taxi driver—a lovely man, but he had no idea where he was going. And I couldn't help him. It's a wonder we found our way here."

Mr. James laughed. "I'm glad you made it. I was just letting the students know that you have kindly and generously offered to direct the production," he said. "Your arrival was timed perfectly." Then he turned once more to the group of us. "Mr. Berman is Shirli's grandfather. Most of you probably don't know that."

My face, which was already burning, now reached inferno temperatures. Sweat was gathering at the back of my neck and creeping across my forehead. I wanted to say something—welcome my grandfather, put him at ease, tell him how proud I was to have him here—anything! But all I could do was stand there with one of those fake smiles planted on my face, the kind where you're grinning on the outside, but inside your stomach is churning and you wish the floor would open up and swallow you whole.

Zayde stared at me and a flicker of worry clouded his eyes. He hesitated a moment, as if he realized something was wrong. I could fool other people but Zayde knew me very well. And then, he just stood there, awkwardly moving his hat from one hand to the other. Mr. James looked as if he was going to say something else. But before he could, Ben stepped to the front of the auditorium.

"Mr. Berman," he exclaimed, grabbing Zayde's hand and pumping it up and down. "It's so great to have you here."

"Ben Morgan. It's good to see you again," Zayde replied. "I bet you didn't think it would be me to walk through those doors."

Ben laughed out loud before turning to the rest of the cast. "You don't know this man yet," he said, "but I can tell you that he's a great musician."

And that's all it took for the entire cast and crew to rush forward and surround my grandfather. Everyone was asking questions all at once.

"How well do you know *Fiddler*?"

"Have you ever directed anything before?"

"Can you sing?"

"Can you dance?"

"Do you play an instrument?"

The questions tumbled over one another like water over a ledge. I hung back, still struggling with my reaction to seeing my grandfather here, and still confused by how conflicted I felt about his presence. Zayde looked a bit dazed and overwhelmed until Mr. James finally silenced everyone by raising his hand.

"I'm sure Mr. Berman will be happy to answer your questions. But first things first. Why don't you tell him your names and what you're doing in the show."

Zayde nodded and, one by one, the cast and crew stepped forward to introduce themselves. I stiffened when Mindi held out her hand to shake Zayde's. Had I told him that we were rivals? I couldn't remember. My grandfather was known for not having a filter, and I was terrified that he'd say something. But he just smiled at her.

When it was Mohammed's turn, I got a bit anxious again.

"What was your name?" Zayde asked, narrowing his eyes and cupping one hand behind his ear.

"Mohammed, sir. I'm playing Perchik, your real granddaughter's stage son-in-law." Mohammed was grinning like a kid with an ice cream cone—although I had a feeling that his smile was more nervous than natural.

Zayde hesitated a moment, and I had a terrible thought—was he going to say something inappropriate about a guy named Mohammed playing a Jew? My hands found my hair and started to wind. But Zayde just nodded and muttered, "Interesting." Then he moved on to the next person. *Thank goodness!*

When he had finished meeting the entire cast and crew, he stood back and faced everyone.

"It will take me some time to learn all of your names. At my age, I'm afraid the names come and go. But thank you for such a warm welcome."

Was it my imagination, or did Zayde stare right at me when he said that last part?

"You've asked many questions about my background and about how well I know this musical. Well, the truth is I just read the play for the first time a few weeks ago."

A murmur passed through the auditorium. Zayde smiled.

"Yes, that's right, only a few weeks ago. But I will tell you something that's more important than knowing this play. I *feel* this play—here, in my heart," he said, tapping his chest with one hand. "I know these characters. I understand them. I could tell you more, but this isn't about words, it's about music. Is there a violin I can borrow?"

Our Fiddler, Thomas, rushed away, grabbed his violin case, and returned to hand it to Zayde.

"Thank you for allowing me to play your instrument."

"It's really the school's."

"Still, it is in your care. Thank you."

Zayde sat down, slowly opened the case, and removed the violin and bow. He ran his fingers along the strings and then inspected the bow. Everybody stood in silence, watching, waiting, as he examined the instrument, running his hand along the side, plucking the strings. He raised it to his chin. Then he took the bow and drew it across the strings, pausing a moment to tune a couple of them. Finally, he took a deep breath, closed his eyes, and began to play the opening song from *Fiddler*. It was as if he had been practicing it for months. His body swayed back and forth and he seemed lost in the music as his fingers flew across the strings.

There were a few seconds of silence, and then everybody started cheering and clapping. My hands hung by my side.

Tash leaned over to whisper in my ear. "What's wrong? Isn't it good that your grandfather's here to help."

I smiled weakly. How could I explain my lack of enthusiasm to her? I was still trying to understand it myself.

Finally, Zayde lowered the violin, opened his eyes, faced the cast, and said, "I think it is time to get started."

CHAPTER TWENTY-SIX

It was quiet in the hallway of the school as I sat with Zayde after the rehearsal. Everyone else had already left, except for the security guard who paced at the other end of the hall, checking now and then to see if Zayde and I were still there. We'd called for a cab so that I could accompany my grandfather back to his home, and now we were watching for it through the window next to the school's front door.

My head was still buzzing from everything that had happened in the last few hours—Zayde walking into the auditorium, the announcement that he was our new director. It was still too much to take in. I had to admit, though, that the first rehearsal under my grandfather had gone remarkably well. He had worked through the opening few scenes with the cast, listening closely to each voice and offering some pretty good feedback about how to adjust the tone and volume here and there to make the numbers sound even better. He'd even made Mr. Nevarez smile a couple of times. Still, I couldn't bring myself to say that I was completely glad he had swooped in to rescue our production.

Zayde was the one to break the deafening silence. "Have I made you angry by doing this, Shirli?"

I sighed heavily. "No, Zayde. You could never make me angry. It's just that I'm so confused. I mean, up until a few days ago, the best you could offer was 'It's not impossible' that you would even *see* me in this play. And now you're my director?"

"But I thought this would make you happy. You wanted the play to go on, didn't you?"

"Of course I did. And I *am* happy. But I also feel a bit . . . ambushed."

"What does this mean?"

"Ambushed. It's when something happens—like an attack—that you didn't expect."

Zayde's eyes widened. "An attack?"

"I don't mean that you attacked me!" This conversation was getting worse by the minute. "I just didn't see it coming, that's all."

Zayde shook his head. "I've done everything wrong, haven't I?"

I could have cried. "No! You haven't. You've just got to give me a bit of time to sit with this. I'll adjust. I promise." Silence filled the hallway once more. And then I asked, "Why didn't you tell me that you wanted to do this?"

"You were so upset the last time you visited, when you told me the play was over. I thought this would be a surprise," Zayde replied feebly. "A *good* surprise."

Didn't he know how much I hated surprises? Almost as much as I hated secrets!

"Besides, I didn't want to risk disappointing you if I found I just couldn't do it after all." He paused. "I wasn't late because of the taxi driver. He got me here early. I stood outside the school, wondering if I could walk through the door, wondering if I could do this thing, to direct the play."

I took another deep breath. "I think I get it," I said. "It's like wanting to go by yourself to buy the violin strings."

"You *do* understand me," he said, smiling.

So . . . what was it that was making me uncomfortable? I was so happy that the play was back on, and that Ben and I were going to be working together again. What was my problem? And then it came to me.

Somehow, Zayde's presence at school felt like a kind of betrayal. When he had taken his first steps back toward music, he had shared that with only me . . . well, me and Ben. I was the one he had opened up to, though, no one else, not even my parents. And now he was suddenly showing that side of himself to everyone at my school. He had *played* for all of them. Maybe I was jealous, I thought with a start. I was going to have to share Zayde and the special relationship we had with everyone in the cast.

Even as I thought that, I knew how ridiculous it was. No matter what happened, he was still my Zayde. He wasn't some snack that I would have to divide up among my friends, the way I did when I was a kid.

"So, Zayde," I said, "how are you going to get to school and back for rehearsals?" I had a mental image of arriving at Zayde's at the crack of dawn and then getting on a bus with him. That wasn't going to happen. "And don't tell me that you plan to walk, or take a bus alone, because that's impossible!"

"Your principal—that nice Mr. James—he said he'd arrange a taxi for me every time. You don't have to worry about that. And I'll be very careful."

No one had ever used the words "nice" and "Mr. James" in the same sentence before. It nearly made me laugh out loud.

"But what about the strain of all of this? It's going to be a lot of hours for you, especially as we get closer to opening."

At that Zayde turned to face me. "Shirli, my darling granddaughter, don't you realize how young this makes me feel? Since your Bubbie died, I sit in my house day after day with nothing but my television—and the hope that you or your parents or your brother will visit. Today I felt useful for the first time in a long time."

I was being such an idiot! And totally selfish. I'd been making this all about me. I took another deep breath.

"I get it, Zayde," I said as the cab pulled into the driveway of the school. "And I'm sorry I made you feel bad when all you're trying to do is help us. I'm really grateful for that. But here's the deal," I added as I turned to him. "I need to tell Mom and Dad about all of this. I'm not going to keep any more secrets from them." Zayde didn't know that I had already told them about his fall. But at this point it was important to lay all the cards on the table.

Zayde nodded slowly. "I knew this was too big to keep a secret. So it won't be one. Yes, it's important to tell them everything."

"Everything?" I asked.

He nodded. "Yes, everything."

"And no more surprises, Zayde," I added as I opened the door of the cab for him. "Please!"

At that, he finally smiled. "That's a deal."

∾

My parents were surprised but remarkably calm when I told them the news.

"I'm glad you'll be able to keep an eye on him," my mother said. "Make sure he doesn't overdo it."

"I promise I won't let him try to demonstrate the choreography!"

And I explained that Zayde had agreed to put an end to the secrets, and he'd said it was okay to tell them everything.

"It's good that everything will be out in the open now," Mom said.

"At least now, we can talk to him about that fall he had."

I didn't respond, and that's when Mom stared straight at me with that look that meant she knew there was more.

"Okay, talk," she said. "Is there something you're not telling us?"

And that's when I blurted out everything. I told them how awkward it had been for me when Zayde first walked into the auditorium, and how torn I'd felt about him being there. They listened and just let me pour my heart out.

"I'm being ridiculous, right? I should have been whooping for joy that we're going to do the play. Instead I was worried that I was going to lose Zayde to everyone else. I sound like I'm five years old."

"No, I get it," my father said. "I have to admit, I was a bit jealous myself when your Zayde played his violin for you, and told you things about his life that he'd never told me. After all, I'm his son!"

I hadn't thought of that! But it made sense. "I think he was only trying to protect you, Dad."

"Of course, I realize that. But in that moment I was jealous that he had chosen you to talk to and not me."

"I understand what you're saying," Mom added. "But I'm sure you will come to realize that there is plenty of Zayde for everyone."

I laughed. "You make him sound like a bowl of chips."

"And you will always be his one and only grand-daughter," my mother said.

I paused. Then, "I'm going to tell you something that you might think is funny. I thought that maybe Dad was going to try to become the director."

Neither of them laughed. They exchanged a look.

"I guess I wasn't as subtle as I thought," he said.

"What do you mean?"

"Your father was trying to make arrangements at work so he could step in," my mother said.

He shrugged. "I just couldn't make it happen."

I threw my arms around him. "Thank you for even trying."

"I had to. After all, you're not the only one with music in your blood," he said. "So, are you good with all of this?"

I sighed. "I'm good. Now I just have to hope Zayde doesn't say anything to embarrass me."

"Who, Mr. No Filter? Oh, I think you pretty well have to accept that there will be something," my father said.

"Your father's right," my mother added. "We can only hope it's not too bad!"

CHAPTER TWENTY-SEVEN

We were now seven rehearsals into the second phase of the show with our new director, and three weeks away from our new opening night. So far, it was going very well. Zayde knew each character, each song, and, maybe most important, each member of the cast and crew.

We were in the middle of our first complete run-through. Zayde sat in the front row, dead center, watching, making notes in a little black notebook. As each scene ended, he would rise, approach the stage, and give feedback to the actors. Sometimes the notes were positive—"That was amazing," "You almost made me cry," "Beautiful voice." Sometimes they were less than positive—"You already forgot the new staging I gave you!" "Couldn't you feel that a bit more?" "No, no, that accent is wrong." And sometimes the comments were borderline inappropriate, to say the least—"Ben, you need to think like a Jew," "Shirli, you'd think you'd know how an old Jewish woman would sound." At least he wasn't showing me any favoritism because I was his granddaughter!

I was nervous all the way through each rehearsal. His comments were so unpredictable! I'd come to accept what my parents had said—sooner or later he'd do something to embarrass me. There was no telling what he might say next—and here at my school, in front of so many people!

I stood off to the side as Mindi belted out her big number with Mohammed. He seemed nervous. Mindi was great. She had a natural flare, a certain élan. She owned the stage, and I couldn't stop watching her.

The scene ended and everybody stayed in place, waiting for Zayde to give his notes. He pushed himself up to his feet and started clapping.

"Everybody, don't you think they deserve a little bit of applause?" he asked.

Slowly but surely, everyone, including me, joined in. Mindi and Mohammed both deserved it.

"Mindi, you are what we'd call a natural . . . and that voice! Up on that stage is where you belong . . . no question."

Mindi was smiling so hard I thought her face would explode.

"But there is something we need from you," Zayde continued. "I need you to let your voice get quieter. You have to let your voice not overwhelm your emotions.

Sometimes less is more. Have you ever heard this saying?" he asked.

She nodded. "I think so." The smile had disappeared,
and now Mindi was looking uncomfortable, even a
little embarrassed.

"Sometimes a whisper is better than a roar. You need
to have confidence in your ability, knowing that you
can impress the audience without having to blow back
their hair."

A couple of people chuckled. Mindi looked even
more worried.

"Remember, you are an artist, not an athlete. It isn't
about who can sing the loudest or hit the highest note
or hold it the longest."

He stopped talking, and Mindi looked relieved. She
shouldn't have been. I knew that look on Zayde's face.
He wasn't done, he was just thinking.

"Where is Shirli?" he asked suddenly.

I felt a chill go up my spine.

"Shirli, are you backstage?" he asked.

I moved out a few steps so I was on the edge of the
stage where he could see me, and I raised my hand. A
sense of dread rose up inside me. He wasn't going to
ask me to sing the song and show her how it should be
done, was he?

"Good. I wanted you to be here when I said this.
You all know that my granddaughter has a magnificent

voice, there is no arguing that. Wouldn't you all agree?"

Oh, please stop, please don't say anything more, please!

He turned back to face Mindi. "But Mindi, your voice may be a little bit better than hers."

That wasn't what I'd expected. I had to stop my mouth from dropping open.

He held his finger and thumb just a fraction apart. "Not much, but maybe this amount. So, Mindi with the magnificent voice, do you think you could give us less so you can give us more?"

"I can try." I noticed that her smile was back.

"Good, but you will not try, you will succeed. You are not only a good girl, but a true performer. Now, I will talk to Mohammed." He turned and motioned for Mohammed to come up closer to him. They met at the steps of the stage. "It seemed as though you were a little nervous up there, is that true?"

"Yes, sir, I was nervous . . . I *am* nervous."

"I thought so. Do you think that maybe part of your nervousness could be that you're playing a Jew?"

Uh-oh! My heart rose up into my throat again.

"You are a Muslim?" Zayde asked him.

My heart stopped.

"Yes, sir."

"I thought as much. That name, Mohammed, it says it all."

I wanted to say something . . . but what?

"It's like my name, Tobias Berman, you sort of figure that I'm a Jew, right? So here you are, a Muslim standing on stage playing a Jew."

"Um, yes, sir."

I looked helplessly to Natasha. "You'd better do something," she whispered.

I nodded and stepped forward. "Zayde!"

"Shirli, please, I need to talk to Mohammed. Just wait. So, Mohammed, do you know what I think about a Muslim playing a Jew? Can you guess?"

A gasp went through the auditorium. I had a vague, random thought that maybe Ben would speak up and save the day . . . or maybe I could just miraculously transport myself to another dimension.

"No, sir, I don't know how you feel," Mohammed said, finding his voice.

I braced myself for my grandfather's answer.

"I feel so happy," Zayde said.

What did he say?

"I feel so happy," he repeated, louder this time. "You know, the Jews, Christians, and Muslims, we are all the children of Abraham. But of course you would call him Ibrahim, wouldn't you?"

"Yes, sir, we would."

Zayde smiled. "You are so polite. My blessed mother who lived through these difficult times, she always made us call our elders 'sir' or 'madam.' When you go home tonight, you tell your parents they raised a very polite young man, okay?"

"Um, yes . . . I mean yes, *sir*," he said.

Everybody laughed. And just like that, I felt the tension drain out of the room.

"So, do you know what all that means? You are playing a Jew, knowing that you as a Muslim are part of the same bloodline. You have every right to be playing a Jew. Up there you are a young Jewish man, full of promise and hope and spit and vinegar. That's a good expression, yes? That is how you must be, filled with confidence."

"I'll try, sir."

"As with Mindi, you will do more than try, you will succeed. I know you will." Zayde paused. He looked as though he was thinking. "Mohammed, may I ask you something?"

"Of course, sir, anything."

"This may be a little, how do they say, delicate, so I hope you don't take offense."

Uh-oh, if Zayde thought something was delicate, it was probably going to be a bombshell.

"Since September, since the towers, has it been harder for you, for your family?"

Unexpectedly Mohammed laughed—nervous laughter, it seemed. He looked down at his feet and nodded.

"Have things happened?"

Again, he nodded. "People have said things . . . called my mother a terrorist . . . people here at school have said things to me . . . I have friends who were beaten up . . . our mosque has received threats." His voice was quavering.

Zayde climbed the stairs and took a seat on one of the two chairs that were stage right.

"Mohammed, come, sit," Zayde said.

Mohammed sat in the chair beside him.

"I want everybody to come out to the stage, everybody!" Zayde called out. "Everybody come, we need to talk."

Stagehands, crew members, and cast members shuffled out from behind the stage and from audience seats and moved right up to the stage. Zayde had taken Mohammed's hands in his. Then, he released his grip.

"I have a new friend," Zayde said when everyone had quieted down. "His name is Amir and his family is from India. He is an American. Mohammed, you're an American, aren't you?"

"Yes, I was born in Newark."

"I thought I heard a little Newark in your voice. Well, my friend owns a store, and people have been vandalizing it. They have written words like 'Terrorist' and 'Taliban' on his wall. He's Indian and he's Hindu. He's not even Muslim . . . not that it would be any less wrong if he were . . . it's just, these vandals, well, they're even stupid."

We reacted with a ripple of laughter.

"How many of you remember exactly where you were when the planes hit the towers?" he asked.

Every hand went up.

"That is my stupid question. Of course, you remember. More important, how many of you remember how you *felt*?"

A few hands reluctantly rose, and then a few more, and finally every hand. I looked around. All eyes were glued on my grandfather.

"It made me feel scared and confused and angry and sad all at once," Zayde said. He paused. "The way all of us felt that day, and maybe sometimes still feel."

Then he turned, searching through the cast, looking for someone. His eyes came to rest on Thomas, our violinist.

"Thomas, can I borrow your violin?" he asked.

Thomas came forward and handed the violin and bow to my grandfather.

"In our play, there is a man sitting on a roof, playing a fiddle."

Zayde played the first few notes from the opening scene and then paused, still holding the instrument under his chin.

"These people you are playing. They felt the same way you felt that day. Their world had been turned upside down. They were uncertain, scared for their lives and for the lives of their children, for their future."

He started playing again. The notes were so pure and clean and full of emotion. I felt myself on the verge of tears, and I could hear others around me sniffling.

Zayde stopped playing. "This is more than a play. This is about lives that were lived. Lives like my mother's. When we say the lines, when we play the music, when we sing the songs, we are remembering them."

He started playing again.

Ben was standing beside me, and he reached out and took my hand. I was shocked. Until I realized that he'd also joined hands with Mohammed. I reached for Natasha. All along, everybody was linking hands until we were one big chain.

We listened as the fiddler on the roof played.

CHAPTER TWENTY-EIGHT

Mr. James looked at his watch—again. Zayde was late. Our principal looked as though he had someplace else he had to be, but obviously he couldn't leave us unsupervised. Zayde was coming by taxi, which was always unpredictable, so I wasn't *too* worried. Still, it was a relief when the back door finally opened and Zayde appeared. And then, I saw Amir trailing behind him!

Mr. James walked up the aisle and they met in the middle, where they exchanged a handshake and a few words I couldn't hear. Then, our principal continued walking and went out the door.

I walked over to Zayde and Amir.

"Shirli, you of course remember my good friend, Amir."

Like Zayde, he was wearing a visitor's badge on his jacket. Everyone arriving at the school other than staff and students had to check in with the office—another consequence of 9/11.

"Of course, hello," I said. It was nice to see Amir, though I couldn't figure out why he was here.

"It is good to see you once more, Shirli."

"Amir drove me to rehearsal. I would have been much later without his help."

"But you would not have been late at all if you had not offered your help to me," Amir added.

This was turning into an even bigger puzzle.

"Shirli, I was telling Amir about the play, and he knew nothing about *Fiddler on the Roof.*"

"Nothing," Amir said. "But I will be coming to the opening night, along with my wife and two of my children."

"That's great!" I said.

"Amir would like to watch the rehearsal, Shirli. No one would mind, would they?"

I wasn't too sure about that, but before I had a chance to answer, Zayde was on his way down to the stage, giving direction to the proper placement of a set piece, leaving me with Amir.

"I could sit at the back and quietly observe," he suggested. "I've never been to a theater rehearsal before."

"Yes, please, you're welcome to stay," I said. I mean, at that point, anything else would have been rude!

Zayde was starting the rehearsal with one of Ben's scenes—one that didn't involve me—so I decided to sit with Amir. That way I could explain the scene to him if he had any questions. I could also ask him why he had driven Zayde, why they were late, and what the help was that Zayde had offered him.

I walked up the aisle. "May I join you?"

"Please, yes, of course," Amir said, getting to his feet.

I sat down in the next seat and he sat back down with me.

"That was kind of you to drive my Zayde," I said.

"It is small payment for making him late to begin with. You see he was doing my books."

"Your books?"

"The store's books. He was showing me a better way to record my accounts receivable and payable. He is very good."

"He's a certified public accountant. He's done that all his life."

"Yes, he told me that. He is very skilled. He has made some changes that will make it much easier and save me money. Speaking of which, I wish he would allow me to pay him for his services."

"He never did like to charge friends or family."

"I am honored that he and I are friends."

Just then, there was a call for silence as the scene was about to start. "This is the opening scene of act 2," I whispered as I leaned closer. "That's Ben playing Tevye, the lead character."

Ben was sitting on a bench outside his house and delivering his monologue, looking up at the sky and talking to God. He finished and exited stage left. Mindi and

Mohammed, who had been standing stage right, now walked to center stage.

"The girl is Hodel," I explained. "She's one of Tevye's daughters, one of my daughters, and that's Mohammed, who plays the guy who becomes her husband, Perchik."

"Mohammed, he is Muslim, and he looks as though he is from Pakistan." Amir was also whispering.

"Yes, he is Muslim. I don't know where his family is from but he was born here in New Jersey, so he's American."

"As my youngest two children, born here, are also Americans."

We sat and watched and listened as they played out the scene. Mohammed as Perchik was explaining that he was going to be leaving their village and going to live in Kiev to be part of the revolution, and he was asking Hodel to marry him.

I quietly mouthed Mindi's lines as she spoke them. I knew all of her lines and all of her songs. But today I noticed that there was something different in Mindi's delivery. The lines were all there, but her voice sounded tired, as though she had been up too late talking. It was a cardinal rule for all of us that we had to get a decent amount of sleep every night, and we had to make sure we didn't overuse our voices when we weren't in rehearsal. Mindi sounded like hers was about an octave lower than usual. And there was a scratchy quality that normally wasn't there—like tires on a gravel road. But as soon as she sang a few notes of her next song, I knew that this wasn't about lack of sleep or too much talking. The girl was coming down with something. I excused myself to Amir as Zayde brought the scene to an early stop, and I made my way to the stage.

Zayde was having a deep conversation with Mindi.

"So, today you will rest and not use your voice too much in the scenes. Yes?"

Mindi looked as though she was going to cry. "I'm really fine, Mr. Berman. I don't need to pull back from anything."

"Of course, you are fine. Did I say you weren't fine? You are wonderful. But today you will rest a little. And then you will be even more fine. Agreed?"

Mindi seemed to want to say something else. But other cast members were beginning to gather around, trying to figure out what was happening. So instead, she just nodded and rushed backstage.

I followed, my mind going a mile a minute. Mindi was getting sick. There was no doubt about that. And if she was sick, then this might really be my chance to take over her part. You had to have a perfect voice to sing that beautiful solo.

I found Mindi sitting in a back corner behind some props and half hidden by costumes. She was hunched over and sniveling into her sleeve. She looked up when I approached, tears streaming down her cheeks.

"So, are you happy now?" she demanded. "This is what you wanted, isn't it?"

I shook my head. I was a little surprised and a little hurt. I'd thought we'd moved beyond just being rivals.

I hesitated. Of course I wanted to be Hodel in this production. I'd wanted it from the moment I knew we were going to be doing *Fiddler*. But did I really want my victory to be at someone else's expense—even if that someone happened to be my rival?

I crouched down next to her. "I just wanted to see if you were okay."

She shook her head. "Stupid cold!"

"When did you feel it coming on?"

"A couple of nights ago. I thought it was just a tickle in my throat. But then it got worse, and now it feels like I've got sandpaper stuck in there. Why, oh why, is this happening now, of all times?" That brought on a second wave of tears.

Okay, she was being just a bit dramatic. But I, of all people, understood her desperation and her drama. "I get it. It's terrible to feel your voice starting to go just before a show."

She looked up again, eyes wide open. "But this has never happened to me before."

I couldn't believe what I was hearing. "Are you kidding me? You've never gotten a cold or lost your voice before a performance?" I could count on both hands and both feet the number of times I had found myself in her shoes.

She shook her head. "This is the first time."

I let out a long, deep sigh. "Well then, let's just say you've been really lucky up until now. But you've got time, Mindi. We're still two weeks away from opening night. By then, the worst of this should be over." Was I actually encouraging her? "And there are lots of things you can do to treat this."

She didn't seem to believe what I was saying. "Like what?"

At that moment, Natasha appeared from around the corner. She stopped in her tracks when she saw Mindi and me sitting next to each other. I could see her sizing up the situation, trying to figure out what was going on.

"Everything okay here?" she asked.

Mindi looked away. I nodded. "It's all okay."

"Your grandfather wants to run the opening again," Natasha said.

I knew I should be out there on stage, but there was no way I could leave Mindi just yet. "Tell him there's been a little emergency. Nothing serious," I added. "Mindi and I will *both* be out there in a few minutes."

Tash took another couple of seconds before she nodded and left us alone again.

I turned to Mindi. "Okay, let me introduce you to every home remedy for colds and throat infections that I've ever heard of." And then I started to list everything from lozenges to steams to lemon-and-honey drinks. My list was long and detailed. By the time I had finished, Mindi's tears had dried up.

I could hear my grandfather calling the cast to the stage. We needed to get out there. I stood up and offered my hand to Mindi. She grabbed it and pulled herself to her feet.

"Thanks," she said. And then she paused. "I appreciate it. Especially because we both know that if this doesn't work, you'll be taking over my part."

I was surprised that I didn't actually feel any happiness at that thought.

"Let's cross that bridge only if and when we have to," I said.

CHAPTER TWENTY-NINE

A couple of days later, I had a plan. I decided to get to school so early I'd be sure to be the first one there. I wanted to arrive before all my castmates, with plenty of time to warm up my voice, look over my lines, and get ready for the rehearsal. I didn't want Zayde to single me out for anything—good or bad!

But Ben beat me to it! I could hear his familiar voice belting out "If I Were a Rich Man" as I made my way down the darkened hall. There were only two other people in the building: the security guard, who greeted me with a nod of his head, and the custodian, Mr. Miller, who was quietly and meticulously mopping the floor in preparation for the stampede of students who would arrive a couple of hours later. I often wondered what he thought about the fact that he had to shine the floors every single day, only to have them trampled on by a horde of students who didn't give a hoot about his work. Maybe he hated what he was doing. Maybe he loved the fact that he could clean up our mess every day. He smiled as I passed and quietly opened one of the auditorium doors just wide enough to allow me to slip in.

And there was Ben, on stage, crossing from one side to the other, waving his arms above his head and singing out as if there were a full audience in front of him. He looked so good—great, in fact—up on that stage, so full of confidence, not to mention the fact that his voice had grown in strength and maturity since rehearsals for the show had begun. I felt a pang—after the show ended, would we ever talk to each other again?

Ben hit the last note of the song and held his position on stage. That's when I started clapping and cheering from the back of the auditorium. I made my way down the aisle toward him.

"You're supposed to let somebody know when you're watching," Ben said, jumping down from the stage and walking up the aisle to meet me. "You can't go around sneaking up on people like that."

I laughed. "Are you calling me a stalker?"

Ben reached me just before I got to the front of the auditorium. And then we just stood there—it felt awkward and nice all at once.

"I wanted to get it right, make your grandfather happy. He's been great, don't you think? I mean, he really understands this play."

I nodded. "I guess it's easier to understand when you're that much closer to it."

"That's true. But it's not just the history. He also knows so much about music." He paused. "Anyway, we're just lucky he came along."

I nodded again. I wasn't going to admit it to anybody, but I still wasn't a hundred percent comfortable sharing my grandfather with everybody. But I had to agree with Ben. Zayde really knew his stuff, and everyone in the cast was looking up to him, taking his direction, asking good questions, laughing at his corny jokes, and just *loving* him.

"So, did that sound all right?" he asked.

"You're great!" I blurted, and then I stammered, "I mean . . . the scene, the scene was great." I felt my face grow warm. Why did this happen every time I stood next to Ben? At least he didn't seem to notice me blushing. Or maybe he was just too polite to say anything.

"You know what's been one of my favorite parts of the whole thing?" he asked, taking a step closer to me. I could almost feel his breath on my face. "Rehearsing with you every day. Seeing you every day."

My heart was galloping at full steam. I gulped. "Yeah, I've loved it too." Oh, my goodness, I shouldn't have used that word . . . I should have said *liked* . . . why had I said *love*?

And then he took one more step, narrowing the gap between us even more. "Shirli," he began.

Just then, the doors to the auditorium swung open and a bunch of the cast paraded in. And at the head of the group was my grandfather, looking like the Pied Piper, smiling and leading the others into the rehearsal.

Ben caught himself and stopped. Then he shook his head and took a step back. "We never seem to be able to finish a conversation, do we?" he said as he brushed by me and went to join the others, leaving me shaken and speechless.

Natasha found me standing still as a statue. "What's up?" she asked. "You look like someone just gave you an electric shock."

Tash couldn't possibly have known how close to the truth that was. What was it that Ben had been about to say . . . or do? My mind was in overdrive, imagining every possible option: He wanted to see me more often. He wanted to see me less often. He felt about me like I was feeling about him. Or he didn't feel it. Was I wrong, or was he leaning in to kiss me, and . . . ? *Oh, stop being so dramatic!* I wanted to shout that out loud. Instead I just looked back at Tash and said, "It's nothing. I had some coffee this morning and I'm not used to it."

She seemed to accept that, and we joined the others, who were gathering around Zayde in front of the stage. I had been so caught off guard by my exchange with Ben that I hadn't even noticed at first that Zayde had brought his violin case with him—the one from his home, the one I had found in his attic. A familiar possessiveness tugged at me. He had only ever shown his violin to me and to Ben. Now I watched as he opened the case, removed his precious instrument, and held it up for everyone in the room to see. I was nothing short of shocked.

"Come, everybody, I want to show you something that is very special to me."

We all gathered around.

"You see these Stars of David that were carved into the wood," he said. "These four on the front." He turned the violin over. "And this one on the back." He went on to explain that many klezmer instruments that Jewish musicians had owned looked like his. "There are only a very few left in the world," he added. "Most were destroyed in the Holocaust." And then he paused. "How many of you know about the events of World War II?"

Most of the people in the auditorium raised their hands, some more tentatively than others.

Zayde nodded. "You've come to learn about what happened to Jews during the pogroms—when your play is taking place—Jews like my own dear mother. But I think it's also important for you to know something about my life and the things that happened to me. Perhaps it will help you understand why the lives in this story are so important to me, and why they should be so important to you."

And then Zayde began to talk. He talked about his childhood in Poland before the war, playing his violin with his family band. He talked about everything changing when laws were introduced to restrict the freedom of Jews in his country. He talked about hiding out in the forest with his parents and his brothers, and about how they had been caught and sent to Auschwitz. He even talked about playing in the orchestra with his friend, Josef, and seeing so many walk to their deaths. And finally, he talked about how he had never wanted to listen to music after all of that. He must have talked for over an hour. Nobody else spoke, or even moved.

I also watched everyone around me—wide-eyed, disbelieving, shocked, and sympathetic. Every emotion in the book was painted across the faces of my cast-mates. Zayde's life story was as hard for me to hear this time as it had been the first time. And somehow it seemed even more real having him tell everybody. But only I really knew how courageous Zayde was being.

"These are not just characters in a play," he was say-ing. "They are real people. I want you to treat them like real people and bring them to life."

And it was then that I suddenly understood all of why it was so important for him to talk about his life. With each part of his story, he was giving each one of us insights into our own characters and our own scenes. He was giving us all a history lesson that would influ-ence our performances.

He looked around the auditorium. "Ben Morgan, when you play Tevye, think about my father. Shirli, when you play Golde, think about my mother. My friends

Mohammed and Mindi and everyone else here, when you are on stage, think about my brothers—think about Josef. Will you do that for me?"

There was silence in the auditorium as everyone nodded their agreement.

"Good," Zayde said. "And now, I have one more thing to tell you that I have not even told my dear granddaughter."

I couldn't imagine what more there was to tell. Zayde held up his violin once more.

"This message is for the young man who will be playing the violin for the show." He searched the crowd, his eyes coming to rest on Thomas. Zayde motioned for Thomas to stand next to him on the stage.

"Other than Josef, the man I met in the concentration camp, this violin was my only friend in Auschwitz," Zayde said, staring straight at Thomas. "And many nights, when others were sleeping, I would hold this violin close to me, whispering to it my fears and my wishes. This violin knows everything that I was thinking at that time—every dream, every prayer—this violin knows it all."

Thomas didn't blink. He was completely mesmerized by my grandfather.

"So, young man, when you play your violin for this beautiful show, I want that instrument to be your friend as well—your very best friend. Can you do that?"

Thomas nodded, still not making a sound. And then, Zayde did the most incredible thing. He placed his precious old violin in Thomas's hands and asked him to play the opening notes of the show. Thomas held the violin as if it were a fragile piece of glass. His face went so pale that I thought he might pass out. But he took a couple of deep breaths, moved the violin up to his chin, and began to play. And the sound that he made was sweet and clear.

"He's never sounded that good before," Tash whispered to me.

I nodded. "I know."

"How does your grandfather do that?" she asked.

I had no answer.

When Thomas lowered the violin, he looked as if he knew that he had pleased my grandfather.

"Thomas, you played with such beauty," Zayde said.

Others nodded their agreement. Thomas smiled broadly in reply. He went to hand the violin back to my grandfather.

"No, you don't understand. It is for you to use in our production."

Thomas looked as shocked as I felt. "You're giving me your violin?"

"Lending. You will keep it safe until the end of our run."

Thomas's eyes had grown as big as full moons. "I'll take care of it, I promise," he said.

"I know you will. You're a good boy."

Zayde then turned to face all of us again.

"I have only recently learned about the importance of talking about my past—a difficult lesson. And I learned this from my granddaughter."

All eyes turned to me.

"She has helped me to find my voice, and now Thomas will help my precious violin to speak again."

My heart swelled nearly to bursting.

"So," Zayde continued, "thank you for listening to me. And now it's time to get back to work."

As we took our places on the stage, I knew that my grandfather was not only a great man, but the greatest director I had ever had.

CHAPTER THIRTY

We raced through the next ten days—waking, rehearsals, classes, more rehearsals, homework, sleep, repeat. Slowly but surely, the show was coming together, and then opening night was just a day away.

"Please turn up the house lights. I would like everybody to come out onto the stage," Zayde called out.

The lights came on, instantly revealing the two people in the audience—my grandfather and Mr. James. In almost complete silence we began to assemble. Those of us in costume were joined by the stage crew, the members of the orchestra, and the tech crew working the lights and sound.

I couldn't help but notice Thomas carrying his violin, Zayde's violin. He never seemed to put it down, not at practice and not even during school. He'd taken to carrying it, in its case, from class to class. He said it was "too valuable" to trust to his locker or even the music room. I could tell from the way he was playing that he'd been practicing a lot more. He was working to make his director proud. We all were.

Finally the entire team was either standing on the stage or sitting on the lip, feet dangling down. Everyone was quiet, but there was a lot of fidgeting and restless energy. We were all tired—close to exhaustion—from the final push. But we were also fueled by sugar, adrenaline, dreams, hopes, and fears.

"You all look so beautiful . . . even the stage crew . . . *especially* the stage crew," Zayde said.

He had insisted that everybody dress "properly" for rehearsals, and the crew members were in ties and jackets or dresses. Zayde insisted that we had to be professional in how we looked. Of course, Zayde and Mr. James were in jackets and ties too, but that was an everyday thing for them. Mr. James had even started to wear a fedora to school some days—a present from my Zayde.

"He's right," Mr. James said. "You all look so wonderful, I'm starting to think we should institute a school dress code."

A groan went through the crowd.

"Kidding, I'm kidding!"

It was a full dress rehearsal—our final rehearsal—so the cast members were, of course, in costume. I could see people wearing clothes that had come from Zayde's attic, things that had belonged to him or to my Bubbie. I wondered if Zayde had noticed them, or seen that the apron I was wearing was one of Bubbie's. It was flowery and bright, and wearing it felt like a way to honor her. Oh, how I wished she could have been there.

With one hand tucked underneath the edge of the apron I was holding a bit of the skirt material, rubbing it between my fingers and thumb. It was my way of not twirling my hair.

"This is our final rehearsal," Zayde said. "How many of you are nervous?"

Slowly a few hands were raised, and then a few more, until finally Zayde and Mr. James put up their hands and everybody started to laugh.

"Nervous is good," Zayde said. "Nervous is normal. Besides, what's the worst that could happen? Somebody misses a line?"

"Or falls off the stage," somebody called out from the back.

Again, more nervous laughter.

"If that happened then somebody might actually break a leg," Zayde said. "I was told it is good luck to say that in the theater."

"Let's avoid breaking legs," Mr. James said. "That's a bit of an insurance issue."

"I was also told, by my Shirli, that a bad final dress rehearsal means you'll have a wonderful opening night, so I wish you all a *terrible* performance."

More laughter and smiles, but this time it felt more natural, as though some of the pressure had been released.

"Now, the one change we've agreed on, for this final rehearsal only, is that Mindi will be performing the scenes and saying the lines, but Shirli will be singing the songs from the wings," Zayde explained. "Mindi, how is your voice?"

"It's better than it was yesterday."

"That's good to hear."

Mindi's voice had broken a couple more times over the past few days, and instead of resting or pulling back she'd pushed it harder. So, in spite of all the remedies I had provided her with, there was a danger that her voice might give out altogether. It was Zayde who had suggested that I step in to provide the singing.

Maybe I should have been rooting for Mindi to lose her voice completely so I could play Hodel, but the truth was that I felt bad for her. It was a stretch to say we were friends, but we were friendly . . . and we'd developed a real respect for one another. We'd even rehearsed a couple of scenes together, helping each other get our lines down and talking about our characters. I really wanted Mindi to have her moment on stage. She'd worked hard and deserved to be there.

"I could *try* to sing today," Mindi said.

"No," Zayde told her. "Better you sing in the performances than in the final rehearsal. The people in this room already know what a wonderful voice you have." He paused. "And Mindi, you know that you are not letting anybody down."

Her expression left no doubt that was how she was feeling.

"We are a family, and each member helps the others. Tonight, you rest, and tomorrow you will be your usual *spectacular* self. Yes?"

She nodded. "Yes."

"Good. Now, before we start I have something for you all." Zayde opened up his jacket and pulled out a letter. "This is from your Ms. Ramsey. She wanted me to read this to you . . . if only I could find my glasses."

He started patting down his pockets. His glasses were right there on top of his head. Everyone saw them; nobody wanted to tell him.

"Wait, wait." He reached up, found them, and brought them down. "You'll have to excuse a silly old man."

And then he began to read.

"*My dearest students, actors, musicians, and stage crew. I do wish so much that I could have been there with you each step of the way through our production. I know from what Mr. Berman has told me that you have put your hearts and minds and souls into your work.*"

Zayde had told us that, since taking over the show, he had talked regularly with Ms. Ramsey. He had even visited her at the hospital, and then again a couple of times since she'd been discharged home.

"*It has made it all so much easier to know that you have been left in the hands of such a capable and competent director.*"

Zayde looked up from the letter and overtop of his glasses. "I want you to know that she did say all of those things." He paused. "Would anybody believe me if I read out that she thought I looked like an older version of Brad Pitt?"

Everybody laughed.

"I assume that would be a no. Back to the letter." He pushed his glasses back up the bridge of his nose. "*I have complete faith that this play will be a tremendous success. I want you all to break a leg because, believe me, that is better than breaking an arm and five ribs! With great admiration and affection, Evelyn Ramsey.*"

There was spontaneous applause around the room.

"Evelyn is such a fine young woman . . . I have enjoyed our conversations and our meetings to discuss the play." He paused. "You know, if I were twenty years younger . . ."

Oh, my goodness, where was this going?

"Then I'd still be old enough to be her father!" Zayde chuckled. "I hope you're not too disappointed that this beaten-up old man has replaced your very experienced teacher."

"No, sir," Ben said, stepping forward. "We miss her, but we've been honored to have you as our director."

Mohammed stepped forward as well. "Yeah, thanks for everything you've done!"

"You're the best!" Thomas yelled.

With that, everybody burst into applause. Zayde shrugged his shoulders and looked away. He then took a small bow and raised his hands to quiet the group.

"I think that it should be the other way around. I need to thank all of you," he said. "You have graciously allowed this old man to enter into your lives and give you a few words of advice. And you have pretended that maybe he still has something to offer to the world."

There were protests from all around me, disagreeing with what he'd just said. Zayde raised his hands again to quiet us.

"I have given you what I have. You have given me your attention, your energy, your love . . . and you have given me something even more important. You have given me back music. For that, I thank you."

I could see that everyone understood what Zayde was saying—what music had meant to him, and how it had been taken away from him for so long.

"I have felt more alive in the last few weeks than I have in, well, a long time," he continued, his voice cracking. "And I have one more piece of advice for all of you," he continued, pulling himself together. "You are young, so the last thing you're thinking about is retiring. But when you do get to that point, I will say this. Don't! Don't ever retire. Keep finding the things you love to do, keep dreaming big, keep looking forward and moving forward. You have all helped me to move forward. And now it is time for the show to go on. Everybody in your places."

As we all headed to our opening positions, I felt a hand on my shoulder. It was Mindi.

"I want to thank you," she said.

"For what?"

"For having my back."

"That's what an understudy is for. Besides, it's just a rehearsal. You save your voice tonight so you'll be there for opening."

"I will." And then she paused. "How Ms. Ramsey feels about your grandfather being there for her is how I feel about you being there for me. I know that if you have to step in then the songs will be great, and nobody will be let down."

"Thanks, that means a lot."

She was just about to walk away when she turned to me once more. "I know he likes you," she said.

Was she still talking about Zayde?

"Ben," she said. "I can see it on his face when you're around."

I could feel a rush of heat rise up into my cheeks.

"He's worth going after." And then she turned and found her place onstage.

CHAPTER THIRTY-ONE

I peeked out the side of the curtain. Fifteen minutes before curtain up. The audience was settling in, and it looked as though there wouldn't be an empty seat in the house. We'd been told every night was almost sold out already.

My family was seated front and center: my mother, father, brother, and an assortment of aunts, uncles, and cousins. They had come to see me, of course, but they were also there to celebrate Zayde. Amir, with his wife and kids, was sitting with my parents, and Amir was beaming, obviously proud of his friend Tobias.

"Do you see her?" Ben had materialized at my side and was looking over my shoulder. He was, of course, talking about our surprise guest—Ms. Ramsey.

"She's there on the left, at the side, and about three rows back." Her arm was still in a sling, but the gash on her face seemed to have faded, and she looked strong. Mr. James had told us that she was still suffering from the symptoms of the concussion—that she needed more sleep and her eyes were sensitive to light and her concentration wasn't right. The important thing was that she was moving in the right direction.

Ben pressed up against me so he could lean over to the side and see out through the curtain. I felt my whole body tingle.

"Funny how the play almost didn't happen," he said as I let the curtain fall closed. "Who would have thought that Ms. Ramsey getting injured in a car accident would have made the show better?"

"Do you really think it's better?" I asked.

"No question. Your grandfather just brought something extra to the production."

I couldn't argue with that. Zayde had made it special. Not just for me but for everybody.

"Think about someone like Thomas. Did you hear how he sounded playing through the opening scene last night?" Ben asked.

"He was amazing. It sent chills up my spine."

"That's because of your grandfather, and because of his violin. It was a gift to Thomas and to everybody in the play," Ben said. "Maybe even an act of love."

I felt a little odd when Ben said that word "love," but really it was true. Zayde was trusting Thomas, a boy he hardly knew, with something that was very precious, the only remaining link to his family, to his past.

"So Mindi is ready to go, right?" Ben asked.

"Definitely. Her voice is in great shape."

"Are you disappointed you won't sing those songs?"

I didn't want to admit that, but I didn't want to lie, either. "A little, but I'm happy for Mindi."

"I heard what you did for her," Ben said. "How you helped her."

I shrugged. "It was nothing. Just some different kinds of tea and a throat spray."

"That's not what Mindi is telling people," he said. "She's telling everybody that she wouldn't be going on tonight if it hadn't been for you."

"That's sweet, but probably not true." I thought for a second and then added, "Mindi has been . . . different from what I expected," I said.

"Yeah, there have been a lot of surprises, starting with your grandfather. I'm really going to miss him."

"I'm sure he'd be glad to see you anytime you want to visit," I said.

"I will, but it's not going to be the same as seeing him every day."

"He's going to miss all of this . . . a lot. And he'll miss you," I said. "He told me how much he likes you."

"I like him, too." He paused. "I like many people in your family."

I turned to face him. "My parents are really nice people."

He laughed. "They are nice, but I was talking about somebody else."

"Well, if you knew my brother better you'd know he can be a little difficult sometimes."

"That, I'm assuming, also runs in the family." He placed his hands on my shoulders, and I felt my body melt under his touch. "I'm really going to miss spending every day with you. I'm going to miss *you*, Shirli Berman."

"And I'm going to miss you, Ben Morgan. Although don't you think we should be on a first-name basis by now?"

"My high school isn't that far away. And I'll have my license in another couple of years."

"That's great. You can come back here and visit. That will make your old coaches happy."

"How about you?" he asked. "Would that make you happy?"

"Well, I'm always glad when a school superstar comes back to visit."

"Are you being deliberately difficult?" he asked.

"You said it runs in my family."

He shook his head ever so gently, and smiled.

"Places, everybody!" the stage manager called out as she burst out from the stage-left wing.

Ben stared at me for another second. And then he bent forward and pressed his lips against mine, softly but firmly. I closed my eyes, leaned in, and melted. It was just as I'd always dreamed it would be. Kissing Ben felt exciting, and natural, and absolutely perfect. We stayed like that, lips together, holding one another for a few seconds until finally Ben stood back and released his grip on my shoulders. He smiled at me.

"It's show time. I'll see you soon, Wife."

With that, he turned and walked away.

I stood there, my mind racing through what had just happened. He had kissed me. And oddly, the whole thing wasn't throwing me at all. I was strangely calm, as if this was exactly what was meant to be—just like the show, and Zayde, and everything else that had happened in the last months.

The stage manager rushed past me once more. "Places, now!" she demanded.

With that, I took a deep breath. We had a show to do. All that mattered right now was the performance. For now, I couldn't fill my mind with thoughts of Ben and Shirli. That would come later. Now it was all about Tevye and Golde.

CHAPTER THIRTY-TWO

Act 2 was about to begin. This was our final night—our final performance. The scene was in front of Tevye's house, and the crew had almost finished setting the stage. In the wings everybody was milling around, trying to stay quieter than the audience, who had started to file back to their seats.

I had been too nervous on opening night to really enjoy performing as much as I should have. It wasn't until the third night that I felt completely at ease—okay, not really completely at ease, but more comfortable. There was always that worry that somebody would blow a line or screw up a song—that *I* would be the one. So far, so good. But the reality was that no matter how good the previous shows had gone, all that mattered was that night, that performance. In some ways, closing night was even harder than opening. If something had gone wrong the first night we'd have known we had four more chances. Now, there was no opportunity for redemption.

I caught sight of Zayde. He was, as always, on the move, offering encouragement, a few words of advice, trying to keep everybody light and loose. I couldn't help but smile, thinking about how wonderful he had been night after night. Somehow, in the face of everyone's stress and uncertainty, he had become more energized. He even seemed younger, if that was possible. Really, though, what was a blown line compared to what he'd lived through?

He saw me looking at him and he gave me a wave and a big smile before walking toward the stage-right wing. He had told me after that first night that he had heard his mother in my performance, and that he knew she would have been so proud of me.

Ben moved beside me and gave my hand a little squeeze. "So, how are you feeling?"

"You know me, I'll be nervous until it's over. You?"

"Funny, during a football game I'm nervous the entire time, but here, well, I feel pretty relaxed."

I shook my head. "I don't know how you can possibly be calm."

"I know my lines, and I'm pretty sure I'm not going to be submarined by a blitzing lineman," he said.

I laughed. "I'm not even sure what that means, but I'm glad at least one of us is breathing easily." It was taking all of my resolve not to start winding my hair around my fingers.

"No fear. So, are you looking forward to next Saturday night?"

"Of course. I still can't believe you got tickets."

"My father has some great connections."

Next Saturday, Ben and his family were taking me into New York City to see a play. We were going to see *The Producers*, the hottest ticket on Broadway! I couldn't help but smile thinking about that. Ben and I were going on a date—well, a date with his family. Sure, we'd been to the coffee shop at the corner a couple of times and eaten lunch together every day this week, and we certainly talked all the time. But this was going to be different.

"Places, everybody," the stage manager called out.

"I guess it's time for me to get out there." He gave my hand another squeeze and headed onto the stage, taking a seat on the bench in front of his house—in front of *our* house.

As he moved onto the stage I was joined in the stage-left wing by Mindi and Mohammed. Ben was opening with his monologue, and then this scene would be theirs.

"Your voice has been perfect," I said to Mindi.

"It's held up. Thanks again for everything."

"You would have done the same for me."

Here we were, almost finished, and Mindi, with some help from my tea and lozenges, had been able to sing every single song in every performance. The voice problems had even worked in her favor. She was singing with more control now that she was following Zayde's advice to "give us less so you can give us more." I was happy for her. She'd worked hard, and she deserved the applause she received every night.

And because I wasn't worried about singing any other parts, I was able to really *become* Golde. I felt her in my soul. She was part of me, and I was part of her. And it was as if, through Golde, I had connected with my past, with my heritage, with my family, with who I was. That character had given me a lot to be grateful for. Who could have imagined that?

The stage manager quieted everybody. The curtain was about to open, the second act was about to begin . . . and the show was going to end. Soon we'd no longer be castmates, team members. We'd go back to our regular lives, and then the school year would be over. And for those in ninth grade, people like Mindi and Ben, it would be the end of their years at this school. They'd soon be gone, off to high school. But at least not gone forever, at least not as far as Ben and I were concerned. I didn't want to think too far ahead. Who knew what might happen next year? But there was still tonight— and next Saturday, and the rest of the school year.

The house lights went down, everybody backstage became silent, and the curtain rose. The orchestra began to play a haunting melody, led by the clarinets, who were then joined by the violins, with Thomas leading the way.

Would I ever hear a clarinet again without thinking of my great-grandfather? Would I ever hear a violin without thinking of my Zayde?

The orchestra finished, the audience applauded, and then slowly the stage lights began to come up, revealing Ben, sitting on the bench. He looked up at the heavens and started talking to God about Tzeitel and Motel's wedding.

"Are you ready?" Mindi whispered to Mohammed.

"Ready as can be."

Ben stood up and pulled his milk cart away. The audience gave him a round of applause. As he left the stage, there was a pause to allow the clapping to stop, and then Mindi strode out, followed quickly by Mohammed.

"Please don't be upset, Hodel!" Mohammed called out.

Act 2, scene 1 had begun.

When the curtain came down, the audience was on its feet in one sweeping wave. We could hear the cheering and shouting that rose to a nearly deafening proportion. Backstage, the entire cast joined in. I found Tash in the tangle of people and we quickly hugged.

"You were great!" she exclaimed above the roars. "You owned Golde."

"And you were fantastic in the ensemble."

She waved my compliment away. "It was fun to do this with you. Let's do it again next year."

I couldn't believe what I was hearing. Was this the same person who had been fearful of even trying out for this show? I laughed and nodded and then searched the crowd for Ben. I spotted him on the other side of the stage, surrounded by other castmates. He looked up and caught my eye. And then we just smiled at one another, and for a second it felt as if everyone else on stage melted away. But a moment later, the stage manager bounded into the middle of the pack, shouting at us to get back into position for bows. Ben gave me one more look and then found his spot.

The curtain rose to even more thunderous applause, accompanied by the orchestra, which had begun its reprise of the song "Tradition." Audience members began to clap in time with the music as the cast began to move forward. First the ensemble members—there was Tash, grinning like I'd never seen before. Mohammed received a loud ovation, which he deserved, followed by Mindi, whose applause was even louder and longer. She turned and looked at me as she moved back into place and I smiled back at her. One after another, the members of the cast stepped forward to bow. And then, finally, it was my turn. The audience roared when I stepped to the front of the stage, and I could hear my brother and my parents above everybody else. My parents had come every night to see the show. I glanced at them—at the whole row filled with my family—as I took my bow and then stepped back.

Finally it was Ben's turn. He bounced onto the stage and the applause became louder again. He took a bow and then a second and then turned to me. His eyes were lit up. He was beaming. He reached back, took my hand, and pulled me to the front. Then he raised his hands to silence the audience.

"Please, please, you should maybe have a seat," he said in Tevye's voice. "Sometimes it's not just a horse that can have a lame leg."

Everybody laughed as they sank back to their seats.

He spoke again, and this time, it was all Ben. "You know, if nothing else, this play is about one thing . . . *tradition*."

Every person on stage starting singing as the orchestra, on cue, began playing "Tradition" one more time. We did one verse and then a second and then joined hands and took one final bow as the audience leapt to their feet once more, and cheered even louder.

Once again Ben raised his hands and silenced everyone.

"I've been told that there is one more tradition in the theater. It's sort of like football players dumping Gatorade on the coach after a victory . . . not that a Jewish man in 1905 Russia would know anything about what football or Gatorade is . . . but still."

That brought a burst of laughter from the cast and audience.

"Could we please have our 'coaches,' our directors, come forward. Please, can we have a round of applause for Mr. James, Mr. Berman, and, of course, Ms. Ramsey!"

There was more cheering from the cast and the audience as Mr. James came out of the wings. Ms. Ramsey slowly rose to her feet from the audience, came to the stairs, aided by her cane, and started up onto the stage. I looked around for Zayde—he was nowhere to be seen.

"I'll go and get him," Ben said. He'd noticed too.

Ben ran off stage and then returned, holding Zayde's arm. All three "directors" met in the middle and gave each other hugs.

Mohammed appeared with three bouquets of flowers. He gave one to Ben, a second to Mindi, and the third to me. Ben walked over and handed his bouquet to Mr. James. Mindi handed hers to Ms. Ramsey, who looked so happy it made me want to cry. That left only Zayde. Everybody else moved aside so he was on his own, at center stage.

I walked up and held out the flowers. "You deserve more than just this." I handed him the bouquet and then wrapped my arms around him, hugging him tightly.

"Your Bubbie would have been so happy, especially seeing you there in her apron," he whispered into my ear.

"I didn't know you'd noticed."

"I noticed. She would have been so proud of you."

"Zayde, she would have been so proud of *both* of us."

I released him and stepped back so once again he was by himself at center stage. He gave a dignified little bow, and then he tossed the flowers into the air and caught them. The audience went completely wild. He was a showman, for sure.

There was one more thing I wanted to do. I was nervous, maybe even scared, but I wanted to do it anyway.

I turned around and there was Thomas, holding the violin, my Zayde's violin.

"I need to borrow this," I said as I walked over to him.

He nodded and handed me the violin and bow. Zayde was still facing the audience when I walked forward and tapped him on the shoulder.

"Zayde," I said, holding his precious instrument out to him.

He turned. He looked at me, and then at the violin. And then his face went pale, and for a moment I worried that I might have gone too far.

"You want me to play?" he asked.

I swallowed hard and nodded. "Everybody wants you to play."

That's when he reached out and took the violin and bow. The audience became silent.

"What would I play?" he asked.

"Play whatever you want. Whatever your heart tells you to play."

Zayde shook his head slowly, and then he stepped toward the edge of the stage and addressed the audience.

"Apparently, I'm supposed to play, if that would be okay with everybody," he said.

The audience answered with cheers and applause. Zayde brought the violin up under his chin and put the bow in position to start. Then he paused and lowered his instrument again.

"But I have a condition," he said, as the audience became silent once more. "When I played as a boy, I always had my family with me. And I think I need to have family perform with me now." He turned. "Shirli?"

At first I was stunned. This was supposed to be Zayde's moment, not mine. But then Ben materialized at my side.

"You'd better get going," he said. And he led me to the front, turning back so it was just me and my grandfather.

Zayde raised his violin once more and started to play. It was "Sunrise, Sunset." The notes were long and full and rich, and as I looked out, the entire audience was standing in silence, eyes wide, amazed and entranced. And in the middle of everyone, there was my father, tears streaming down his cheeks as he heard his father play for the first time. It made me want to cry, too!

I turned back to Zayde. His eyes were closed. I wondered what he was thinking. Was he blocking out the world the way he had when he had played at Auschwitz?

No, his expression was so calm, so serene, so joyful. He was lost in the joy of the music. I knew he was thinking about his family—about his mother and father, his brothers, about Bubbie, about my father and mother and brother. He was thinking about me.

He opened his eyes and gave me a slight nod. That was my cue. And I started singing.

AUTHORS' NOTE

While all of the characters in *Broken Strings* are fictional, there are parts of this story that are based on real events.

During the Second World War, the Nazis created concentration camps, a series of enormous prisons that consisted of labor camps, transit camps, prisoner-of-war camps, and, of course, the death camps. The largest and most infamous of these was Auschwitz.

Auschwitz was really a network of prison camps. The main camp, Auschwitz I, was built in 1940 in what was an abandoned Polish army barracks. In 1941, Auschwitz II, also known as Birkenau, was opened a few kilometers away from Auschwitz I. Birkenau was the site of the most active gas chambers. It was also the place where arriving Jewish prisoners would disembark from trains onto a long gravel ramp, and where the selections would take place—the process that determined which Jews would go immediately to their death, and which would be granted life for some short period of time longer.

The conditions for those who were granted life were brutal. Many died from cruel treatment, harsh working conditions, overcrowding, and starvation. But in the midst of these inhumane circumstances, the Nazis established a number of orchestras in Auschwitz. The orchestras consisted of Jewish musicians, both men and women, who had been sent there from across Europe.

The primary duty of the orchestra was to accompany the Jewish prisoners to their daily work details. This was almost a form of torture. The musicians were ordered to play quickly, and the prisoners would have to march in time with the music, at an impossible pace. Their bodies were so wasted from illness and starvation that many dropped on the spot.

The other responsibility of the orchestras was to play music on the ramp while prisoners were arriving and getting off the trains. This musical greeting was meant to fool the arriving prisoners into believing that everything would be fine for them in this terrible place. In this way, the Nazi guards could control the unsuspecting prisoners and move them in an orderly fashion wherever they wished, including toward the gas chambers. Many members of the orchestra were overwhelmed with emotion while they played, knowing that their music was accompanying the arriving prisoners to their deaths.

Here is what Coco Schumann, a survivor of the Holocaust, once said about the experience of being a musician in Auschwitz: "The music could save you: if not your life, then at least the day. The images that I saw every day were impossible to live with, and yet we held on. We played music to them, for our basic survival. We made music in hell." (A helpful resource for more information about this subject is the website Music and the Holocaust at www.holocaustmusic.ort.org.)

Approximately 1.1 million people died or were killed in Auschwitz during the course of the war. Nearly 1 million of those were Jewish prisoners.

ACKNOWLEDGMENTS

Huge thanks to Lynne Missen and all the folks at Penguin Random House for taking this book on. We sat down with Lynne to talk about this project a couple of years before we finally signed with Penguin. It seems like this was the place that it was meant to be! Thanks also to Catherine Marjoribanks for the thorough and meticulous edits. We love your attention to all the details!

When this book was still in manuscript form, we had the opportunity to have it read by a couple of school groups. We asked for their detailed feedback, and we got it! The final product has been shaped by the thoughtful responses from the students of Associated Hebrew Schools, Danilack Campus, in Toronto, Ontario, and by Ms. Green's grade eight English classes at Baynon Fields P.S. in Richmond Hill, Ontario. Special thanks to Jessica Ruzhytska for coming up with the perfect title for the book!

—Kathy and Eric

First and foremost, my deepest gratitude to Eric for bringing this book idea to me and for wanting me to write it with him. Eric is a generous writing partner and, from start to finish, it was a joyful experience to be part of this collaboration.

My ongoing love and gratitude to my husband, Ian Epstein, and my children, Gabi Epstein and Jake Epstein. You provide the love and laughter that I need in my life!

—Kathy

When the initial idea came to mind—and that idea was only an acorn from which this oak grew—I knew that there was only one person to approach: Kathy. She is a world-recognized writer of fiction related to the Holocaust, and her children are both accomplished professional performers, which covers the twin themes of this novel. This was such a seamless collaboration that it was, at times, impossible to see where my words ended and Kathy's started.

This book is for my grandchildren, Quinn, Isaac, and Noa. I hope this book can offer a window onto the world I want them to live in—one filled with understanding, acceptance, kindness, caring, forgiveness, and love.

—Eric

ERIC WALTERS is one of Canada's best-known and most prolific writers of fiction for children and young adults. His books have won over 120 awards, including thirteen separate children's choice awards, and have been translated into thirteen languages. He lives in Guelph, Ontario, and is the co-founder of Creation of Hope, a charity that provides care for orphans in the Mbooni district of Kenya. His most recent novel is *Elephant Secret*, which is his hundredth published book. Visit him online at ericwalters.net and on Twitter: @EricRWalters.

KATHY KACER's award-winning list of Holocaust fiction and non-fiction for young readers includes *The Secret of Gabi's Dresser*, *The Diary of Laura's Twin*, *Hiding Edith*, and *To Look a Nazi in the Eye*. Her books have been published and translated in twenty countries. She is the child of Holocaust survivors, and the parent of two actors and musical theater performers. For more information, please visit: www.kathykacer.com.

Permissions Acknowledgments

Praise for Ian Manuel's

MY TIME WILL COME

"A stunner. . . . Manuel's account, told in prose and poetry, is gritty and unflinching . . . and poignant throughout. The result is a gripping narrative about a man's struggle to prove his discarded existence still has meaning."
—*Publishers Weekly* (starred review)

"Manuel's book depicts a carceral system that is brutal through and through, from judges seeking 'retribution' rather than justice to corrupt, violent and petty prison workers and mental healthcare that ranges from lackluster to dangerous."
—*Los Angeles Times*

"An honest and vulnerable depiction of life in one of Florida's toughest prisons."
—*Indianapolis Recorder*

"[Manuel's] story is heartbreaking and hopeful and needs to be told."
—*Booklist*

"Both heart-wrenching and uplifting. . . . A disturbing, vital, necessary eyewitness addition to debates about the mass incarceration epidemic in the U.S."
—*Kirkus Reviews*

Ian Manuel

MY TIME WILL COME

Ian Manuel lives in New York City. He is a motivational
speaker at schools and social organizations nationwide.

Ian Manuel is available for select speaking
engagements. To inquire about a possible
speaking appearance, please contact
Penguin Random House Speakers Bureau at
speakers@penguinrandomhouse.com or
visit www.prhspeakers.com.

MY

TIME

WILL

COME

MY
TIME
WILL
COME

A MEMOIR OF CRIME, PUNISHMENT, HOPE, AND REDEMPTION

Ian Manuel

Foreword by Bryan Stevenson

Vintage Books
A Division of Penguin Random House LLC
New York

FIRST VINTAGE BOOKS EDITION, APRIL 2022

The Library of Congress has cataloged the Pantheon
edition as follows:
Name: Manuel, Ian, author.
Title: My time will come : a memoir of crime, punishment, hope,
and redemption / Ian Manuel ; foreword by Bryan Stevenson.
Description: First edition. | New York : Pantheon Books, 2021.
Identifiers: LCCN 2020045133 (print). | LCCN 2020045134 (ebook).
Subjects: LCSH: African American prisoners—Biography. | African
American criminals—Rehabilitation—United States—Biography. |
African American juvenile delinquents—Biography. | Restorative
justice—United States. | Discrimination in criminal justice
administration—United States. | Discrimination in juvenile justice
administration—United States.
Classification: LCC HV9468.M26 A3 2021 (print) |
LCC HV9468.M26 (ebook) | DDC 365/.6092 B—dc23
LC record available at https://lccn.loc.gov/2020045133
LC ebook record available at https://lccn.loc.gov/2020045134

**Vintage Trade Paperback ISBN: 978-1-9848-9798-5
eBook ISBN: 978-1-5247-4853-1**

Book design by Betty Lew

vintagebooks.com

Printed in the United States of America
1st Printing

I dedicate this book to Linda Johnson,
for loving me unconditionally.

To Peggye Manuel for giving me life.
All I needed was a chance.

To Debbie Baigrie for forgiving me.

To Bryan Stevenson for my freedom.

And to all of those who told me that I'd never
amount to anything, that I'd die nameless,
just another number in prison, I hope my
story helps you believe in miracles and
magic. It was you, the naysayers, who gave
me the motivation to seek the impossible,
to keep clinging to the faith in my darkest
hours, to know that My Time Will Come . . .

Foreword by Bryan Stevenson

WHEN I FIRST MET IAN MANUEL IN A FLORIDA PRISON, HE was not allowed to be in the same room with me. As an attorney meeting a client, I could have a contact visit with almost any other prisoner at the facility but that would not be possible with Ian because he was barred from direct contact with other people. He would have to be on the other side of a thick glass wall in a separate room; we would have to talk through a tiny hole. In preparing for the visit, Ian and I had both hoped that prison officials would relent and allow a proper visit but that request was repeatedly denied.

They brought Ian into his glassed room restrained in a chained outfit I'd never seen before. He was bound in a jumpsuit made of heavy-duty nylon that opened from the back but was padlocked at the neck and waist. It was a full-body straitjacket that so confined his ability to move that he couldn't walk, he had to waddle from side to side. I'd had hundreds of contact visits with death row prisoners before my meeting with Ian but this was new to me. It took me a while to get over the spectacle of such violent restraints on such a young person inside a secure facility.

Ian and I had exchanged several letters and spoken on the phone many times before we met. Our calls were some-

times emotional because Ian was trying to understand what was happening around him or what he was experiencing, I often heard pain and anguish in his voice. I would frequently tell Ian I was proud of him and he told me later that this sometimes confused him.

At our first visit, Ian told me he was nervous about meeting in person. I asked him why and he said he didn't want to disappoint me. I tried to reassure him but he said he was still nervous. Then he told me he'd written a poem he wanted to recite, so I, of course, said I would listen. It was at that peculiar moment in our first meeting, in that unforgiving, cold prison, that Ian, constricted and absurdly bound with chains and restraints, spoke his poetic words. His poem spoke about grief and sadness, strength and resolve, and most important, hope and love. His words tried to make sense of things that were overwhelming and complex. His poem was about his existence and what he seemed to provoke in the people around him; it was a lament for freedom and forgiveness. I was very moved by his words. I told Ian that his poem was beautiful and he smiled. It's the smile that I remember most about our first meeting.

It is cruel to say to a child of thirteen that you are so beyond hope or redemption, your life is so irredeemable and without value, that you must die in prison. What we've done to children in this country—condemning them and throwing them away—is shameful. Ian Manuel is one of thousands of kids who have been sentenced to life imprisonment without parole for crimes they were accused of when they were children.

Ian's conviction was followed by torturous imprisonment. He was too small to be housed in general population at the adult prison where he was sent, so they placed him

in solitary confinement for nearly two decades. His abusive isolation was justified by misguided protocols and a devastating lack of understanding about adolescent development, mental health, or behavioral science. What happened to Ian is beyond cruel but sadly not unique. We have traumatized tens of thousands of unaided children who have been incarcerated in adult prisons for decades; we still do it today.

I'd read Ian's file and it was clear he was being abused and abusing himself and others in response. But, at our first visit, he still managed to recite his poetry. Despite the humiliating and degrading cloak of bondage he was forced to wear, you could still see resolve and compassion in his eyes.

I left the prison with great hope for Ian.

Children are magical. Nothing in the human experience affirms the gift of life, the beauty of our existence more than our children. Infants have an extraordinary ability to make the most hardened of us feel inexplicably joyful when they smile. Small children have a curiosity and capacity for affection and love that can uplift, move, and transform us. So much of what we do in life is organized around protecting, caring for, and loving our children.

But we don't all mean the same thing when we say "our children." For some, that's a much more specific and narrow universe. For me, "all children" are "our children," but after representing hundreds of kids in jails and prisons, I've come to realize that's not everyone's view.

Americans have long embraced the priority that children represent which makes the story of Ian Manuel so critically important and simultaneously hard to understand. We've done something terrible in this country to a generation of our children, something we've yet to fully acknowledge or

address. Our poorest and most vulnerable children—those born into extreme poverty, violent neighborhoods, or violent families, those in greatest need of assistance have largely been abandoned in many communities.

Hundreds of thousands of children in this country live in spaces where they are neglected, abused, and mistreated. They are forced to grow up without consistent love and affection, without safety, without guidance or direction. Many of these children suffer from trauma disorders by the time they're five years old.

Any human being will be traumatized if they are subjected to constant danger, shouting, anger, and violence that causes fear. Our brains begin to produce cortisol and adrenaline when we are threatened or stressed. When we're constantly menaced, our brains overproduce these chemicals, flooding our bodies with stress hormones even when there is no immediate threat. Like the thousands of combat veterans whose symptoms led to greater attention to post-traumatic stress disorders, thousands of American children develop trauma disorders before they start school. Of course, these toddlers and young children never signed up for violent combat and their plight has received far less attention.

We have done very little to help these children. In fact, when these kids go to school we aggravate their condition by threatening them. We tell many vulnerable children they'll be suspended or expelled if they don't behave like healthy kids with no trauma or disabilities. We deny these young people critically urgent mental health care and too often, we deprive them of safety, which is the most effective treatment for children coping with trauma.

Many of our children get worse and develop all kinds

of problems. Some children try to manage the feeling of always being imperiled by using drugs or seeking unhealthy stimulation or dangerous escape. Some kids join gangs to feel less alone in their struggle to survive. We harshly punish traumatized children for making these kinds of choices even though extreme punishment just makes things worse. Most judges, prosecutors, lawyers, and advocates fundamentally misperceive the nature of the problem—and as a result, they repeatedly make decisions that add to the burden of our most vulnerable kids. This brutal system is part of Ian Manuel's story.

There are serious consequences when we fail to respond effectively to extreme poverty and the abusive and unhealthy living conditions found in rural and urban communities across this country. Children suffer, engage in dangerous behaviors that undermine health and safety, and lives are lost.

We live in a nation that has failed to prevent guns from being placed in the hands of traumatized, unsupervised thirteen-year-old children. That, of course, inevitably leads to tragedy. Debbie Baigrie became a tragic shooting victim as a result of Ian's struggles. His painful story reveals a cycle of dysfunction and neglect that exposes our flawed system and our collective failure to help people with great needs. But Ian's story is also inspiring; a story of hope that should compel us to recognize we can and should do better.

It turns out that Debbie Baigrie is an extraordinary human being. She is remarkably strong, compassionate, and thoughtful. She forgave Ian and became his ally and champion.

It turns out that Ian is also extraordinary despite his vio-

lent act. He searches for beauty and purpose in the midst of great suffering. He struggles against certain death in an obscure prison cell mandated by the courts to win freedom. Both Debbie and Ian have made powerful statements to the world.

Debbie Baigrie has said to the world that there should be nothing "ordinary" about thirteen-year-old children shooting adults and that we need to do extraordinary things to help address the horrific problems in American society that allow child trauma and violence to be so poorly managed.

Ian is now able to say to the world that it should never be "ordinary" or acceptable to condemn a child to die in prison. Through his remarkable spirit and resolve, he has survived a cycle of abuse and violence, a saga of tragedy and dysfunction and still held on to his humanity.

Ian is magic. His story is difficult and heartbreaking, but he takes us places we need to go to understand why we must do better. He survives by relying on a poetic spirit, an unrelenting desire to succeed, to recover, and to love. Ian's story says something hopeful about our future.

We remain the nation with the highest rate of incarceration in the world. We have condemned thousands of children to die in prison who are still incarcerated today. Our prison system is notoriously cruel, and we have shown a shameful unwillingness to help the most needy, disabled, and traumatized people in our nation. But, Ian's story affirms that we can turn things around. His journey reminds us that we are, in fact, more than the worst thing we've ever done.

I used to tell Ian I was proud of him not because he was succeeding in prison or even because he was gifted and talented. I was proud of him for believing he was more than a

crime despite what everyone around him said. I was proud of Ian for refusing to surrender his humanity in the face of horrific, inhumane conditions of confinement. I am proud, because as this book dramatically illustrates, Ian has held on to his magic.

MY

TIME

WILL

COME

1

MY STORY HAS BEEN TOLD MANY TIMES. YOU CAN READ it in police files and court records, case notes and daily logs. The story of my birth, for example, told by a judge sentencing my mother to prison soon after my arrival in this world. And there's the story of that day when I was five, in the case notes of a social worker who drove me to a foster home and then, a few days later, drove me back to the projects, to the room I had shared with my abuser. The story of my childhood was told multiple times by juvenile probation officers who found me to be a problem best managed inside the walls of institutions. In the illustrious space—cold and intensely bright in my memory—of an adult courtroom, it would be the robed and sober voice of a judge who would foretell my death when I was thirteen. Relying on the stories of police officers, lawyers, and other accomplished professionals, he would send me to Florida State Prison, never to be released. As I said, my story has been told many times and by highly regarded experts in their fields. But today, if you'll bear with me, I would like to try to tell it to you myself. I have reason to believe the experts may be wrong about me. You see, today, thirty years later, I am neither in prison nor dead.

In the stories told of my life, each begins with a crime.

A crime by my mother against a neighbor, crimes against me, crimes committed by me. My stories are defined by legal codes and diagnostic categories. To tell you the truth, I struggle to shake these, to describe myself to you as I am, in all that I am. My sense, though, is that this is an experience true to millions of people who, like me, happened to be born into poor neighborhoods at a time in history when the intervention of choice is arrest and incarceration—even for mothers of infants, even for young children. I would like not to begin my story as the experts have done, with the story of a crime. But that is, in fact, the reality of this life. So I will begin with the story of the worst thing I have ever done, the crime I was sentenced to die in prison for. But I begin here not because, as the experts have said, this defines me. I begin here because I hurt someone very badly during a time in my life when I was blinded by my own hurt. And I want to admit to it. I want to state the truth of it. I think I owe it to her. And to the child that I was. I think we need to speak about harm, what we've done, what's been done to us, because that is what will open doors, what will air out and begin to heal the wounds we carry and have caused. And that is what will allow for new stories to begin to be told. I am telling you my story today because I want to tell a story of hope and meaning, of being one among a human family.

I SHOT DEBBIE BAIGRIE ON JULY 27, 1990. I WAS THIR-teen and, along with a group of older boys, I was trying to rob her and the man who was walking her to her car. He, of course, was walking her to her car out of concern for her being a woman, alone at night, in a parking lot. My friends and I were the embodiment of his reasons for concern and I

believe that night I only confirmed any beliefs he had about kids like me.

At the time, my mom and I were homeless, staying with a family friend in the housing projects I had called home most of my life. Central Park Village had been a prosperous, entrepreneurial black community before I was born. But after deadly riots and looting there in 1967, the neighborhood had fallen on hard times. It was now a complex of run-down, low-rise buildings, riddled with poverty, gang violence, drugs, and crime. Because Mom had let the rent on our place fall behind, she and I were staying with a lady known to me as Aunt Louise, though she was no relation of ours. During my childhood, Central Park Village was a place of comings and goings, among family, friends, and acquaintances; the place was full of people like us—roamers.

GUNS WERE NOT NEW TO ME. WHEN I WAS ELEVEN, MY friend Marquis and I had gone jacking, committing our first crimes together—robbing people, seventy-five cents here, two dollars there—only to be arrested. The gun we had brandished turned out to be an old, rusty, empty Colt M1911, the standard-issue sidearm of the U.S. Armed Forces from 1911 to 1986. Toward the end of that school year, during a conflict I had with a classmate, Marquis's cousin had pulled the gun out, pointed it at my opponent, and insisted that I fight him. The gun I would end up using to shoot Debbie was a .32 revolver.

On the night of the crime, I met up with Marquis, who was fourteen at the time, and two older boys from the neighborhood and we walked downtown. Downtown Tampa was my stomping ground for a couple of years. I knew where

police cars were stationed; where it was too crowded to pull off a robbery; where it would be unlikely for us to get caught.

We continued downtown, searching for the right place at the right time, but I was nervous.

Marquis was stern in a friendly way: "Man, Jim-Jim, look it done turned nighttime and we ain't done nothing yet. The next people we come across, we jacking, whether it's too open or not." Everybody agreed. We didn't have far to go before an opportunity presented itself: as we were walking across the parking lot, we turned to see a white man and woman, leaning against a car, rapt in conversation.

One of the boys cooked up a plan on the spot. "Jim-Jim, I'm gonna go over and ask 'em for some change. When you see one o' dem reach for dey money, do your thing." "All right," I said. Marquis and the other boy stood right behind me. "Do one of y'all have change for a twenty?" the boy asked. I thought I heard either the man or the woman say yes. At the top of my lungs I yelled, "It's a jack, y'all, give it up," pointing the revolver at them. The woman stared at the gun and screamed, which startled me. Before I knew it I had pulled the trigger and she took off, running.

TAKE IT BACK

Her mouth opens as she inhales her scream.
The bullets are reloaded because the trigger was never
*   squeezed.*
We're back at the start when we first asked for change.
And her face is the same because she never felt that
*   pain.*
He isn't on his knees—looking me in my eyes.
Like I'm the last thing he'll see for the first and final
*   time.*
The song self-destruction isn't resounding in my mind.
We're just standing at the scene. Before it became a
*   crime.*
If I could see into the future. Sitting on that porch on
*   India.*
When my codefendants came to visit. I'd've chosen to
*   stay with Lydia.*
I'm back in Central Park. Two-story apartment
*   building.*
Never knowing where I'm going . . .

I stared down the man and barked, "Get on the fucking ground." He stood motionless, terrified. Ever so slowly the man got on his knees. For a moment I stood trembling, shaken to the core. As the woman ran I aimed the gun at her fleeing figure, and squeezed the trigger. She screamed but kept running, disappearing around the corner.

I turned back and started sprinting toward Central Park. The other three boys running behind me, I could hear Marquis say, "Jim-Jim, hold up, man, hold up, wait for me, don't leave me here." When I asked the three "How much y'all get?" Marquis answered, "He ain't have nothin' on him, Jim-Jim, nothin'."

THAT NIGHT, CENTRAL PARK VILLAGE WAS ABUZZ WITH rumor and gossip about what had happened. People I had known all my life in the neighborhood—people who had given me rank and praise for jacking in the past—were now clearly intent on keeping their distance from me.

"No, boy, get away from me. I heard what you did downtown."

"Say what?"

"Man, Marquis told us you just killed two people downtown."

A police car pulled up on State Street and called me over.

"You been in the park all night?"

"Yeah, why?"

"Because you fit the description of somebody who took part in a shooting downtown today. A woman was shot."

I couldn't be seen downtown wearing the Bulls shirt that had matched the description of a young black shooter on the loose. I turned to a little boy on a bicycle. He was a few years

younger than me, about eight or nine. He had been sitting on his bike with one foot on the curb quietly watching us.

"Lil Cal, trade shirts with me until I come back." He had on a gray and blue Georgetown Hoya T-shirt. Without hesitation, he said, "Here you go," and began pulling the shirt over his head.

I WAS BORN MARCH 29, 1977, IN TAMPA GENERAL HOSPITAL to Peggye McClendon Manuel. When as a child I asked her why she named me Ian Einar Manuel (Ian being Scottish Gaelic for God's gift; Einar, Old Norse for lone warrior), she told me it was pure serendipity: she claimed to have pulled Ian and Einar out of a bag of names. "If your sorry-ass daddy would've showed up at the hospital and signed your birth papers, you would've had his no-good-ass name (Jimmy Reese, Jr.). He told me he was going to get some Pampers and milk; I ain't seen him since." I would learn much later that Ian is a variant of Sean, the name of my older brother. As to Manuel, after divorcing my brother's dad, Robert Manuel, Peggye had kept his name.

Soon after I was born, my mother was sent to a prison for shooting a woman with a .32 revolver. As the story goes, Sean, known as "John-John," had taken to wandering through the woman's yard and she had sternly reprimanded him, prompting my mother to warn her that she had better leave Sean alone, that is, if she knew what was good for her. Now the woman had gone so far as to slap my brother, who ran home and told our mother. Enraged, Peggye pulled her gun from its hiding place, walked over to the woman's property, and shot her at point-blank range but didn't kill her.

After Peggye was arrested, her best friend, Lynn Creal,

whom we called "Aunt" Lynn, borrowed money from a neighborhood loan shark, Joe Upshaw, to bail her out of jail. When it was time for my mother to be sentenced, she grew angry: "I'm here for protecting my son. If you gon' send me to jail for that, then go right ahead . . . I don't give a damn."

Judge Coe didn't either. He sentenced her to three years.

With Mom in prison, I was shunted to and fro among Peggye's friends, who did the best they could to take care of me. But it was my paternal grandmother, Linda Johnson, who conclusively stepped up. She constantly worried Lynn, begging her to let her look after me until my mother was released. Lynn ended up taking me to visit my mom at Lowell Correctional Institution. "Ian's grandmother won't leave me alone about this boy," she told Peggye. "I can't take no more! I'm going to give him to her till you come home."

GRANDMA LINDA WAS BORN IN DECEMBER SOMETIME between 1911 and 1920. She was raised in Cordele, Georgia. She bore two children, a daughter and a son. In search of a livelihood, my grandmother had migrated to Tampa, forced to leave both of her children behind. She found work as a cook in Morrison's Cafeteria at the Tampa Bay mall. She would hold that job for more than twenty-five years before retiring. I recall little of my infancy spent with Grandma Linda, but I have the dearest memories of her from age six on, years after my mother's release from Lowell. While Peggye could express her love only in sometimes hard-to-fathom ways, my grandmother adored and spoiled me as only a grandparent can.

The first of every month, Grandma would receive a social security check, a retirement check, and free food coupons

from Morrison's, and she'd say in her singular southern drawl, "Come on, boy, we're going out yonder." "Out yonder" was the Tampa Bay mall.

We'd walk downtown and sit on a bench to wait for the Hartline bus. When it pulled up—the orange, yellow, and red Hartline strip painted along its sides—its doors would swoosh open, inviting us in. Grandma Linda would give the bus driver two quarters and two dimes to pay our bus fare, thirty-five cents each for the trip to "out yonder." The bus would roll away from downtown along Main Street, through west Tampa, past Macfarlane Park, toward Tampa Bay mall. I always eagerly anticipated passing, and staring through the window at, the Old Sombrero—Tampa Stadium. The bus would eventually roll into the parking lot and stop at the mall's entrance.

Sometimes we'd walk past Morrison's Cafeteria as we stepped through the mall's glass entrance to go cash Grandma Linda's checks. At other times we'd head straight for the cafeteria. I still remember my usual haul there: fried shrimp, mac and cheese, sweet potato pie, and sweet tea. Grandma never ate much herself.

After our meal, if we still had to go to the bank, we'd walk up to the counter, and Grandma would take out her checks and give them to the teller. Then I'd wait for my inevitable embarrassment when the teller would turn the checks over and say, "Just sign right here, Mrs. Johnson, and we'll get you your money." Grandma would always have to say, "I don't know how to spell my name!"

The teller always responded: "It's OK, ma'am, just put an X and that'll be good enough."

With relief, I'd exhale and watch Grandma carefully mark her two Xs; the teller would count out and give her her

money, between eight and nine hundred dollars, which to my mind meant that she was rich. Before returning home from "out yonder," Grandma Linda would often load me up with goodies—toys, clothes, shoes, sweets, whatever I wanted.

IF I TOLD MY STORY

If I told my story . . .
Would you believe a word I said?
Or would the truth be like a square root—
too deep and difficult to understand.
If I told my story . . .
And all the times I've bled.
How I played hopscotch, over blood drops.
A result of a childhood, curtailed in a cell.
If I told my story . . . of the water—
splashing closed eyelids like a dam.
One million tears that never spilled.
A wounded heart just waiting to heal.
If I told my story . . . of courage.
And my will to act in spite of my fears.
How I survived being buried alive—
You probably wouldn't believe your ears.
If I told my story . . . of guts and glory.
Without sugarcoating the facts.
It would be obvious, without much argument.
That I've lived a miraculous life.

. . .

LATER, THE NIGHT OF THE SHOOTING, ALL HELL BROKE loose at the Hall in Central Park Village, the game room. To get there, you had to step through a hole in a wall, a passageway through a blockade of brick and concrete that was big enough for a man to go through. When I found myself standing on the other side in a sandy area, I saw two Central Park kids rounding a corner, running from the game room. They were carrying a bounty of candy and other sweets, which struck me as odd, because the game room was closed at night. I yelled, "What y'all doing?"

"Jim-Jim, we just broke in the Hall," they excitedly replied.

I walked around the corner to the front of the Hall and pushed the door open.

Word must have spread swiftly. The press of the crowd was intense. Pure mayhem. Men with crowbars were busting up the videogame machine for quarters. Women were arguing over cases of cigarettes and food. People were running back and forth, in and out the door, hauling cases of beer and jars of pickles. Behind the counter I saw a big pig's feet jar full of pennies. I grabbed it and ran.

No sooner had I stepped through the hole in the wall headed back to Central Park than I heard the all-too-familiar sound of police sirens, the cars pulling in off Nebraska Ave. toward the Hall. I took off as fast I could, the heavy jar of pennies slowing me down.

After the police left, I was standing on State Street and saw Tammy, a girl I knew who was pregnant with the baby of legendary Tampa fighter Frank "Baldy" Green. I looked

at Tammy's bulging stomach and thought of a way to give her the pennies.

"Tammy," I said, "I'm a give you these pennies, but after you have that baby, I want to hold that baby as many times as there are pennies in this jar."

Tammy smiled brightly and said, "OK, Jim-Jim."

BUYING TIME

If I could buy time
I'd pay for the past
Reach into the glass
And pick memories out of the sand
I'd spend money on moments
I was interacting and laughing
Subtract loneliness and sadness
Then add up the balance.
I'd watch how I spend it
Because time is precious.
Be very selective
And buy times I was happy.
If time could be purchased
I'd bring back my family
Roll back all of the hearses
And open their caskets.
I'd alter results
Because I'd know what would happen
And would feel it's my fault
If I just sit back and let it
I'd break a bill
And ask for change
So this time things
Wouldn't turn out the same.
If I could buy time
I'd pay for some smiles
Recreate all of the days

They've destroyed as a child
If time could be bought
I'd purchase moments I lost
Every tick tock on the clock
No matter how much it cost.

. . .

"WHEN THE NURSE CLEANED YOU UP AND BROUGHT YOU to me, I said, 'That ain't my baby; I don't know what y'all did with my baby. You better take this black motherfucker back where you got him from and bring me my child.'" For as long as I can remember, after her release from prison, my mother often recounted this. Often absent, she had a mean streak. All the same, my love for her was stubborn, even though her capacity for cruelty ended up damaging me in ways that I'm still trying to figure out. When I misbehaved, she would whip me with an extension cord or switch, but her words hurt even more. Insults flew from her mouth like bullets.

"Jim-Jim, you make me sick. The more I teach you, the dumber I get," or "You ain't my son, I found you on the doorstep." Sometimes, she compared me to a neighborhood boy named Corey. "I wish you had been cute like Corey. That was a beautiful baby." Once she told me, "Ian, go outside and play." I went and looked out the window, only to see that there were no other children around. "There's nobody outside to play with." "Jim-Jim, you came out of my pussy by yourself. If God wanted you to have somebody to play with, I would've had twins."

Peggye McClendon Manuel was born in Belle Glade, Florida, the gateway to the Everglades, a wild and rough place near Lake Okeechobee, where a lot of migrant workers gathered before fanning out all over the state, following crops that needed picking. She didn't stay in Belle Glade long. She and her brother, George, were taken from their mother and sent to live with her mother's sister and husband in Orlando when she was a little girl because her mother, my grandma Betty, was a single parent and an alcoholic. I don't

know if my mother ever knew her father. She lived with her aunt and uncle until she finished middle school, when she started fighting with her uncle. After one fight too many, when she was around fourteen, she was sent alone to Tampa to rejoin her mother, who had married the man I knew as Grandpa Sonny. Peggye made it clear to me from an early age that I was unwanted, a mistake. When she became pregnant with me, my brother, Sean, was nine years old, and the last thing she wanted was another child to feed and clothe. I remember asking her once if I could have a sister, to which she responded: "I ain't having no more damn kids. You better ask your sorry-ass daddy to have you a sister. Your black ass ain't supposed to be here, let alone a sister. If I would've followed my first mind and got an abortion instead of listening to Big Momma, Ian Manuel wouldn't exist." Big Momma—at least five foot ten and more than three hundred pounds—was the neighborhood matriarch, whose proclamations were definitive.

My mother hated the darkness of my skin so much that, as a child, I wished I were of lighter complexion. There was a time when I had heard that chlorine could change pigmentation, so I'd sit in the shallows of the neighborhood pool (I couldn't swim) and repeatedly submerge my body. When I'd get out of the pool, I'd purposely ignore the lifeguard yelling, "Boy, wash that chlorine off of you." Later, when I was eight or nine, I started taking bleach baths. I'd get Clorox from the basement laundry room and walk back up the twelve concrete steps. I'd stop the tub up, turn the hot water on, and wait for the tub to fill. I would always have to decide how much bleach to pour in—not because I feared damage to my skin but because I worried that my mother would beat me for using up her bleach. Sometimes

I would risk as much as half a bottle. If the water was too hot, I'd adjust the temperature by briefly turning on the cold water faucet. Slowly I'd sink into the tub and slide down to my neck, sometimes losing track of time as I soaked. In my child's imagination, I was trying to achieve the color of a son that my mother would be proud of and love.

STRETCH MY IMAGINATION

If I could stretch my imagination
and split my thoughts apart—
I'd reach past our separation.
And pull you closer to my heart
If I could stretch my imagination
I'd disintegrate these bars.
Reach upwards with my arms.
Until my fingers touched the stars.
If I could stretch my imagination.
like the muscles in my legs.
I'd be the chest where you rest.
Every time you're scared.
If I could stretch my imagination
like a thousand rubber bands.
I'd pull the strings of your heart
until they popped me on my hands.
If I could stretch my imagination.
like a rainbow in the clouds.
I'd navigate icebergs and glaciers.
For the radiance of your smile.
If I could stretch my imagination.
And bend the stiffness of my mind.
I'd see past my limitations
Until I could stare into your eyes.
If I could stretch my imagination. . . .

. . .

WHEN I WAS FIVE, MY MOTHER, BROTHER—SEAN PIERRE Devon Manuel—and I lived in a two-bedroom apartment in Central Park Village, a family of three on Burden Court—at once all too aptly and ironically named. If I had a family portrait of the three of us at the time, one glance at it would make you think we weren't related. I was the runt of the family. I didn't really start to grow until about the sixth grade, and I never got to be more than five feet, ten inches. Peggye was a big woman, but short. She weighed more than 220 pounds and was only five foot two. Sean was a giant next to both of us. He was always tall for his age, and by the time he was sixteen, was more than six feet tall and about 230 pounds. On my birthdays, I would sometimes put on his forty-two-inch-waist pants to see how much I'd grown. They always swallowed me as easily as a whale might swallow a minnow. Sean, "John-John," was my idol. He was an excellent fighter and well respected, not just in our neighborhood but in others throughout Tampa. I was proud to be Lil Jim-Jim, John-John's little brother. I wanted to be as big and bad and respected as John-John.

When my mother was home, she liked to sit on a brown wooden dining room chair on the porch next to the front door. She always had a yellow box of Argo cornstarch, her snack of choice, and a clear tumbler filled with RC cola and ice cubes. She'd finish her RC and then crunch and suck the ice cubes, before lighting up a Winston 100s cigarette. When she was not at home, she more than likely could be found at Momma Dump's, near our project. The actual name of the bar was Blue Light, but it belonged to Momma Dump, so that's what everyone called it. There, Peggye drank beer after beer.

The front door of the bar was propped open by a chair most of the time, unless it was too cold or rainy. Inside, to the left of the front door, was a jukebox and to the right a phone booth. Straight ahead were a couple of green pool tables. The bar was at an angle to the left. It wasn't that long; it had only five or six barstools. Aside from the expected kaleidoscopic panorama of bottles of liquor on the shelves, there were jars of pig's feet and pickles as well as boxes of candy. Even though we kids weren't supposed to be there, occasionally I would wander in looking for my mother, and sometimes Momma Dump would hand me some candy and say, "Now, Jim-Jim, you know you're not supposed to be in here. Get on out of here before I lose my license."

IT WAS DURING THAT TIME THAT JOHN-JOHN SEXUALLY abused me. While the details are sparse in my mind—for self-protective reasons, no doubt—I remember enough to know I didn't need or want to remember any more. Mine was a painful initiation into sex and the streets' supposed sacred code of silence. When he would finish he would tell me, "Don't tell Momma! Understand?" And I would nod yes. Little as I was, I was full of shame and fear; I didn't break the code of silence for a long time. But one day Peggye and I were downstairs in the dining room of our apartment. Sean wasn't there. Momma and I were getting ready to leave for an outing. While tucking my shirt into my unbuttoned pants, my mother said, "Boy, where your drawers at?" I stood frozen, speechless, in a daze. I couldn't think of a lie fast enough. Louder, she repeated the question. Her mother's intuition must have told her something was terribly wrong. I began crying. Now she knew something was grossly amiss. She grabbed me by the shoulders: "What hap-

pened? Tell me! Tell me!" Through tears, my voice cracking, I said, "John-John."

My mother buttoned me up, got on the phone, and called the police. The police came and interviewed my mother and me; they arrested my brother. Child welfare services spirited me off to a shelter home; they temporarily took custody away from my mother as they conducted their investigation.

Even in the home of concerned, friendly white people, I was in shock at being separated from my family. I had a nightmare my first night at my new foster parents' home. I woke up screaming my dead "uncle's" name, "Bobby! Bobby!" I was comforted by unfamiliar faces. Sean was sent to a juvenile facility for six months or so. After he came out, we returned to our life together, John-John and I back in our old bedroom. It was never spoken of again.

TWO DAYS AFTER THE SHOOTING, I WENT DOWNTOWN and retraced the woman's steps as she had frantically run from the crime scene—from the car that she had been leaning on while talking to the man to the corner where she had turned. On the sidewalk around the corner I spotted what I took to be dried drops of blood. For the first time it dawned on me that I had actually shot someone. I remember it was a hot afternoon and the sun was in my eyes. Maybe it had been a while since I had eaten. But I walked into a fire station and told them I thought I needed help, shortly before fainting. I woke up in the hospital to my mother yelling at the nurses.

As I would later learn, I had shot Debbie Baigrie, a twenty-eight-year-old mother of two girls, in the face. She had survived.

I DON'T KNOW HOW TO SWIM AND I'M SCARED TO DEATH of deep water. The night after the shooting, I dreamt I was thrashing about at sea to avoid drowning. I slept worse than fitfully. Time and again I woke up anxious, terrified. I was full of regret, though remorse for what I had done would come later. The next morning I went to work, as I did on occasional weekends, for Bob Gilbertson at the Tampa Young Men's Christian Association—as close to a father as I have ever known.

My biological father had been a blur in my life. He cropped up sporadically when least expected. Jimmy Reese was a hardworking trucker for the Fogarty Brothers; he drove a green and white truck. As a young man he had earned the nickname "Rock Jaw" for a reason lost to time. My very first memory of him is of a drunk stumbling into his mother's—Grandma Linda's—house to watch wrestling on TV, around the time my brother molested me. On another occasion there, annoyed by my behavior, he tried to beat me. Grandma Linda would have none of it and chased him out: "Don't you hit my baby; you drunk, get out." Two or three times a year, he would come around to my mother's house, I assume to give her a little something to help take care of me. His idea of fatherly time was to say to her:

"Lemme get that boy for a little bit." And he would take me to the outskirts of Central Park Village, where he lived, toward Tampa Heights, to places like the 8-Ball, a bar where older men hung out and gambled. It had videogames. Or he would say to my mom: "Lemme get that boy for the weekend." And I would have to go spend time with him and his girlfriend, Beverly. He would babble to me about inconsequential matters like a man with a guilty conscience. He would dole out pocket change as if to buy my affection. He once bought me a boom box, which I ended up selling or pawning. I didn't need a boom box. He told a story about me, when I was between ages one and four, which still haunts me: he, Beverly, and I were in a house. They were asleep; I was not. The house caught fire. I must have woke to the smell of smoke. I crawled, screaming, waking them up. My father said I had saved all of our lives.

IAN-GREDIENTS

Sprinkle seasons of solitude
in a crockpot of confinement.
Chop the hottest jalapenos
and rub'em in the wounds of your body.
Burn family members like tinder
that died in the 2000s and '90s.
Choke down hard times past your larynx
like a toddler swallowing solids.
Open bottles of ketchup
from the tomatoes beneath your pigments.
Turn up the gas behind the glass
and let'em bake you like a biscuit.
Or sleep inside a freezer
with nothing but your skin.
Then fidget inside a mixer
as they beat you like an egg!
Then you'll begin to understand
how difficult my life has really been
and the ingredients that it took
to make me everything I am.

. . .

WHEN I WAS SIX, GRANDMA LINDA LEARNED THAT HER daughter, my aunt, had died. Grandma Linda packed a suitcase and she and I headed downtown to the Greyhound station to catch a bus for Cordele, Georgia, to attend the funeral. This was my first and only visit to my grandmother's birthplace. Cordele was a rural, predominantly black and desperately poor town in southern Georgia, inhabited by the descendants of sharecroppers, in a region known as the Black Belt. We stayed with my cousin Isora, a sweet, young brown-skinned woman. I remember meeting my cousin, Ken, only a few years older than I was. He took me out in the house's backyard, where the family had pigs locked in a pen and rabbits in a cage. He showed me how to feed the animals. I stood in stunned amazement as he poured two buckets of slop into the pen; the pigs rushed toward it, greedily slurping, and devoured it. Later, we went to the church for the funeral. I watched as they lowered my aunt's casket into the ground, Grandma Linda holding my hand.

Soon after Grandma Linda and I returned home to Tampa, we were standing at a bus stop where she was seeing me off to school as she did every morning. I don't remember what brought things to a head, but Grandma Linda started yelling at me in front of the other kids waiting for the bus. I yelled back. She slapped me hard across the face. I slapped her back, knocking her down. I blurted, "Grandma, I'm sorry." As she rose to her feet, she said, "Come on. I'm taking you to your momma." I began to cry and beg: "Please, Grandma, don't tell Momma. I'm sorry."

When she told my mom, I was ordered to my room and I was certain I was about to get the beating of my life. But, instead, I heard Momma blame Grandma for what had hap-

pened. "You treat that boy like a king. Buying him this and that, everything he asks for. Stop and I bet he'll straighten up." I heard Grandma Linda say, "I is," in a small voice. I think back now on all of the humiliation my grandmother faced as she struggled to pull herself and her children—and now her grandchild—out of poverty, all of the courage it took to travel as a young black woman from Cordele to this city, so different from what she knew. It is a sharp wound in my heart to remember how I treated her in that moment, how I hurt the person I loved most in the world, who loved me and made love possible for me even now.

LINDA'S LOVE

I want a woman that can hold me—
like the little boy I am.
The one incarcerated as a kid.
And forced to be a man.
A lady that will cradle me—
arms around my head.
As I cry for the little boy—
the world just left for dead.
I want to be loved for who I am—
particularly the darkness of my skin.
Because I've been abused and ridiculed—
for something I had no choice in being.
I want a woman to be that something—
I haven't had since Grandma Linda.
To be my partner, and my pillow.
A place I can just surrender.
Someone who treats me special—
like Grandma did when I was a kid.
Someone I can trust, take off the mask.
Relax and just be Ian.
Maybe I'm just a dreamer.
Asking for the impossible.
Somebody to love me devoutly—
A woman like Linda Johnson.

. . .

GRANDMA LINDA LIVED ACROSS THE STREET FROM THE
St. Peter Claver Elementary School. She paid for my tuition
to attend, starting in first grade, and for the next two and
one-half years, sat on her front porch each day, watching
me like a hawk through the schoolyard's fence when I was
at recess.

St. Peter Claver's school was established in 1893 to serve
children of the black community. It was soon destroyed by
fire; the notice tacked on an oak tree in front of the ruins
read: "the late fire on these grounds was not caused by any
ill feeling to the Catholic Church, but because the citizens
do not propose to submit to a negro school in the midst of
the white and retired resident portion of the city." Despite
threats of violence, it was rebuilt by brave black men and
women determined to educate their children, in a setting
of prayer, worship, and learning. At St. Peter Claver when
I went, little black children were resplendent in crisp uni-
forms: girls in long-sleeved white shirts under dark blue tar-
tan pinafores, and boys in short-sleeved light blue or white
shirts and dark blue pants. Thanks to my grandmother, it
was here that I developed a love for school, especially for
the care and devotion of teachers whose praise I craved.

At the end of the school year awards were handed out in
the auditorium where proud parents sat with their children.
As the ceremony neared its conclusion—kid after kid had
been called to the stage—I began to fear embarrassment
next to my mother and her friend Linda Wright. Finally, Mrs.
Yvonne Fort, a middle-aged black teacher, called my name:
"And to Ian Manuel for excellence in reading and writing." I
walked up, beaming, accepted my certificates, and thanked
Mrs. Fort. When I returned to my seat Mrs. Wright said in

a hushed voice: "Jim-Jim, lemme look at those certificates. Reading and writing, baby, that's all you need in this world. As long as you've got that, you can be anything you wanna be."

There was also the issue of the Eucharist. I remember sitting mesmerized by the rite as I watched Father O'Keefe refer to the communion bread and cup of wine as the actual body and blood of Christ. "Jesus said, 'Do this in remembrance of me.'" Father O'Keefe then fed the little white discs to the children who stepped up to the altar, each accompanied by his or her parent. I was excluded from the sacrament. When I mustered the courage to ask a teacher why, she told me that only kids with parents in tow could participate. After school that day, I joyously hurried home.

"Momma, listen, I need you to come to my school's church with me next week."

"For what?"

"Well, they gave kids this thing to eat today and I asked why I couldn't get none and they said my parent had to be there."

"Boy, I ain't going down there for that shit. That ain't nothing but some damn bread. If you want some bread, drag your ass into the kitchen and get it."

Grandma Linda developed dementia over the next few years. I remember when she could no longer control her bowels. Her embarrassment and confusion—and my own. Isora came one day to take Grandma Linda back to Cordele, where she would be placed in a nursing home for the remainder of her days. I would never see her again. I'm not even sure when she died. It is hard to even begin to estimate this loss for me. It was as if, at eleven years old, it was time for me to grow up—no one to care if or what

I ate, no one to walk me to and from the bus, no one to wonder where I was or what I was doing or with whom. It was at this moment that I first understood what it meant to be homeless, to be without anything to hold me in place and offer shelter and comfort—and was pulled fully into the chaos of Central Park Village.

In the middle of the school year, I would have to start attending my district's public school, Morgan Woods Elementary, located in the Tampa upper-middle-class suburb of Town and Country, a twenty- to thirty-minute bus ride from Central Park Village via the interstate highway—twice as big as St. Peter Claver and consistently ranked among the lowest performing public schools in Florida.

IN CENTRAL PARK VILLAGE, THE ONLY OPTIONS FOR AN eleven-year-old boy like me to earn real money were to mug people or become a drug runner for the major players in the 'hood. I wanted no part of that, regardless of how much I had glamorized my brother, Sean, who at this point in my life was serving time behind bars. I decided with my friend Ron that we would just head downtown and secure gainful employment. I don't know why but I was confident that if I could get somebody to listen to me, I would be able to convince them to give us jobs. "Who's gonna give us a job? We're kids," Ron objected. I told him to let me do the talking.

After a few fruitless encounters, we ended up at the YMCA beneath the monorail to Harbour Island, a mall built along the Hillsborough River. I said to the lady at the front desk, "Me and my friend are looking for a job; do you have an application that we can fill out?" She looked at us amused, obviously finding our bravado cute. "You'll have

to speak to Sandy, my manager, over there." Sandy ran the YMCA gym. "Sir," I began and repeated what I had said to the woman. "Why don't you go next door to the administrative office and see if they have anything for you?" he responded. I was fierce in my determination. Once she knew why we were there, Bob Gilbertson's secretary walked into his office and returned to say that her boss was busy but that we should wait. Soon we were ushered in and found ourselves standing before Mr. Gilbertson, CEO of the YMCA, who had ultimate authority to hire us—he was an affable, clean shaven (except for a mustache) white man about six feet even, weighing more than two hundred pounds, and of business casual style.

"Where are you guys from?"

"Central Park Village; we're looking for something to keep us off the streets, to help us with school clothes and things like that, you know, to support ourselves a little bit."

"Well, what can you do?" he asked as we all sat down.

"Clean windows, wipe down the exercise bikes, sweep."

"Gosh, guys, I can't very well give you a job, but I'll tell you what, I'll buy you lunch and then let's talk."

Bob gave us a twenty-dollar bill and directed us to a pizza joint up the street. He told us to come back with the change, which we did. Unbeknownst to us then—but as we would later learn—Bob knew as much about Central Park Village as anybody. He was aware of the poverty and danger permeating the 'hood. He understood how lack of hope could shatter lives, and how Central Park was toxic to children, forced as they were from an early age to conform to the unforgiving code of the streets, where respect is earned by never allowing oneself to be dissed without consequence. The more he had learned about Central Park,

the more he had wanted to connect with it and nurture the potential of its children and teenagers, but logistics had posed a problem: the nearest Y with youth programs was in the suburbs. Years later, after exhaustive fundraising, Bob was able to build a YMCA branch closer to the projects. For me, what stood out about Bob when I first met him was that he didn't treat me like a child; he didn't blow me off. He saw something of value in an eleven-year-old boy who had had the courage—the courage, I like to think, of my Grandma Linda—to walk into his office and ask for work.

To be sure, Bob could never have put us on the Y's payroll, which I didn't know at the time; there are child labor laws after all. We chatted about what might be possible—maybe summer camp one day—and unexpectedly Bob proposed that we do odd jobs around his house for pay. From the start, Bob was always challenging us: "Ian, if you saved one penny and doubled your savings every day, how much money would you have in ten years?" Bob was always talking about the importance of budgeting. He lived in a world apart from Central Park Village, in the prosperous area near Bayshore Boulevard in Tampa, with its elegant houses, freshly cut grass, and nice cars. Going there for me was both pleasurable and disorienting; it inspired me to dream but also to worry about whether I could or would ever truly live in Bob's world. When word got out in Central Park that Ron and I had "jobs," other kids wanted in, and eventually two other boys our age, Jose and Donte, ended up joining us.

Soon we settled on a routine: many a Saturday our group went out to Bob's house to perform chores such as trimming hedges and weeding the yard. Afterward Bob would take us to lunch in the neighborhood. We would then do fun things, for he treated us much the same way he treated

his own children, who were older than we and who, more often than not, were off doing their own thing. For instance, he had a boat anchored at a sailing club on Davis Islands and he took us sailing. The first time the boat tilted all of us boys gasped in horror, worried that it was about to flip and we, who didn't know how to swim, would land in the water and drown. Once Bob asked us if we had ever gone fishing and we said: "Yeah, yeah, sure!" But our comical inexperience during our fishing expedition made clear that our yeses were more than exaggeration.

Bob belonged to a yacht club of sorts, and we would sometimes go there for meals and recreation. What was extraordinary about the place, for me at least, was that its members were diverse in a way that I had never known: Asians, African-Americans, Latinos, whites, women and men, all of a certain class and seemingly to the yacht-club born. Everything about the place felt so near yet so far away: Bob wanted us to know what might lie in store for us if we stayed out of trouble. We would talk about things that immediately concerned us, eager as we boys were for the insights of a father figure.

Sometimes Bob would drive us back home from our Saturday outings and we would caution him not to take us all the way into Central Park Village, where a white man driving a white Volvo would have been a magnet for grief at four o'clock in the afternoon. Once we told him about one of our exploits, acting like tough guys and scaring people at gunpoint. He told us that we weren't being smart and would most assuredly find ourselves in harm's way if we kept that up. "Somebody's gonna hurt you. You can't do that. That's not even kidding around. It's got downsides you can't even see." Bob tried to instill in us the core values of the YMCA:

to have sincere concern for the needs and well-being of others; to tell the truth; to treat others as we would have them treat us; to do what is right.

The Saturday after the shooting, when I went to visit Bob, I was by myself for some reason and I told him nothing about what had happened. I went about things as usual. I washed his Volvo. He told me to do it again, as I had done a poor job the first time. We then went to the yacht club and wandered around. Late that afternoon he dropped me off at a safe space near Central Park Village—no drugs, no crime—a little grocery store across from the parking lot of the Tampa Fire Department. This would be my last afternoon with Bob for nearly thirty years. The whole time, I felt the weight of what I had done, the shame of my betrayal of all that Bob had tried to offer me.

THE YEAR GRANDMA LINDA LEFT FOR GEORGIA WAS ALSO the year my mother tested positive for HIV. I found it difficult to wrap my head around her living with an infection that most assuredly would one day claim her life. It was intolerable to imagine that I was going to be motherless— and I didn't know when. I knew the man she got it from, Herbert. He used to come around and stay with Momma sometimes and play with me when he wasn't up in her room behind closed doors. Years later, she would drive me in her gray Pinto to the cemetery. We would walk to his tombstone; she would kneel and put flowers on his grave, and whisper things to him that I couldn't make out.

At Morgan Woods Elementary, I was in Mrs. Kean's third-grade class. I found it now impossible for me to sit still. I was constantly fidgeting at my desk. Unbidden, I would blurt answers out. Often, when assigned a reading or writ-

ing exercise, I would finish way ahead of everyone else. I would begin tapping, sometimes even banging, on my desk, trying to get the attention of other students, who were concentrating on completing their assignment. I would raise my hand to go to the bathroom with a suspicious frequency. Sometimes Mrs. Kean thought I was faking it, merely being a nuisance, and would ignore me. In anger, I would show her up: I would pee on myself right then and there, sitting at my desk. The piss would soak through my pants, wet my seat, and spill onto the floor. Furious, Mrs. Kean would order me to the bathroom to clean myself up as my classmates whooped and hollered. It didn't take long for me to be labeled "emotionally handicapped" and assigned to the EH class, where there were five or six other students.

OVER THE NEXT FOUR YEARS, I WOULD ATTEND FOUR DIFferent public schools, where I would be routinely removed from classrooms, receive paddlings, detentions, and suspensions, and be given work far below my intellectual abilities—because of my inability to sit still. It has only been in recent years that I have learned that what I was dealing with was likely the profound dysregulation commonly seen in children living in contexts defined by chaos, violence, and abuse. The symptoms of the trauma and terror of my life at home were met with punishment, rejection, and ridicule in the school context. And by sixth grade, I was brimming with hurt, anger, and resentment. In the sixth grade I began to get into serious trouble and ultimately spent more time in facilities than in my mother's home. Prior to sixth grade, I had grown accustomed to getting picked on and beat up for my looks and manner by other kids in the neighborhood. All of that would change in 1988 and '89 when my body

went through a sudden growth spurt and, for once, I was bigger and stronger than the kids who targeted me. I gained respect among the older boys and was included in their robberies and drug deals. Robert E. Lee Elementary was on Columbus Drive in the middle of Tampa Heights, a short walk from Central Park. This is where I became Jim-Jim, no longer Lil Jim-Jim. In my memories, I seemed to spend more time fighting and suspended than in the classroom.

My first arrest was in sixth grade when, during one of my suspensions, a group of older boys and I attempted a series of stick-ups that resulted in a gain of maybe five dollars. All of us were sent to W. T. Edwards Juvenile Detention Center. At age 11, this was my first time in detention and my sentence was twenty-one days—an eternity to me at the time. W. T. Edwards was on West Buffalo, the street that was later renamed Martin Luther King Boulevard. It sat in front of Hillsborough Halfway House, near Tampa Stadium. As we were being processed, a staff member said, "I hope you know how to fight, because you're going to have to get down in here."

"Even if we don't mess with nobody?"

"This is W. T. Edwards. You're going to fight whether you mess with somebody or not. Because if you don't mess with somebody, best believe somebody is going to mess with you."

THREE DAYS AFTER THE SHOOTING, I STOLE A WHITE, four-door Cadillac Fleetwood, with two friends, ages fifteen and sixteen. We had never stolen cars to sell them; we simply wanted the feeling of being free and easy as we drove through all kinds of neighborhoods.

Now I could never figure out the mechanics of car steal-

ing, though I had seen guys do it. All I knew was how to start the car. I had done this on a few occasions.

Soon the blare of sirens seemed to be coming from everywhere. We jumped out of the car, each running in different directions. Once out of sight, I began walking calmly to appear uninvolved. But all of a sudden a police car pulled up next to me and an officer leapt out with a K-9 barking violently (I am terrified of dogs).

"Get on the ground. Get on the ground."

He called for his partner to handcuff me, which the partner did aggressively, before leading me to the back of another squad car, which had just screeched to a stop. Now both cars gave chase to my friends. We were arrested near Hyde Park, on the west side of Tampa.

At the police station I said I was "Ian Emmanuel" because "Ian E. Manuel" was on a one-week home pass from a juvenile program. The police ran my name and it came back clean—otherwise I would not have been eligible to be released to parental custody. Obie, Ron, and I were each allowed one phone call. Ron called his mom, as did Obie. I called Momma Dump's, where my mom was often to be found.

"Is Peggye there?"

"No, Jim-Jim, she isn't here but she was here earlier."

"I'm in the police station and I need her to come get me."

"OK, Jim-Jim, if I see her I'll tell her."

I said OK and hung up. By now Obie's mom had come to fetch him. So now it was down to Ron and me.

"Ron, when your mom comes in, tell 'em we're kin so I can go with you."

"My mom won't do that, Jim-Jim."

I was allowed one more call, and I tried Momma Dump's again. Peggye was still not back.

Hours later, while sitting in one of the holding cells, I spotted the white police officer who three days earlier had thought I fit the description of the suspect in a shooting downtown.

"Excuse me, Officer, do you remember me from the other night?"

He looked at me for a second: "Yeah, why?"

"Just wanted to know if y'all caught whoever shot that lady."

"I don't think we ever did."

My conscience was gnawing at me.

OBIE, RON, AND I WERE ARRESTED AT AROUND SIX O'CLOCK, an hour and a half or so after we had stolen the Cadillac in Hyde Park. It was between nine and ten o'clock when I found myself handcuffed in the back of a squad car shooting the breeze with a police officer on our way to W. T. Edwards, twenty minutes away, where I would be held until my mom could be found.

"Boy, what you doin' stealing cars? What you doin' with those older hoodlums?"

"I grew up with those guys. We do this all the time."

The officer and I chatted about all kinds of things. I regaled him with tales of my life as a child criminal. When we reached the detention center's parking lot, he put the car in park and turned the ignition off.

"Is there anything else you wanna tell me before we get out of the car? It'll stay in the car."

"Are you for real?"

"Believe me."

"You know that lady that got shot downtown the other night? I did it."

In his deposition, the officer would claim that he then proceeded to read me my Miranda rights. He did not. What he did do was tell me that I had to remain in the car while he made a quick call in the detention center. This was not what I wanted to hear: Ten minutes or so later, the officer reappeared, turned the car on, and threw it in reverse.

"Hey, man, what you doin'?"

"I've got to take you downtown. There's a detective that wants to see you."

"Man, I don't want to go back downtown to talk to nobody. I want to go inside and sleep!"

"I'll get you back here as soon as we're finished. It won't take long. You hungry?"

"Yeah."

"I'll stop and get us something to eat on the way to the station. Relax, get some sleep until we get there."

He stopped at a Popeyes drive-thru for chicken and biscuits; I could no longer keep my eyes open and fell asleep in the back of the squad car until arriving back at the police station. When we got back downtown, we walked through the back of the station, where I was introduced to the detective: he was standing in front of a table with stacks of hundred-dollar bills, presumably in the wake of a drug bust. The detective and officer led me upstairs. The officer took my handcuffs off, gave me the box of chicken and biscuits and a soda, and asked me to sign a waiver of some kind. After the detective read me my Miranda rights, I reconstructed the shooting for him—he had said that the faster I told him what happened, the sooner I would be able to get some rest. The interrogation over, I was driven back to W. T. Edwards. The next day, I was taken to juvenile court and sentenced to twenty-one days for grand theft auto.

. . .

A COUPLE OF WEEKS WENT BY AND I STILL WASN'T charged with the shooting. I frequently stopped by the open classification window in W. T. Edwards and asked Ms. Matthews to check if I had any pending charges or holds. She would look through paperwork and at her database and reply, "Nope, you're fine. You should be out soon." I didn't know what was going on. I was fearful police were waiting until the very end of my twenty-one-day sentence to charge me so that I would have to serve an additional twenty-one days.

Around my eighteenth day in W. T., I asked the supervisor, a middle-aged brown-skinned man who wore thick glasses, to assign me to clean the hallway. Sweeping the long expanse with a wide broom allowed freedom of movement from dorm to dorm. Soon a staff member approached me.

"Manuel, the supervisor want you. He around there waiting in front of classification."

I hurried around the corner and saw him talking to a black detective wearing a sharp suit.

"Manuel, I'm forgetting your brother's name. What's it again?"

"Sean Manuel, but they call him John-John."

The supervisor said to the detective, "Yeah, that's it, Sean Manuel—you remember him?"

"Oh, yeah, I remember that boy."

I said, "I'll go get the broom and start sweeping."

"No you ain't. You going to jail. Detective Dessau is here to arrest your ass."

"Man, stop playing. What you got me out here for?"

"Nigga, I ain't playing. I'm as serious as cancer. You going to the county jail. You done made it to the big time now."

FOR DAYS AFTER I SHOT HER, DEBBIE BAIGRIE SAT AT HER front window, terrified and fearful that I might show up to finish her off. A petite, pretty blonde, Debbie, then twenty-eight, was mother to two daughters, a toddler and an infant. Debbie had grown up in a nice Tampa neighborhood, the scion of a family with Orthodox Jewish roots. She was now married to an electrical engineer and had been living a relatively comfortable life.

On the sweltering evening of July 27, 1990, Debbie met up with two girlfriends in downtown Tampa for a rare dinner out—her first such night after the birth of her one-year-old. As she left the restaurant to go to her parked car, she ran into a fellow gym member; he advised her that the neighborhood was unsafe and offered to accompany her to the parking lot. It was then that calamity struck, causing her to wonder what kind of face she still had. As she would later tell a reporter:[1] "The sound of that gun was louder than I could have ever imagined. A bullet entered my open mouth, tore through my teeth and went out through my cheek. Staggering back into the restaurant, blood streaming from my face, I screamed, 'Help me! I've been shot!' I was too panic-stricken to be conscious of any pain; the only thing I felt was fear.

"My wound was not life threatening. But five teeth had been shot out, a portion of my gums was destroyed and there was a small bullet hole in my cheek." So began Debbie's decades-long ordeal—more than forty oral surgery interventions—to reconstruct her mouth. When days later she found out that she had been shot by a thirteen-year-old, she was incredulous: "Why, he's just a child!" she exclaimed. At thirteen years of age, I was charged as an adult with multiple offenses: robbery, attempted robbery, and two counts of attempted murder in the first degree. Florida law allowed for a child of any age to be tried as an adult if indicted for a life-or-death felony. As I would later learn, no allowance was necessary. Because of my juvenile record and the gravity of the charges I now faced, state law mandated that I be sentenced as if I were an adult. Assistant State Attorney Hank Lavandera put it this way: "As it now appears, based on his prior record, he could face a life sentence if convicted of these charges."[2]

THE MORNING OF MY SENTENCING HEARING I WOKE UP in Morgan Street County Jail, to which I had been remanded on August 17; it sat right across from my old neighborhood. I had spent most of my confinement on the juvenile floor (juveniles, ages thirteen to seventeen, were housed away from adults). We were on the third floor, where they used to incarcerate women, whom they had moved to a newly constructed facility—Orient Road Jail. On the juvenile floor there were six cells numbered from 3A1 to 3A6. I spent most of my time in 3A2; it was packed with kids from Central Park Village, there for robbery, grand theft auto, drug possession, and trafficking. Each cell had eight bunk beds, though each more often than not housed twelve to sixteen

inmates. This meant that now and then some of us had to sleep on mattresses placed on tables in the TV room and on its floor.

Our cellblock was riddled with fighting and cruel juvenile mayhem. Kids asleep might wake up wrapped in toilet paper and on fire (the contraband matches having been secured from an adult inmate). Or toilet paper would be rolled into tight wicks, which were jabbed into their nostrils or between their toes and lit.

I had seniority, after my numerous stints in juvenile detention centers, and a reputation for backing down from no one. I got respect for my fighting skills. Now and then I would look out for kids who were slated for rough times. I'd sneak up and tell them, "Listen, they going to try to jump you after chow. You need to ask for a cell change." Some listened and saved themselves. Some didn't and left on stretchers. I took a liking to one white kid in particular— William Bartfield, and did not allow anybody to mess with him. William told his mom I was looking out for him and she began putting money into my account. I was surprised and grateful for the gesture, but I naturally gravitated toward those I considered underdogs like myself.

All the same, seniority and fighting skills aside, I still pissed on myself while sleeping. This didn't stop until my fourteenth birthday, two weeks before my sentencing. It just stopped abruptly.

SINCE AROUND THE END OF JANUARY, I HAD BEEN IN solitary confinement. I had flung, through the bars into the wing, a cup of water with which I was supposed to have gulped down some kind of medication (it may have been

a painkiller; the drugs administered to me were not yet psychotropic). At first, the guards didn't know who was responsible for the vandalism, but when they threatened confiscation of the cell's TV, I had no choice but to confess, resulting in a fiery dispute with the deputy and a nurse.

The cell I inhabited was minuscule. If I had to estimate its dimensions, I would say that at its widest I could take no more than five steps in the size eight shoes that I wore at the time. There was a narrow bunk bed near the window; I fit it comfortably as I was only five foot seven. That window became a source of fascination to me. Soon after I found myself in solitary, the Super Bowl took place in Tampa, and believe it or not that night I could see the lights of Tampa Stadium from my cell. They shone exceedingly bright. I imagined the rampant excitement of people from all walks of life in the stadium and watching the game on TV all over the world. I later learned that Whitney Houston had sung the national anthem, this during the Desert Storm war. I stared at the window and was overwhelmed by a longing for home; I don't know if you can realize how it feels to be so close to home, yet so very far away. I was gripped by sadness and cheered myself by imagining attending a future Super Bowl.

LATE FEBRUARY I HAD AN APPOINTMENT WITH MY COURT-assigned attorney downtown for a motion to suppress my confession, which was the only hard evidence connecting me to the crime. A deputy escorted me into the cold court-room and led me to the jury box, where juveniles usually sat away from adult prisoners. I found a seat among the sparse crowd of spectators. My lawyer, Brian Gonzalez,

hobbled over to me (still on crutches from a torn Achilles tendon, I believe) and said, "Hey, Ian, how are you doing this morning?"

"I'm good. Just ready to go to trial so I can go home."

It was February 22, 1991, and I had been arrested on July 30, 1990. Nearly seven months had passed; I had never been locked down for this long.

"Yeah, that's what I want to talk to you about."

"What's up?"

"I need you to consider changing your plea to an open plea of guilt."

"What's that?"

"It's a plea where you throw yourself at the mercy of the court and let the judge decide what your sentence should be. Not the state. I've already talked to the judge and he has assured me that you won't get more than fifteen years."

"Fifteen years!" I said. Was this dude crazy? I didn't want to go to prison period, let alone for fifteen years.

"Yeah, I know it sounds like a long time, but it's better than life. And I'm going to argue for a youthful offender sentence, which is far less than that. All you have to do is plead guilty."

"I don't want to go to prison. Can't you try to get me life probation or something like that?"

"Ian, you're going to have to do some time, but if you go to trial, you'll make the judge mad and he'll give you life for sure. So what's it going to be?"

I shook my head no; I wasn't pleading guilty.

While my lawyer and I went back and forth, my mom had been sitting among other spectators, watching us. My lawyer hobbled over and sat down beside her. They whispered to each other intensely.

After about five minutes, my lawyer escorted my mom over to the side of the jury box.

She said, "Baby, do what your lawyer say and plead guilty so you'll get a chance to come home. I don't want you to get life. That would break my heart."

"Ma, I don't wanna go to prison, period."

"Please, Jim, do it for me. Do this one thing for me. Don't think about yourself just this one time."

At that moment it seemed to me that every time I had gone against my momma's wishes and done things my way, I had come up short. I looked with my tear-filled eyes at hers and said, "All right, Ma."

ON THE MORNING OF APRIL 11—AT AROUND 5:30; IT WAS before dawn—juveniles at Morgan Street County Jail who were to be sentenced or who had court appointments were herded, handcuffed, into a van that would take us to the courthouse downtown. Anxious as I was about what would happen, I was certain about two things: the worst-case scenario, which to my teenage mind was no different from a life imprisonment, would be the fifteen-year sentence that my attorney had promised—with good behavior I would serve no more than ten; the best-case scenario would be my fantasy of life probation, which I had asked my attorney to request. I had heard too many horror stories about life in prison from grownups to want to spend even a single day there. At the courthouse, we were ushered into holding cells corresponding to our respective judges. Mine was the Honorable Manuel Menendez, Jr., renowned for his severity. In my holding cell was a guy I used to call "cousin," though we were unrelated. We grew up in Central Park Village; my mom and his, whom I called Aunt Louise, were very good

friends. When I had gotten out of juvenile detention the previous year, I had stayed at his house. His name was Sam. He was facing a petty trespassing charge. When they came to get me for sentencing, hours after I had arrived, he said, "Good luck, I'm praying for you"—or some such thing.

It was before 8:30 a.m. when I was led into the court-room and assigned to the jury box with another juvenile to await the beginning of the hearing. In the audience were my mother; Betty Walker, my maternal grandmother; Bob Gilbertson; Debbie Baigrie; and the man who had walked Debbie to her car that night. "I went to the courthouse to see him sentenced," Debbie would later recall.[3] "After my initial fear had passed, I'd become plain angry. But when I saw him in court, my rage seemed to leave me. He looked so young and alone, among all the attorneys and law-enforcement officers who were there." The State of Florida was represented by Karen Cox, and I, the defendant, by Brian Gonzalez. My public defender began the proceedings by reciting the difficult circumstances of my background and upbringing—emphasizing that I had never had a strong male role model—not to excuse my run-ins with the law, my criminal history, but to explain my actions as perhaps caused by my environment and warranting leniency. "No one can argue,"[4] he said, "with the seriousness of these offenses. It's a horrifying situation that we stand before the court and we're not here to make excuses. There is no doubt Ian Man-uel has failed at his attempt regarding juvenile sanctions."

Karen Cox, the assistant state attorney, agreed that I had a terrible background and had been unresponsive to juve-nile sanctions. Rather than leniency, however, she called on the judge to dispose of me. At thirteen, I was a problem with no solution. Cox concluded: "It may be a comment

on our society that we can have a thirteen-year-old who comes to us with this type of background and no prospect of rehabilitation . . . There is no solution to this problem and the only thing we can do is protect the citizens from the future criminal conduct that Mr. Manuel will engage in if he is released. I would ask that he be sentenced to life in prison as the sentencing guidelines call for."

Cox was advancing a prevalent view at the time about boys of color, a view that would achieve enduring notoriety with Hillary Clinton's infamous 1996 remarks at the apex of anxiety about high rates of crime and violence during her husband's administration: *"They are often the kinds of kids that are called super predators. No conscience. No empathy. We can talk about why they ended up that way but first we have to bring them to heel."*[5]

Cox then inquired whether Debbie Baigrie wanted to address the court. Debbie said, "No, not right now."[6]

The court invited my mother to speak. She said, "I really don't know what to say. I have done the best I can for Ian and I don't believe there is nothing that can't be done. Something has to be done for my child. Like the lawyer, I agree it's the environment. These people take these things for every day occurrences. They feel like this is what people do.

"I tried to tell him this isn't the way. Maybe now it will sink in. There is another side to life. The first time he was arrested, I was at HCC [a community college] in a juvenile course trying to see what's wrong with my children because both of them had gone astray. I don't know.

"Something has to be done, not be locked away for the rest of his life. I don't feel that's the answer. He can't get away with it, because that wouldn't be the right answer either. If someone shot me, they would be ready to call them

up. I feel like—I don't know. I don't want him locked away for the rest of his life, but he has to be punished."

My public defender prefaced his presentation of Bob Gilbertson as a character witness by saying: "Judge, there is another side to Ian Manuel. Unfortunately, what the court has heard so far, it would indicate that he's a human being with not one ounce of good within his body."

Bob, whose support of me was undying, and who had been sending me a few dollars now and then while I was in the county jail, recalled my dealings with him:

"During this time, there was never really any—I understood there were things going on with Ian. I wasn't privy to exactly what was happening with regard to other criminal activity, but all of the time that he spent with us and at the Y, he acted just like any of the other kids that we have.

"His interaction with other kids on field trips, of which he took a number, was always excellent and there were never any problems with other kids, never any problems with authorities relative to complying with what he was asked to do.

"I would draw from that to some extent that if Ian were kept active and were at the point—kept supervised, he knows how to behave and he knows how to do the right things. It's the less supervised kind of setting it appears he has difficulty in . . . . We work with a lot of kids all the time from a lot of different environments and it would be our hope that there could be something done where he could continue to get some education and some trade so that if he is released, he would have something he could do with his life from that point on."

Brian Gonzalez then pleaded to the judge for leniency:

"If Mr. Ian Manuel is sentenced as the State or the PSI

would suggest, I believe we would be disregarding his last chance although it would be his first chance as an adult at the age of fourteen to allow him to function among us, among you and I and everyone else that exists in this community.

"Apparently, it's become quite obvious to all of us that he cannot function right now. We are resolved in that matter and we don't attempt to sit here and tell the court he should not be going to Florida State Prison. I believe his crimes suggest he should go to Florida State Prison. It is obvious he does have good within him. There is no doubt in my mind in my interaction with him that there is something there. It's obvious his values have not been molded properly. It's too young for him to be etched in stone, to be disregarded to a life or substantial amount of years in prison."

Something then happened that has haunted me ever since. The juvenile prisoner sitting next to me in the jury box said something funny, and I laughed. Debbie saw this and it understandably angered her. She felt that I did not understand the gravity of my actions and the impact they had and continued to have on her. She was right. I did not understand. I was fourteen years old and I just wanted to go home. It would take years for me to understand.

Debbie decided to address the court:

"Your Honor, I was listening to the Public Defender talking about how Mr. Manuel didn't have a father as a role model. Neither did I. It didn't make me go out and shoot people. They said the gun went off by accident. It was aimed in my face. I don't think it went off by accident.

"From the time this started, I should have been angry. I should have been angry at him and angry at his parents. I wasn't angry. I felt like he was as victimized as I was because

of where he came from. He was a product of his own environment and he is as much of a victim as I am.

"I kept speaking to everybody, please rehabilitate him. He's young. I have two children. I know it takes work constant every day—every day I do something with my children. I think this is going to affect them for the rest of their lives. He's still a child.

"Until yesterday, I kept thinking, I wish he could be rehabilitated. I wish that he could be made an example of. If he could go from doing this to making something of himself, getting an education and doing something with his life instead of spending the rest of his life in prison, it hurts me to think that somebody should have to do that at such a young age and have no chance of a life.

"But after hearing everything that's been going on, he doesn't even care. He doesn't care what he's done to me. He doesn't care that he's going to spend the rest of his life in jail. And if he doesn't care, well, I don't care."

There was a hush in the courtroom. I have no way of knowing whether Judge Menendez was at all swayed by Debbie's remarks. He seemed already to have made up his mind when he took command and pronounced his stern judgment:

"The prospects for adequate protection of the public and likelihood for reasonable rehabilitation of the child if assigned to juvenile services and facilities considering all these factors, I find would be none, absolutely no chance of that happening for juvenile sanctions . . .

"I do find at this time and determine that adult sanctions are suitable and should in fact be imposed against the Defendant in this particular case.

"With regard to each of these offenses at this time, it is

the judgment, order and sentence of the Court, first of all, that you be adjudicated guilty of each of these offenses of robbery, attempted robbery and two counts of attempted murder in the first degree . . .

"Your attorney has indicated and asks the Court to consider imposing sentence because of the fact of your age and your environment.

"I think that in one sense, while your environment may have played a part in the situation you're finding yourself in, I cannot for the life of me understand how anyone could actually say the environment is the cause of your conduct.

"If that was the case, there are a number of other people that live in your environment, your mother, for example, and she's not going out there and committing the atrocious acts that you've committed.

"Our society, I think, does require incarceration for some period of time, a substantial period of time, if for no other reason than to protect itself from you. A comment was made here that perhaps would provide for one last chance, one opportunity to allow you to prove that you can become a productive member of society.

"As you might have noted here, you've been given a number of chances. After a while, you run out of chances. There are some acts whether you've been given prior chances or not, there just is no second chance available. I think you've crossed that line."[7]

For count one, robbery, Judge Menendez sentenced me at age fourteen to life in prison without parole. For count two, attempted robbery, he sentenced me to fifteen years incarceration to run concurrently. For count three, the attempted murder of Debbie in the first degree, he sentenced me to life without parole. For count four, the attempted murder of the

man who walked Debbie to her car, Judge Menendez sentenced me to life probation on top of my life without parole sentences, "in the event the Department of Corrections for some reason should release you from incarceration."

I was struck by my helplessness in the light of his omnipotence. In retrospect, I feel that I was being tried not only for the crimes that I had committed but for proof that I had a right to exist.

When you are a kid being sentenced, your mom can stand with you. When my mom heard the judge's declaration, she understood the enormity of his intention. She hugged me tight. She was crying. My face pressed against her, I refused to cry, not in front of strangers. My own tears would come later. As the bailiff gently, but firmly, pulled me away from my mom toward the fingerprint area, little did I know that that would be the last time my mother and I would touch.

AS I WAS LED BACK TO THE HOLDING CELL, I WAS ROBOTIC, a chaos of feelings churning inside of me—anger at the judge, terror at not knowing what lay ahead, fear of what could happen to me in prison. Not used to—perhaps incapable of—showing vulnerability to strangers, or anyone else for that matter (a danger where I came from), I numbed myself to the overwhelming hurt I felt.

When I walked into the holding cell Sam said: "Man, what did they do, Jim? What did they do?" For some reason in my mind, I don't know why, each life sentence didn't mean my whole life, didn't mean I would die in prison; each meant twenty years, already an eternity to me. So I told Sam they gave me forty years.

"What? Stop lying. You always playing, man. What did they give you?"

"They gave me forty years."

"What? You for real?"

"Yeah, man."

Sam was the only inmate left in the holding cell, and I was glad he was there. I needed a familiar face, someone around whom I could be myself. He repeated, "You for real, Jim?" and he just started crying. He kept pounding his fist into his hand and saying, "I'm gon' kill all them crackers when I get out." His tears gave me permission to release my pent-up emotions. I cried as well; we hugged. I was surprised: I had never seen Sam cry except when his mom whipped him. Now both of us were sobbing in the holding cell before we were handcuffed together and returned by van to the county jail. Most days, I still think about that moment with Sam, the way my sentence, and the hopelessness of it hurt him too. What does it mean for one child to see another sent—deliberately, methodically, and under the moral authority of the adults in charge—into the heart of darkness?

OCEAN SHELL

I press my ear canal—
against the interior of my ocean shell.
Just longing to hear the water.
But my attempts all fail.
And what comes through my ears—
are Echoes of Torture from the hopeless.
I hear coughs & gaggings
from multiple gassings.
And boots & fist against flesh.
Sounds of desperation.
From victims of devastation.
Releasing another exasperated breath.
I hear the sound of shivers—
from prisoners in the cold of winter
with nothing to cover their bodies.
I hear the cardboard fan—
in the prisoner's hand.
To combat the sweltering summer.
I hear the groans & mumblings.
And the goings & comings—
of past occupants who remain anonymous.
I hear the ultimate suffering.
Hunger reminiscent of thunder
An orchestra of grumbling stomachs.
I hear noises & voices.
From unknown sources.
And the unmistakable sound of crying.
I hear prisoners taunted.

and tormentors confronted.
By those with nothing to lose but their minds.
But where is the water?
The wonderful ocean—
I originally longed to hear.
With this cell by my ear.
The only water I hear—
is the repeated patter of tears.

.   .   .

WHEN I AM LED TO THE THIRD FLOOR (I'VE BEEN ORDERED out of solitary confinement), cell 3A2 is packed with my homeboys from Central Park, one of whom is Marquis, who had participated in my crime but was never arrested for it. He was in the county jail for another robbery.

"Jim-Jim, what'd they do, what'd they do?"

"Nothin' but life, nothin' but life," I said, chuckling, recovering bravado. I refused to show the pain I was in. I was implying as loudly as possible "I can handle this." Marquis and I, of course, had grown up together, and he regarded me as someone with a lot of heart, a lot of courage; I didn't want to show him my fear. By law, after my sentencing, I was no longer a juvenile but an adult and would soon be put among the adult men on the first floor. I had only a few hours to prepare for the transition, and I tried to visualize how I would defend myself against what might face me there. Adult inmates sharing cells, after all, were renowned for viciously beating each other up. Stretchers were always being carried in and out of those cells. I hoped to be placed among older homeboys who might know, and look out for, me.

When the officer came to fetch me, he announced that I would be transferred to Orient Road Jail. He was leading me to a holding cell where, by myself, I would wait for the van that would take me to my new prison. The officer and I took the elevator down, I, dressed in a light blue jumpsuit and toting my sheets, cup for drinking water, toothbrush and toothpaste, and, inside my pillowcase, letters my mom had written me. As I walked slowly toward the holding cell before heading to Orient Road Jail, a sergeant barked: "Uh-uh, don't be walking all slow now. You goin' with the big

boys. You wanted to be a big boy? You a big boy now. They got somethin' for you over there."

At Orient Road Jail, I didn't have to be processed; I was already in the system. I was shocked. The first floor of Orient Road seemed like the biggest hotel lobby in the world, wide enough to fit two tractor-trailers side by side and as long as a football field—or so it seemed to me. Men and women inmates commingled there, sitting around chatting. I was led down the hallway to 6 Charlie; I had no idea what 6 Charlie was, but it turned out to be solitary confinement. I was uncuffed and put alone into a single cell. It was brand-new, the paint was so fresh you could smell it. It was cold in there. They kept it cold in there. That was OK. What disturbed me was that everything was purple. The door was purple. The walls were purple. The rails were purple. The concrete slab that you put your mattress on was purple. Perplexed, I asked the first officer making his rounds: "Sir, please can you tell me why I'm in confinement and why everything is purple?" I learned from him that I was in solitary because of my age, fourteen, and because of the length of my sentence, life imprisonment. As to why everything was purple, psychologists had decided that the color had a calming effect on inmates.

It was now around 9:30 p.m., twelve hours or so after I had been sentenced. I was numb, interred in all that purple—in solitary confinement as I had been when I woke up, but with a life sentence now hanging over me. I dwelled on the events of the day: I thought about my impulsive laughter in the courtroom, wondering if that was what sealed my fate; about Debbie's heartfelt remarks; about my mom, who was HIV positive, and whether she would be

alive when I got out. I held on to a glimmer of hope. My lawyer had said at sentencing: "Don't worry, we're going to appeal; don't worry, we're going to appeal."

I fell asleep from exhaustion.

ABOUT TWO WEEKS AFTER I WAS SENTENCED, I WAS TAKEN by surprise and hurried back to court. I thought the appeal my lawyer had mentioned was at hand. Before the hearing, I asked him: "What am I doing here? Is this the appeal you told me about?"

"No, no, Ian, that'll come later. You're here because the judge forgot to give you three years mandatory. The law in Florida says that because you carried a firearm you have to be sentenced to a mandatory minimum of three years. The judge doesn't have a choice in this, so since he forgot, I let him know. I brought it to his attention so it'll look good on your appeal."

I now found myself standing before the man who had already condemned me to die in prison, waiting for him to give me more time.

"HEY, BOY, WHAT'S YOUR NAME?" A FAT WHITE CORREC-
tional officer seated behind a desk at the Reception and
Medical Center asked me.

"Ian Manuel."

"How old is you, boy?"

"Fourteen, sir."

"Fourteen. One of y'all call K Wing and tell 'em we got
another one of them pop-eyed ass jitterbugs for 'em. Sign
this paper here and stand down there at the end of the line
away from the grownups."

The Reception and Medical Center is a state prison in
Lake Butler, Florida—a part of Union County—about one
and one-half hours from Tampa (I would not see Tampa
again for nine years). On May 10 I had been transferred to
Lake Butler. Offenders are taken there not only for medical
treatment but for initial classification and processing into
the state correctional system. Lake Butler was well known
as an exceptionally brutal place. Even as young boys in Central Park, we had heard tales from returning ex-cons about
its viciousness: how the guards hated blacks from Miami
and inmates who wore red Converse sneakers; how they
had a jar filled with gold teeth that they had kicked out of
inmates' mouths. Some of these gold teeth had supposedly

been implanted into the mouths of K-9s. And if you got caught committing a minor infraction in open population, sometimes the guards would make you sweep the sun off the sidewalk, that is, push a broom across an already spotless sidewalk until sundown. "Driving a Cadillac" meant walking around the sprawling Lake Butler compound with a butt can, picking up cigarette butts all day long as punishment. Widely notorious guards, like "Nigger Johnson," and K Wing Freddie, were said to have beaten and killed many an inmate over the years in the cellblock known as K Wing—the confinement wing of Lake Butler. Because of my age, I was assigned to K Wing, where adolescents were segregated, to begin the rest of my life in prison.

"THE LAW TREATS ADOLESCENTS DIFFERENTLY BECAUSE they are different," says the Equal Justice Initiative's landmark report *Cruel and Unusual: Sentencing 13- and 14-Year-Old Children to Die in Prison*.[1] "Using state-of-the-art imaging technology, scientists have revealed that adolescents' brains are anatomically undeveloped in parts of the cerebrum associated with impulse control, regulation of emotions, risk assessment, and moral reasoning. Accordingly, the neurological development most critical to making good judgments, moral and ethical decision-making, and controlling impulsive behavior is incomplete during adolescence." The study, published in 2007, identified seventy-three children in the United States sentenced to life imprisonment without the possibility of parole for crimes committed when they were thirteen or fourteen years old. Of those sentenced for nonhomicide crimes, I was one. Among the report's key findings are these:

The United States is the only country in the world known

to have condemned thirteen- and fourteen-year-old children to imprisonment until death.

Most of these children were accomplices to adults or older teens who were more culpable for the crime.

Seven, or roughly 10 percent, of the seventy-three children were convicted of crimes in which no one was killed. In one case, no one was even injured. All seven are children of color.

Six states have condemned thirteen-year-old children to imprisonment until death. All but one of these children are racial minorities.

Most of the seventy-three children suffered years of severe abuse and neglect. Some tried to commit suicide as young as age eight.

Judges in the vast majority of these cases were forced to impose mandatory death-in-prison sentences without considering the child's age or background or the circumstances of the crime.

Children of color are disproportionately sentenced to die in prison. Of the seventy-three children identified, roughly two-thirds are people of color; nearly half are African-American.

Most of these kids are from poor families and received grossly inadequate legal representation. Court-appointed attorneys failed to file postconviction appeals and never challenged the death-in-prison sentences in most of these cases.

All of the seventy-three children have been sent to adult prisons, where many are targets of horrendous physical and sexual assault by adult inmates. One Equal Justice Initiative client attempted suicide three times after being repeatedly raped by adult inmates.

. . .

I WALKED THE LINE TO THE END OF A LONG BROWN BENCH by an open gate. Grown men, my fellow passengers on the sheriff's bus to Lake Butler, stood side by side along the bench. At the end of the line, several feet away from the last adult, I found my place. Corrections officers ordered us, the men and me, to strip and to open our mouths wide and run our fingers inside in a circular motion as they walked up and down the line, peering into our mouths for contraband. They commanded us to pull our ears back and to run our fingers through our hair, then to turn around and wiggle our toes, one bare foot at a time. Finally, they forced us to bend over at the waist, pull the cheeks of our buttocks apart, and cough loudly three times. The cacophony of coughs was at once horrific and disgusting. They handed us prison garb— mine way oversized for my adolescent frame—and ushered us through a gate to some more benches, where we waited to be called to the property counter before going to see the nurse for the first time.

You have so many days to get your vaccinations and shots for diseases like tetanus. They draw blood to make sure you're not carrying diseases. They perform psychological evaluations. Dental exams. They process you supposedly to ensure placement in the most appropriate adult prison. If you have serious medical issues they'll put you in one that can offer the needed treatment, or so they say. If you have severe mental illness, they'll put you in one that can provide mental health care. (Twenty-five percent of all prisoners suffer from a mental illness, the most common being clinical depression, bipolar disorder, schizophrenia, and psychotic breaks.) You are at Butler for your overseers to develop a profile of you; theirs is an ongoing process of collecting

and assessing information to determine the level of risk you might pose, the kind of confinement right for you, and other prison-related matters.

To get to K Wing a guard escorted me through the first-floor door and instructed me to jog up two flights of stairs to another door, which led to an administrative station. There was a board with slots for different-colored slips of paper. This was the housing board, and the color of a slip indicated an inmate's status: red for youthful offenders, yellow for those being disciplined; white for troublemakers causing administrative conflict, and so on. The point was to prevent officers from mixing colors, that is, housing inmates of different statuses in the same cell.

I was led to K Wing's shower, down some steps, and off to the left. I was locked in the shower for about thirty minutes before a short, fat, white corrections officer arrived. "Strip," he demanded. I said, "They already searched me." He said, "Boy, don't motherfucking back-talk me. Just do as you're told."

I went through the motions: I took my clothes off, opened my mouth wide and circled my fingers in it, pulled my ears back. But this time the rest of the examination would be different. The guard pulled latex gloves out of his pocket and made a show of slowly putting them on and stretching the latex up to his wrists, snapping them loudly against his skin. Then he said, "All right, boy, turn around and bend over and open your ass up, and I mean real wide, and keep 'em spread until I tell you to turn around. If you don't open up wide enough for me to see if you got anything up in there, I'm going to stick my hand up there and see for myself."

Overcome with anxiety, I recalled my brother's molestation of me as a child, yet I complied with the officer's

sick command. After having been bent over as the guard inspected me for about a minute, I was finally allowed to stand up straight. The guard ordered me to dress and led me to my cell.

K WING CONSISTED OF TWO TIERS OF ABOUT FORTY CELLS, twenty on the first floor and twenty in the basement. There were two steel bunks in each cell, except for the last two cells downstairs, which had none. These two cells were called "the hole," where inmates deemed unruly were sent to be broken into submissiveness. The hole was a cell with bars and an outer door that could be shut to close off all sight and sound outside.

I was placed on the second floor, in cell 4. During the twenty-three days I spent at Lake Butler, two fellow juvenile cellmates came and went; one was fourteen like me, the other older, seventeen years old, I believe. We were locked down on K Wing twenty-four hours a day; if we had to leave the building for any reason we were chained and shackled and escorted by an officer. My cellmates and I slept, ate, and did our business in a cramped four-by-eight cell with a stainless steel latrine.

We all woke up early because early morning was when transfers were announced, Mondays through Fridays. Everyone would get up hoping his name was on the list to leave that dangerous place. Back then they were killing people in Lake Butler. In confinement. They were beating people. I heard tales of gassing, though I myself didn't witness any actual instances.

At first my main preoccupation was to do nothing that might antagonize guards so I wouldn't be beaten. They, especially Officer Wilson—a slim black guy—used to slap us.

If he caught you falling asleep against the wall late at night before count time was clear, he would become enraged. He'd sneak down the catwalk, trying to catch you nodding off. If you were unfortunate enough to be sleepy, he'd make you come over to him so that he could reach through the bars and slap you five or six times.

I grew severely anxious at always being at the mercy of Officer Wilson, at the prospect of being assaulted by him on the one hand and on the other because I was always hoping that when I heard them rolling the doors and telling people to pack it up I would hear "Hey, Manuel, roll it up," which meant I would be on my way out of Lake Butler. As I was having trouble falling asleep and staying asleep at night, a psychiatrist put me on Vistaril, a sedative to relieve anxiety and tension—even now, I recall the foul taste of the oral syrup. What I didn't know at the time was that taking this psychotropic medication, prescribed chiefly to induce sleep, was raising my psychiatric grade and so the risk to myself and others that prison authorities imagined I posed.

Because we hadn't committed any serious disciplinary infractions, we were allowed to order from the canteen weekly, and my mom was sending me money at the time. Of course, we bought food and snacks, but a loophole in the ordering system allowed adolescents to buy tobacco products—here in confinement we were getting away with something that would have been impossible in open population. I didn't smoke, but in prison, tobacco is big commerce. I'd order Tampa Jewels cigars and packs of Bugler tobacco. And then I'd trade my haul for extra sweets—cookies and honey buns. We traded with adults farther down the wing. Upstairs only the first six cells were for juveniles. Tobacco was so valuable that you could double your money with

it. When the officer wasn't on the wing, you'd get on the bars and shout, "I got a pack of cigarettes for four packs of cookies, who call that?" Someone would say, "Hey, I call that." An adult could roll at least thirty-six cigarettes from a single pack of tobacco, so to him, trading four packs of cookies for three dozen cigarettes was a great deal. I loved peanut butter cookies then, especially when I could wash them down with a carton of Yoo-Hoo. By the way, the food at Lake Butler was good. We ate breakfast at around six, lunch at twelve, and dinner at five. Big old biscuits, scrambled eggs, bony fish—considered a delicacy by some—and slop, noodles drowned in unrecognizable sauce.

AT LAKE BUTLER I READ THE BIBLE INTENSIVELY TO WHILE away the hours. When I was a little boy, Grandma Linda used to take me to New Salem Baptist Church, and it was there that I first became acquainted with the book through Sunday school. Now a certain Mr. Norman—aware of the notoriety of my case—visited the prison. A Seventh-Day Adventist, he took a liking to me and ended up giving me this big black Bible. He taught me that the Book of Proverbs has thirty-one chapters, so if I read one a day, I would complete it in a month. I read around in the Bible and felt the tug of religion, felt the comfort it offered. One of my favorite passages is from Proverbs 30:

> Four things on earth are small,
> yet they are extremely wise:
> Ants are creatures of little strength,
> yet they store up their food in the summer;
> hyraxes are creatures of little power,

yet they make their home in the crags;
locusts have no king,
yet they advance together in ranks;
a lizard can be caught with the hand,
yet it is found in kings' palaces.[2]

Regardless of my hazy understanding of what I read, these passages seemed vaguely to speak to my condition, and for this I cherished them. Looking back now, I think this was where my interest in poetry may have begun. These words and images and the comfort and strength they gave me was powerful in a way I don't understand—but they planted a seed of hope in me that I would find my way out, back to my mother, back to my home, and—most dangerously—that I was somebody.

ONE SATURDAY, I HEARD AN OFFICER YELL "CLEAN UP," as a cellblock trusty walked down the tier sticking brooms through the bars. When he got to my cell, I told him I didn't want the broom. The officer said, "You got to clean up." I said, "Sir, today is the Sabbath and it's against my religion to do any work on this day." He said, "Boy, is you crazy? Today is Saturday. The day of rest is Sunday. And what you talkin' about? Inmates work seven days a week up in here. Sweep the fucking cell." I refused. He went and got the sarge, who took his turn ordering me to sweep the cell. Again I refused. I felt this was what Jesus wanted me to do. Stand up for him despite the consequences. I explained my reasons to the sarge. The sarge left. About thirty minutes later, the officer returned to my cell with handcuffs and said, "The captain wants to talk to you." My hands were cuffed behind

my back and I was escorted down the steps of the tier onto the quarterdeck and into the sergeant's station. The door closed behind me. The sarge was seated at the desk, and I was ordered to stand in front of the black captain who was also in the office. I read his name tag. It said "Jones." I was standing before the notorious officer everyone referred to as "Nigger Johnson."

The sergeant said: "Boy, tell the captain what you told me."

"Sir, Sunday is the first day of the week, Saturday is the last. Today is the Sabbath day and it's against my religion to sweep my cell today."

Without hesitation, Captain Jones swung a heavy-handed slap my way. I ducked. Captain Jones then swung again with his left hand; again I evaded his attempt. As I bobbed and weaved, my hands cuffed behind my back, I made a calculation I would need to make repeatedly over the coming years as I learned to navigate the labyrinth of Florida DOC power games. I realized that if I kept embarrassing "Nigger Johnson" in front of his staff he would make a point of hurting me as bad as he could. When the captain swung again, I stood my ground. He slapped me hard on the left and right sides of my face four or five times. I said nothing. I just stood there, crying silently.

"Boy, where you from?"

"Tampa."

"How old you is?"

"Fourteen."

"Fourteen!"

"Yeah, and I'm a get my momma to call HRS on you." (That is the Florida Department of Health and Rehabilitative Services.)

"Boy, I don't care nothing about no HRS. Is you gon' clean that cell now?"

"No sir," I said.

"If you don't clean up, boy, I'm a put you in the hole. And when I put little motherfuckers like you in the hole, I likes to beat 'em while they choking on the gas I done sprayed on them. So what you gon' do?"

"I'm not cleaning my cell on the Sabbath, sir."

"Put his ass in the hole."

An officer led me out of the sergeant's station, down the steps of the first-floor tier, past the shower, and down the long hallway to the second to last cell on K Wing. I walked through the outer door and then the cell bar door, which the officer manually closed. He uncuffed me, then walked out, closing the outer door behind him. I sat down on the bare mattress, wondering if I had done the right thing and waiting for a beating and gassing that never came. That night, I woke up to huge cockroaches crawling over my body. I jumped out of my sleep and brushed them off my torso onto the floor of the dark cell. I couldn't go back to sleep because I didn't know if rats would show up next. What showed up next, though, was a white corrections officer with what looked like a permanent crook in his neck. Entering my cell, he began slapping and punching me in my face and on my head for two to three minutes. Cowering, I tried to cover my head with my arms. He exited the cell as quickly as he had entered it, closing the outer door behind him.

In my rage and fear, I got up off the mattress where I'd sunk, took two steps to the front of the cell, grabbed the bars, and began screaming, "Medical emergency! Medical emergency!" The officer who had just assaulted me returned, opened the outer door, and stepped into my cell.

"What's your problem?"

"You know what my problem is. I got a medical emergency. My head hurt."

"Listen, you're scheduled to leave Lake Butler in the morning. If you report this, I'm a take you off the transfer list and you're going to be stuck here with me. So you'd better be quiet if you know what's good for you."

THE WASP IN THE WINDOW

The wasp in the window
that once buzzed full of life.
Lies still on the sill—
face first in a crack.
I wonder how it got here—
to rest before my sight.
Wings stiff & extended—
as if still in flight.
Did it fly into a web—
while still alive.
Before dying in a cell—
with holes that resemble hives.
What happened to its barb?
Does it still reside inside?
If I squeezed it with my thumb—
will I be stung if I tried?
Does it somehow feel the sun—
everytime it rise?
Or has death taken its soul—
like it did its yellow lines?
I wish I could pick it up—
and give it a proper burial.
Even an insect's cadaver—
shouldn't be kept in confinement.
But there's a barrier between us—
that prevents me from touching.
So let poetry be the button—
to open the window that I couldn't.

. . .

BY FLORIDA LAW, I HAD TO BE TRANSFERRED TO AN ADULT prison. Juvenile facilities were for adolescent criminals with youthful offender sentences of up to six years, including probation. I had been tried for a life-and-death felony as an adult and sentenced to life in prison without the possibility of parole. I arrived at Apalachee Correctional Institution, one of Florida's oldest prisons, in the Panhandle, near a little town named Sneads, in June 1991. This facility has a mix of custody levels: minimum, medium, and closed. It has two units: ACI West and ACI East, the latter supposedly featuring less stringent custody. Not long after I'd stepped off the prison transport bus, Mr. Maybury, an affable, heavy classification officer, said, "Manuel, your name, DC number, place of birth, and birthday." Your DC number is your prisoner identification number given to you when you're processed. You memorize it the way you memorize your telephone number because you have to say it every night during count. Mine was 518907. By now I hated being asked my birthday: I'd say "March twenty-ninth, 1977," and the response would be "Are you sure about that?" Thirty years later, my file still states my birthday as March 2, 1977, because the deputy who picked me up from the juvenile detention center the night of my arrest made the error.

At Lake Butler I had been classified for ACI East Unit. Having inspected my file, Mr. Maybury reassigned me to ACI West because of the nature of my sentence and the fact that I was on medication: He said, "Well, you can't stay here, Ian. My fences ain't ready for you." ACI East didn't have gun towers. I was quickly processed and escorted to M dorm, at the time the west unit's orientation dormitory. M dorm,

like the others, had an open-bay layout, meaning all eighty bunks were out in the open—no cells, no doors, no privacy.

As soon as you stepped through the dorm's inmate entrance, you were in the dayroom area, which had about twenty chairs, two tables, and a thirty-two-inch TV positioned above the wall directly in front of the doorway, about fifteen feet away. Another door led to the inmates' sleeping area, which consisted of about eighty bunks. If you walked through the sleeping area doorway and turned immediately left twice, you entered the bathroom area, with its white porcelain sinks and toilets. At the back of the bathroom was the shower area. I was assigned to the top bunk of a bed on the right side of the dorm. My bunkmate was a black man about fifty years old named Mr. Stafford. He drew portraits for money.

I had received a Super II radio (like a miniature boom box but with only one big speaker) in a permitted package from my mother, and as I lay on my bunk, listening to the *American Top 40* countdown with Casey Kasem one afternoon, he said a girl had written in about her relationship with a boy that had to end because she was moving to another city. She asked Casey to play "Anything for You" by Gloria Estefan to serenade her boyfriend. I felt a twinge when I heard these lyrics: "But don't even think that I don't love you/That for one minute I forgot you/But sometimes things don't work out right/And you just have to say goodbye." I thought of my mom and my guilty plea. I rolled over on my side, my back toward the grown men of the dormitory; I stared out the window and recalled another lyric of the song: "And though inside I feel like dying/You know you'll never see me cryin'."

THE WATER

Sitting on a damp blue bench.
upset by unchangeable events . . .
In the distance there's a- swish!
Farther still, there's a silent steel fence.
I look down where I sit.
Where there's rain gathered in drips.
I see my eyes, nose, and lips.
The breeze makes them blink, breathe, and wish.
The image makes me reminisce—
of a different series of events.
Where I couldn't see any of this.
Or hear the ball bounce before it . . .
Or feel the brisk breeze, at its clip.
It was just me, back and knees bent.
Looking at crimson gathered in drips.
Seeing my eyes, nose, and lips.
Asking myself—
why-are-you-doing-this?
Like a camera that clicks—
the images switch.
I return to the damp prison bench.
I see the fence, feel the wind, hear the swish.
I reach out and touch my face in the water,
I taste freedom for a moment.
And I, I appreciate it.

. . .

THE COMPOUND WAS FULL OF MEN FROM TAMPA WHO had read about my case. The *Florida Sentinel Bulletin,* a newspaper popular among black people, had zealously covered "13-Year-Old Black Boy Sentenced to Life in Prison." I became everyone's little brother. Some would say: "Man, if it had been a black person shot they wouldn't have given that boy all that time. You know how many people I've shot?" The men I met were largely protective of me. Sometimes people assume the worst about a situation like mine: a black adolescent around older, more mature male prisoners is going to be sexually taken advantage of. That wasn't the case with me. I made friends, attended school (there were no grades), and spent hours on the basketball court.

I felt relatively safe, at least among the other prisoners and at least compared to the chaos and violence I experienced growing up in Central Park. But now and then trouble would erupt. I remember an older guy in his forties who thought I had broken into his locker; someone had told him as much. I had not. One day he walked up behind me, grabbed me, and punched me in my face. I wrestled him to the ground and fought with him like my life depended on it. Other inmates struggled to pull me off him. After that, I started sleeping with a weapon under my pillow, even though I never had occasion to use it. It wasn't really a knife but a piece of one of those lightning rods you sometimes see attached to the roof of buildings. The prison's maintenance staff used to sell these instruments of self-protection for ten dollars apiece.

Now and then Sundays I attended church, and one weekend that summer I elected to be baptized in the prison's chapel. Matthew 7:12: "So in everything, do to others what

you would have them do to you, for this sums up the Law and the Prophets." This was the fundamental precept of the religion I accepted, the religion the institution that held me espoused and promoted. But the tension between this precept and the realities of daily life in an environment controlled by a brutal combination of deprivation and neglect on one side, and raw, unchecked power on the other, was more than I could get my mind around.

ONE DAY I WAS SUMMONED TO PICK UP LEGAL MAIL. I fairly ran to retrieve it. I had been anxious to hear from my lawyer about the appeal to get my sentences overturned. Sure enough, I received a letter and some legal documents from him. I read the letter as I walked back to the dorm: Judge Manuel Menendez, Jr., had denied my motion to mitigate my sentence; he had reached his decision after considering my character. My lawyer had enclosed all the transcripts and depositions in my case and wished me good luck in getting my sentences overturned by other means.

"By other means?" I had none. I walked back to the dorm in a fury, especially angry with my mother for having encouraged me to take the advice of a lawyer who had misrepresented matters to us and had no intention of appealing my case. Did the denial to mitigate my sentence mean that any appeal on my behalf would be forever out of the question? In a letter to Peggye I was unsparing in blaming her. She responded: "Don't try to lay that guilt trip on me, boy. If you would've had your ass home like a normal thirteen year old, instead of downtown shooting people, none of this would have happened."

5

CENTRAL PARK VILLAGE IS NOT THE KIND OF PLACE
where people expect a white Christmas. In the dead of winter there are no treetops glistening or children listening to
hear sleigh bells in the snow. The last time the temperature
had plunged into the thirties and snowflakes had fallen was
in 1977, the year I was born.

In its usual tropical weather, we children of Central Park
Village—regardless of how impoverished or crime-ridden
the 'hood was—always looked forward with building excite-
ment to Christmas Day. Grandma Betty used to go around
Central Park Village every Christmas morning shouting,
"Merry Christmas, everybody." It was so embarrassing.
For Christmas, Uncle Alvin and Uncle Lewis would come
home, on leave from the military, bearing gifts for all of
us. Grandma Linda would get me train sets, He-Man dolls.
Once she even got me the Snake Mountain from the bad
side of Skeletor's Island. Another year she got me an Atari.
Uncle Alvin, who was stationed in Okinawa, bought a Sega
in Japan and had it shipped to me—this was one of the best
presents I ever got.

Now, age fourteen, as Christmas approached in Apalachee
Correctional Institution, I was feeling numbed by the intensity of incarceration. The touch of Christmas spirit in jail—

the dispensing of a five-dollar canteen gift certificate (the Christmas Five, as it was called) to each inmate a week before the blessed day did little to ease my longing.

My depressive mood about the Christmas behind bars prompted me to do something I had not planned, much less foreseen. Going through the discovery related to my case that my lawyer had sent after the motion to mitigate sentence had been denied, I noticed in the police report Debbie Baigrie's address and telephone number. On Christmas Eve I decided to call her, not knowing exactly what I was going to say but knowing what I wanted to say, which was that I was sorry for what I had done. At Apalachee, if you were in open population on the adult side and the compound had not been shut down, you could walk outside and use the phone to call collect; there were also phones in the day-room strictly for nighttime use. You could use the phone for fifteen-minute intervals whenever you wanted to, or rather when one was available. There were two phones on either side of the compound and in the middle, near the canteen, a bank of ten—so there were ten telephones for more than a thousand men, meaning that traffic was always heavy. You always had to be eagle-eyed for an opportunity.

The last time I had heard Debbie Baigrie's voice was at my sentencing when she expressed her belief that I did not care about what I had done to her. I was nervous. When I picked up the phone, before dialing the outside operator, I wondered whether I should assume a false identity, whether I should pretend to be the officer who had arrested me or the detective who had interrogated me. Debbie knew their names and would be more likely to accept a collect call from them. I was making no sense though: why would law

enforcement be calling Debbie collect? My fourteen-year-old mind was desperately searching for a way to ensure that I would have the chance to apologize. Something inside me said, "Ian, if you really want this to work you're going to have to tell the truth and say who you are." I dialed zero and waited a few seconds that felt like an eternity before the operator picked up.

"How may I help you?"

"I'd like to call this number collect from Ian to Debbie."

"OK, hold on."

As the telephone rang, my heart was pounding furiously. A woman picked up and said hello.

"You have a collect call from Ian for Debbie. Do you accept the charges?"

"Can you ask him his last name?"

"Sir?"

"Manuel, I'm Ian Manuel." I didn't say I was calling from Apalachee Correctional.

"Yes, I'll accept the charges."

It was then all on me: what do you say to somebody you've shot? I spoke from the heart.

"Miss Baigrie, I called to wish you and your family a Merry Christmas and a Happy New Year and to apologize for shooting you in the face."

"Ian, why did you shoot me?" she asked in a soft, tremulous voice.

"It was a mistake," I said. "It all happened so fast."

"Maybe the first shot was a mistake, but then you shot at me again. Then you shot at my friend."

I think I repeated, "It all happened so fast."

I was too young to realize how unlikely it all was, that

only a uniquely special person would accept a call from the child who shot her. All I knew at the time was that I had done something necessary.

We spoke for the fifteen minutes allotted us by the prison phone. Just before it cut off, I asked her, "Can I call back?" She said yes.

I proceeded proudly to tell my homeboys at Apalachee that I had called Debbie, and they teased me: "You better leave that woman alone before you get another charge." Later on, during my intermittent correspondence with Debbie Baigrie, older convicts would say cynically: "That lady's trying to trick you to get you out of prison so she can kill your ass." For now, they looked at me with skepticism; they thought my excitement at connecting with my victim would simply blow over as a bout of craziness. Some even thought I might be lying: "You didn't call no lady you shot. What's wrong with you, boy? You always playing games."

Between my call to Debbie on Christmas Eve and February 1992, I wrote three or four letters to her about what was going on with me. I wrote that my lawyer had let me down; that I was trying to better myself as a person; that I was improving my basketball skills. For nearly two months, I waited anxiously every evening during mail call for a response, but none came. I was now resigned never to hear from Debbie again, and, with my legal options for appealing my life sentence seemingly exhausted, I began to rack up disciplinary reports (DRs) for infractions that in prison were criminalized but that on the outside would have warranted grounding as punishment or even psychotherapy. Instead, I was shoved into a revolving door of disciplinary confinement for stretches ranging from a few to thirty days. Over the next year, I would receive over thirty DRs for bad

behavior, roughly three per month. Yet, as many times as I was written up for infractions, I never thought about the consequences they would bring. I didn't know any better.

THERE WERE VARIOUS LEVELS OF DISCIPLINARY PUNISH-ment. There was your walking DR, which meant that you remained in open population, in a position to get into even more trouble and amass more DRs, until your appearance before a disciplinary court. A classification officer and a lieutenant would then determine your guilt, whether you should be given probation, or whether your recreation time should be limited. Actual physical confinement was limited because of space. In the west unit there were only about twenty cells for more than one thousand inmates. There were times when you would be sentenced to forty-five days and you would do only a week because they had constantly to rotate inmates in and out. That is how I was able to accumulate so many DRs: no sooner was I let out of confinement than I was back in.

When not in confinement I was often gambling in dormitories off limits to me, incurring even more DRs, which were clearly not serving as a deterrent. There was a lot of money to lose or win in those games. My mom was sending me about forty dollars a month at the time as canteen money. I would buy a case of shrimp soup, or a case of peanut butter cookies, and Tang. What she didn't know was that I was gambling with the money left over.

IN FEBRUARY OF 1992, I WAS TRANSFERRED BACK TO ACI East Unit after spending my first eight months in prison at ACI West. The ACI population held many inmates I knew from W. T. Edwards and the Tampa County jail. Mario Gil-

bert, Antonio and Pookie and Scope. Even Marquis, who had enlisted me on the fateful day of the shooting, was there, but on the west side in G+H dorm. I went to pay him a visit. I snuck through a gateway that separates the east and west compounds and walked the short distance to his dorm. I stood outside the dorm's doorway and told someone who was entering to tell Marquis somebody was looking for him. I heard his voice and saw him through the screened windows, walking down the middle aisle. When he pushed the door open, came out on the porch, and saw me standing there, he screamed, "Jim-Jim, what's up, boy?" We hugged and he jokingly said, "Jim-Jim, you don't look like Monkey Man no more, boy." He ran into the dorm and brought out pictures of people from Central Park. Even though I had only been off the streets about a year and a half, people looked different and I was beginning to forget names and faces.

We talked for about thirty minutes. Marquis, who was only sixteen at that time, explained that he had gotten ten years, three mandatory, for the armed robbery he had been in the county jail for. He told me that his job at the prison was outside-the-gate garbage detail. He rode around on the back of a garbage truck, throwing trash bags and dumping the contents of waste containers into the truck. His route took him to the officers' living quarters, and he told me about all the contraband he found and brought back.

As for me, I had been assigned to work in the main laundry room. Because I found washing and folding clothes about as much fun as adding and subtracting fractions, I requested schooling, which meant half day at school and half day inside the grounds behind the kitchen, dumping swill and keeping the area clean. The swill was kept in

huge steel bins in a freezer that sat outside the kitchen. When the swill truck arrived, we'd walk up a short concrete ramp, enter the deep freezer, and tilt and roll the heavy bins toward the back of the truck. The work was grueling. On the back of the truck, there would be an officer with a seventy-five-inch steel pole. He would go around to each swill bin and stab hard and repeatedly into it, making sure that no inmate had buried himself in an attempt to escape.

"BOY, WHAT'S YOUR MOTHERFUCKING PROBLEM," SAID the officer. I had been transferred briefly back to Lake Butler because I had complained about pain in my wisdom tooth and was supposed to have oral surgery. With a new mindset, I wasn't the timid little kid they had beaten and humiliated at Lake Butler around a year ago. Instead, I now regarded myself as a fifteen-year-old student of prison life, stronger, more sure of myself and my ability to defend myself.

I was put in open population because I had come from an adult camp. One night in the dorm, one of the officers and I got into an argument. He told me to step into the officers' station, which was connected to an inmate dorm laundry room. And this is where inmates were taken and beaten into submission before being sent back to their bunks. Inside the station, the officer began cursing at me. To his surprise, I began cursing back.

The officer looked shocked by my response and seemed to rethink whatever his plan for me had been. He got on his walkie-talkie and called for help. Two sergeants arrived, and the officer explained what had happened. One of the sergeants looked at me and said, "Inmate, how old are you?"

"Fifteen."

"Fifteen! Man, turn around and cuff up. You ain't supposed to be on the compound no way. You trying to get all of us fired?"

As I turned around and allowed handcuffs to be placed on my wrists, I said, "I ain't no youthful offender. I come from an adult camp. I'm at ACI. I'm just down here for dental."

"It don't matter—Lake Butler policy is anybody under eighteen can't be on our compound."

Once he got me in handcuffs, the sergeant confronted me. "Boy, what is this about you disrespecting my officer?"

He pulled a quarter out of his pocket and said, "Listen, I'm going to flip a coin. Heads, we're going to beat your ass and take you to jail with a DR, or tails, we're just going to beat your ass and take you to jail."

I said, "I don't care how many times you flip it, you ain't fit to put your hands on me."

I went to K Wing in the cellblock untouched, but soon I was back in the hole for a seven-day stint.

No sooner had I returned to ACI than Marquis told me that our friend and former classmate had been killed. Marquis called me to the fence one day and said, "Jim-Jim. Patrick dead."

Patrick had come to Central Park to buy a gun from a female named Caffeine. Caffeine, not knowing the gun had one bullet in the chamber, had pulled the trigger while passing the gun to Patrick. Patrick was struck in the head or chest. Marquis said that his last words were "See, I told you, girl," before he closed his eyes and died. I reminisced about our friend. I thought about our class race when we attended Robert E. Lee Elementary and how at the start I stopped to tie my shoe only to come in second. Patrick came

in first. We had joked afterward about who was the fastest. The argument was moot: he was.

Patrick and I were the same age. And now he was shot dead and I was in prison. This would be the first of many reports of the death of someone I knew as a child, each related second or third hand, the details confused—was it a bullet to the head or the chest?—all of them stark for their brevity and finality, leaving no room for indulging in grief.

IT WAS NOW AUGUST 1992. I HAD TURNED FIFTEEN AND was housed at Apalachee Correctional Institution. I was summoned to classification and asked to sign a consent form for an interview. Channel 10 of Tampa was doing a TV show called "Kids That Kill" and wanted to interview me. Though fortunately Debbie had survived the shooting, I had been sentenced as if she had not. That must have been good enough for Channel 10.

Debbie saw the interview, and I received my first letter from her. She was furious at my account of the crime. In a childish effort to minimize what I had done, I told the reporter, "She kept going for the gun." Debbie wrote: "I can't believe it's been two years later and you're still lying about the crime." This began a five-year period during which Debbie and I exchanged letters frequently, sometimes as often as once a month. I was ashamed that I had misrepresented my crime, but I was grateful to have Debbie back in my life.

IT WAS ALSO AROUND THIS TIME THAT I WAS CALLED TO Colonel Harrison's office. I had been to his office so many times that it felt like my home base. Colonel Harrison had pictures of himself hunting on the walls of his office; he used to tell me stories of his hunting trips and travels. He

reminded me, in many ways, of Bob Gilbertson, because Colonel Harrison also treated me like the kid I was. He told me that he had been promoted to assistant superintendent and would be transferred to Holmes Correctional Institute; he wanted me to know. This was ominous: the man who had looked out for me would no longer be there to spring me from confinement, as he often had. I felt more alone at ACI than ever.

As it sank in that he would no longer be there to protect me, I asked, "Why can't you make assistant superintendent here?" He explained that the opportunity was elsewhere; he had to go where his promotion assigned him.

After Colonel Harrison left, whenever I went to the hole, my stay would be extended, and when I got out, staff would try me in ways they never had before. One day, after I'd served a stint, a heavyset officer assigned to the back gatehouse (where inmates were counted) saw me passing through, my property in two pillowcases.

"Manuel, I'm glad to see you out. Come down and report to work this afternoon."

It was an unwritten rule in Florida's prison system that inmates leaving confinement did not have to report to work until the next day.

"Man, I'm just getting out of jail. I ain't got to go to work until tomorrow."

"That ain't no rule, that's some inmate made-up bullshit and I'm giving you a verbal order to report to work and if you don't, I'm writing you two DRs, one for disobeying an order and one for refusing to work."

When treated unfairly, I often impulsively responded and found myself right back in solitary confinement. This time

I was focused on the things I had been dreaming about during my stint: I had a package waiting for me in the mail-room, plus I wanted to go to the canteen and load up on some sweets.

"All right, sir, I'll be there."

By the time I had reached the mail room, the same officer had called the female officer there to remind me to come to work. I did not fall for the harassment. I picked up my package, returned to my dorm, and then ran off to work. When I arrived at my kitchen workstation, the same officer told me that there were enough inmates back there already and that he was assigning me to Mr. Hatchet's lawn mower squad for that day.

Previously, I would have given him exactly what he was looking for: a reason to lock me back up. But not that day. Not on my first day out.

Still, I was full of anger and took it out on the lawn mower Mr. Hatchet gave me. I ran with it full speed, pushing hard into the lawn. There was a loud boom. Fire shot out the side of the red-paneled frame and I let it go. Mr. Hatchet and the other grass cutters looked at me incredulously. Mr. Hatchet ran over to check on the lawn mower. He looked at me and said, "Manuel, what's wrong with you? You don't cut grass like that!"

The exploding lawn mower was too obvious an analogy for the anger building and always on the verge of erupting in me at age fifteen. With nothing to hold me steady, no hope anywhere on my horizon, and needing all my energy to contain my rage at the chronic insults and capriciousness of those in power over every detail of my life, I began to accumulate more DRs for "disrespect." While serving yet

another stint in confinement during this period, an older boy and I got in an argument in the shower that led to an exchange of blows.

AT DISCIPLINARY COURT, I PLED GUILTY TO THE DR BUT asked the officers to sentence me to a concurrent thirty days so I could get out in time for Christmas. They told me to step out of the office while they deliberated.

After a few minutes, they called me in and told me I had been given thirty days disciplinary confinement. When I saw the yellow hearing worksheet, I noticed that neither the concurrent nor consecutive sentencing box had been checked.

"I need y'all to check a box so I can get out for Christmas."

The male classification officer said robotically, "You have fifteen days to appeal our decision."

When I repeated my request, Sergeant Nobles reached out and with a stroke of her pen checked the consecutive box, before tearing off the carbon copy to give me. I could not bear the thought that I was not going to make it back to open population for Christmas. As she slid the carbon copy across the table to me, I turned around and was walking out as she yelled behind me, "Manuel, come back here and get your papers!" I kept walking as if she hadn't said a word.

She rushed in behind me. "Manuel, didn't you hear me calling after you to get your report?"

Unable to contain the pain and anger, the disappointment and outrage—this one small thing that I wanted, to be out of a confinement cell on Christmas, this one small comfort so arbitrarily taken from me—I rained down a storm of curses and insults on the officer standing, dumbstruck, before me.

Shaken, she turned from me, and walked quickly back to the hearing room. For this, they recommended that I, age fifteen, be remanded to another facility for close management. Long-term solitary confinement awaited me at Union Correction facility. The solitary confinement of children is a form of torture routinely practiced by the American correctional system. As the American Civil Liberties Union puts it:

Humans are inherently social animals; we crave community and connection with others. Being deprived of it can anguish even the most independent individuals. Solitary confinement—the practice of isolating people in closed cells for 22–24 hours a day, virtually free of human contact, for days to decades—violates this fundamental need, causing extreme suffering.

People in solitary confinement descend to a psychological and emotional state that is deep and dark. The "hole," as solitary is often called, is an apt description. Even when a person is freed from solitary, its effects may not go away. Research has shown solitary confinement causes serious, long-term harm, which is why courts across the country recognize that it should be used only sparingly, even for adults serving years in prison for violent felonies.

For children, solitary confinement is especially dangerous. Because their brains are still developing, children are highly susceptible to the prolonged psychological stress that comes from being isolated in prisons and jails. This stress can inhibit development of parts of the brain—such as the prefrontal cortex, which governs impulse control—causing irreparable damage. In other words, children subjected to solitary

confinement are forced into a hole so deep they may never be able to climb out."[1]

A few days before my transfer, Marquis was released from his own confinement. He had heard that I wasn't coming back to the compound and was awaiting transfer to a close management facility. On his way out, he stopped by my cell and reached through the bars so we could embrace. As I released him, I saw tears in his eyes. We both knew—and couldn't even begin to imagine—what awaited me.

IMAGINE THAT YOU, AT AGE FIFTEEN, HAVE BEEN SEN-
tenced to social death, life without parole, in a space nine
feet by seven—the size of a freight elevator—where for
twenty-two to twenty-four hours a day you are trapped;
where in a deadly daily routine you sleep, wake up, shit,
piss, eat—food slipped through a slot as if you were an
animal; where you are denied the possibility of human contact except as physical or mental abuse; where visual and
sensory stimuli—the stuff of life—are only a memory or
a dream; and where who you are is defined only by your
willingness or unwillingness to be disciplined and punished.
Imagine life without hope in a brutal hellhole of sameness
designed to break your spirit and challenge your sanity. The
United Nations considers solitary confinement for more
than fifteen days torture. It was my condition for eighteen
consecutive years. Scientists have shown that solitary confinement, especially of juveniles, can damage the brain, pro-
voking panic, anxiety, depression, loss of control, and even
suicide. I managed to endure it and survive.

As early as the mid-nineteenth century, the writer Charles
Dickens denounced the barbarism of the practice when he
visited a prison in Philadelphia: "I believe that very few
men are capable of estimating the immense amount of tor-

ture and agony which this dreadful punishment, prolonged for years, inflicts upon the sufferers, and in guessing at it myself, and in reasoning from what I have seen upon their faces, and what to my certain knowledge they feel within, I am only the more convinced that there is a depth of terrible endurance in which none but the sufferers themselves can fathom, and which no man has a right to inflict upon his fellow creature. I hold this slow daily tampering with the mysteries of the brain to be immeasurably worse than any torture of the body."[1]

The tampering with the mysteries of my own brain by prison authorities was aided and abetted by psychiatry and pharmacology. From the start of my incarceration I had trouble sleeping because of anxiety and was prescribed medication that sometimes worked and sometimes didn't. Soon, in response to my behavioral liabilities as they saw them, psychiatrists were quick to diagnose me as suffering from a form of mental illness, bipolar II disorder, which develops during the teenage years. Like bipolar I, it's characterized by a fluctuation of moods high and low, but its elevated moods—hypomanic episodes—are less intense than bipolar I's full-blown mania, and depression is its more characteristic state. But I have never suffered extended periods of highs and lows, so I have always been skeptical of this diagnosis. Bipolar depression and attention-deficit/hyperactivity disorder can sometimes be confused, though, because they share symptoms. I am certain that—because of my inattention, hyperactivity, and impulsivity—I've suffered from ADHD since childhood, but ADHD was not at the time recognized as a form of mental illness by the Florida Department of Corrections.

It is a curiosity that a state-funded institution, run by

professionals, would systematically place human beings in the most toxic of settings and then, when this made them sick, conclude that the problem was coming from inside of those human beings. There is likely no diagnosis that accurately captures the range of harm and its consequences for the mind and body of someone subjected to solitary confinement. The diagnoses given to me and the drugs used to bring them under control all seemed ultimately aimed at keeping me there longer.

Among the psychotropic drugs used to treat me, or forcibly injected into me—to put me at ease for management—were Benadryl, Remeron, Depakote, Sinequan, Geodon, Seroquel, Abilify, Tegretol, Vistaril, Valproic, lithium, Trilafon, Ativan, Thorazine, and Zyprexa—regardless of their onerous and sometimes debilitating side effects. In short, I was a constant object of pharmacological experimentation, at times shackled spread-eagle on a bed, the objective being to render me insensate, to nullify me with mind-altering drugs.

EARLY ON, I HAD LEARNED FROM OLDER INMATES THAT you could now and then get relief from the savage sameness of solitary confinement—the feeling that the walls are closing in on you—through a change of scenery. All you had to do was shout, "I'm going to kill myself," and so initiate a psychiatric emergency. Guards would rush to your cell, strip you of your clothes, and take you to the infirmary, where they would lock you in a cold room with a concrete bunk for three days at a time. I have a vivid memory of sitting naked in such a room, shivering on a stainless steel toilet, hugging myself for warmth, my chin slumped on my chest, as I drifted off.

I later learned from a book that the origins of solitary confinement can be traced to a Quaker prison experiment at the Walnut Street Jail in Philadelphia at the end of the eighteenth century, which aimed to do away with corporal punishment and to rehabilitate offenders by completely isolating them from human society. As the *Solitary Watch* blogger Mary Hawthorne notes, solitary confinement was "ironically and perversely, a reform attempt, based on the notion of 'penitence' (hence 'penitentiary') conceived by the Philadelphia Society for Ameliorating the Miseries of Public Prisons."[2] Inmates at Walnut Street Jail were isolated in their cells to do assigned work and read the Bible with a view toward repentance. Whenever they were led from their cells, hoods were placed over their heads to prevent them from knowing where they were and from seeing other inmates. In less than fifty years, solitary confinement would become a terrible mode of punishment, recognized by the U.S. Supreme Court as inhumane. Its aim was no longer to foster rehabilitation.

AT MARTIN CORRECTIONAL INSTITUTION, INMATES WERE stabbing each other with regularity throughout the overpopulated compound. Things got so bad that the prison started gassing inmates for surreptitiously talking to each other on the cellblock. For me solitary confinement early on was curiously a blessing—it kept me out of harm's way. I wasn't stabbed and I wasn't gassed. When I was first committed as a teenager, I spent a lot of time fantasizing, stuck in a time warp, from 1990 to 1992, when I was full of dreams. I wanted to be a superstar professional basketball player, rapper, or actor. I thought of being arrested the summer after I'd completed seventh grade. I was looking forward to

eighth grade; I envisioned playing basketball for the junior high school team, the Madison Mustangs. Even though I was small, I was athletic. Would I have made the high school team? Would I have played college basketball? Would I have landed in the NBA? Might I have become the next Allen Iverson, the next Michael Jordan?

Most children's dreams are tested by the realities of their expanding world as they grow into adulthood. They learn that they will not be Michael Jordan, or president of the United States, and they find where their true talents lie. My dreams remained untested, as my world had shrunk to a cell.

I recalled the raps and poetry that I wrote while serving time in juvenile detention, sharing them with my homeboys and reveling in their encouragement. I thought that if I could deeply affect these young men, who came from tough circumstances and were hard to reach, I could move audiences outside of prison. My hero was Tupac Shakur, who rose from poverty to worldwide fame as a rapper and actor. For me he was extremely influential. Everything about him—his take-no-shit attitude, his dignified demeanor, the power of his rhymes—appealed to me. I was as much astounded by his first album, *2Pacalypse Now,* as I was by his acting debut in the movie *Juice,* about the trials and travails of four young men in Harlem dealing with the harsh realities of inner-city life. I wanted to be the next Tupac.

Once a week the library cart would come around. Inmates from the general population working in the library would bring you books that you had requested. I was drawn to gritty, hard-edged stories about the black urban experience that celebrated criminal swagger and bravado. My two favorite authors were Iceberg Slim (*Pimp: The Story of*

My Life; Trick Baby; Long White Con) and a writer Iceberg Slim profoundly influenced, Donald Goines (*White Man's Justice, Black Man's Grief; Black Gangster; Street Players*). Both career criminal writers were hugely popular in prisons at the time—their books were a snap to read—and both remain popular among rappers today for keeping it "real," for championing thug life.

SOLITARY CONFINEMENT THROUGHOUT FLORIDA IS A complex, infernal, multitiered affair. According to the Florida Administrative Code, "close management" is "the confinement of an inmate apart from the general population, for reasons of security or the order and effective management of the institution, where the inmate, through his or her behavior, has demonstrated an inability to live in the general population without abusing the rights and privileges of others."[3] Florida, the third largest prison system in the country, is at the vanguard of the mass incarceration of black Americans. Whereas black people constitute less than 20 percent of Floridians, they amount to nearly 50 percent of the state's prison population, and 60 percent of inmates under close management are black. Yet in some important respects Florida is indiscriminate in assigning offenders to close management: it is heedless of age, developmental disability, or mental illness. Even children and juveniles in state prisons can come under close management.

There are three levels of close management housing: CM 1, CM 2, and CM 3—ranging from most to least confining. Assignment to one or another supposedly depends on your record and behavior. In CM 1, offenders are imprisoned alone in around sixty square feet for twenty-two to twenty-four hours each day. Solitary confinement in CM 2

and 3 may involve a cellmate, compatibility not guaranteed. Good behavior supposedly earns greater freedom, leading eventually to integration in the general prison population. While CM 2 and 3 are said to offer more leniency than CM 1—participation in work and educational activities outside of your cell—prisoners in these categories are often denied privileges they are due. All CM 1 inmates are at the mercy of corrupt or vengeful corrections officers who, with a false or petty disciplinary report, can either retard or void progress.

A vicious cycle often ensues when prisoners who find it impossible to conform to behavioral expectations are condemned to solitary confinement: the restrictiveness reinforces and heightens their malady, resulting in the inevitable lengthening of their stay. For eighteen years, I was such a prisoner. The longer I was in solitary, the harder it was for me to meet their behavioral expectations. And the harder it was for me to do as I was told, the more forceful the prison became in attempting to ensure that I did. Looking back, I know that it is a universal human experience during adolescence to seek to assert independence, to insist on defining one's own personhood. In the context of a solitary confinement cell, this stage of my life was received as defiance and met with brutal force aimed at crushing it. My journey through the arbitrary and cruel CM system was that of the rider of an elevator that is out of control, ascending and descending seemingly with a mind of its own. No sooner would I seem to be completing a six-month sentence in CM 2, on my way to CM 3, for example, than I would find myself, after, say, five months and twenty-nine days, guilty of an infraction, real or concocted by corrections officers, that prevented me from achieving greater freedom.

Over the course of my incarceration, as I was shuttled back and forth among prisons throughout the state—Lake Butler, Apalachee, Martin, Union, Columbia, South Florida Reception Center, Florida State Prison, Santa Rosa, Suwannee Annex, Charlotte, Northwest Florida Reception Center, and Hillsborough—I amassed more than two hundred disciplinary reports. Most fell into the category of disobedience or disrespect of officials.

IN 1996 PRINCETON POLITICAL SCIENTIST JOHN DILULIO sparked widespread social panic when he put forth a novel theory about juvenile delinquency—which he has since retracted given how stunningly wrong all of his predictions turned out to be—sounding an alarm about the advent of a "new breed" of black inner-city youth whom he called "superpredators." "Fatherless, Godless, and jobless," they are "radically impulsive, brutally remorseless youngsters, including ever more teenage boys, who murder, assault, rob, burglarize, deal deadly drugs, join gun-toting gangs, and create serious disorders."[4] This was the media landscape in which an interview with Debbie Baigrie ("I Forgave the Guy Who Shot Me")[5] was published in the now defunct *McCall's* magazine.

Debbie described the excruciating toll my crime had exacted—the shooting had ripped up her mouth and gums, requiring years of painful reconstructive surgery. But with dignity and empathy, she added:

[A] glimpse of Ian's bleak life made me reflect on my own circumstances, the reasons I have to be thankful: a husband with a good job as an electrical engi-

neer, a great family, a beautiful home, many caring friends. So, hoping I could make Ian's life a little better, I began a correspondence with him. My husband didn't approve. "Forget him!" Stephen said. "He can just rot." . . . It would be wonderful to end this story with the news that Ian has been completely rehabilitated. But reality is seldom so neat. What I am grateful for is that Ian seems to be finding himself, that I have not only recovered but have been able to develop a relationship with my attacker and that I have found a new direction for my life. I still get a lot of pressure to stop bothering about Ian, but he needs a friend. And for reasons I don't fully understand myself, I intend to go on being that friend.

From 1992 to 1995 Debbie and I wrote to each other perhaps as much as once every other month. From 1995 to 1997, the frequency slowed to once every three or four months. By then Debbie had carved out a successful career for herself as a nonsteroidal bodybuilder and personal trainer, which she regarded as therapeutic, and of course she was busy raising her two daughters and running a bodybuilding magazine. It is hard for me to remember in great detail my letters from Debbie over the course of six years; with the exception of a few, they were all destroyed in a prison fire. I can recall only bits. I remember her caring, motherly tone best: she was always imploring me to stay out of trouble and encouraging me to study for my GED/High School Equivalency exam. For my part, I wrote of teenage matters as I had read about them in magazines, and of my need to get out of prison so that I could pursue sports in college. I asked her if she could send

me copies of *Sports Illustrated* and *People* that she had lying around her house, but prison policy prohibited that, fearing the slipping in of contraband.

Debbie's caring for me was shown by her willingness to drive two and one-half hours each way from her home in Tampa, on the opposite coast of Florida, to visit me at Martin; she knew that no one had come to see me in prison in nearly six years. Her request was sharply denied. A letter sent to her by a Department of Corrections functionary dated May 8, 1996, said in part: "This is in response to your letter and phone conversation requesting a visit for Ian Manuel. While you have been quite clear in your interest to help Ian, I am hopeful you can understand the position of the Department of Corrections. It is the policy of the Dept. not to permit visits by those persons known to be victims of those who are incarcerated. Such permission would not be in the interest of security, in maintaining care, custody and control of the system."

In 1996 after the *McCall's* article appeared, *The Maury Povich Show* got in touch with Debbie. It wanted to devote a full hour to our story; it wanted to have her on the set and to interview me via satellite. She told me they said that if I stayed out of trouble for thirty days I would be allowed to do the interview. She was adamant that I keep my nose clean. I explained to her that I was in the most restrictive confinement, CM 1, and that, regardless of good behavior on my part, there was no way Martin Correctional Institution was going to permit my appearance on the show. I made the mistake of telling older convicts what had happened, and they poured poison in my ears: they claimed that she was being paid for the interviews she was doing. "Boy, that lady's using your dumb ass to get rich. And here you in

prison broke." Debbie was righteously offended, indignant at being the object of my suspicion when I challenged her, asking for money: "I have forgiven you for shooting me in the face, and now I'm going to forgive you for slapping me in it. And that's where it ends."

Debbie had previously considered cutting off our correspondence—before the *McCall's* article, before the Maury Povich invitation. She had reached out to my mother, presumably to bond with her, and things had not gone well. In a letter from April 1995, she wrote:

> Dear Ian:
>
> I just got off the phone with your mother, and it was a very bad idea to call her. You see, I have been trying all this time to help you and I never realized that all of you think I should be dead. I wasn't the judge that put you in there. I was the victim. As the victim I tried to get you rehabilitated before you went to prison and have been fighting for you ever since. Only because I really care. I tried to explain that and she sees it differently. I think all she sees is some rich, blond girl that couldn't begin to understand her situation. I'm far from rich but I do have children and I believe they need attention, guidance and love. I always felt sorry for you because it was beyond my understanding why someone that young could be with a gun. I felt you were a victim too . . . I don't need her approval or understanding, but I also don't need her contempt. Right now, I'm scared . . . No one has ever wanted me dead before. You didn't. You didn't even know me. She doesn't appreciate anything I've done and

I'm scared Ian! I really am. I think I must just forget about this . . . You are a special guy and I believe that everything will work out.

> All the best,
> Debbie

I've really enjoyed corresponding with you. Good luck, Ian. My thoughts are with you always.

ON JUNE 8, 1996, I WAS SITTING IN MY CELL AT MARTIN staring ahead; I had a cellmate at the time, a guy named Terry. I was on runaround status, which meant that now and then I was allowed to leave my cell to retrieve supplies at the officers' station to hand out to inmates, and today was supply day. The cell door clicks open and I see the officer in his booth waving me over. I get dressed and join the other runarounds, grabbing stuff: toothpaste, soap, toilet paper. I lunge for some toothbrushes.

"What are you doing? You ain't passin' out nothing today, you're comin' with me. We need to take a walk."

Inmates aren't supposed to go beyond the small area near the officers' station without being handcuffed, shackled, and chained, and here I was walking free in prohibited spaces with Sergeant Adams. An improbable thought raced through my mind: was I about to be released from CM on some technicality?

"Where are we going?"

"To the chaplain's office. Anyone in your family been sick lately?"

"My mom."

"OK."

The walk felt much longer than it was; the distance be-

tween confinement and the chapel was only fifty yards or so. There, before a black chaplain, we sat. In a deep, calm voice, the chaplain said: "Ian, I got a call from your brother. I must regretfully inform you that your mother, Peggye, has passed away. I verified it with the hospital where she died." The chaplain allowed me to call Sean, who confirmed that AIDS had put an end to our mother's life. She had for a while been sending me alarming pictures of herself with her letters. She'd been a big woman, five foot four, 220, 230 pounds. Now she was getting skinnier and skinnier. I had been mentally preparing myself for the inevitable, but the fact was still devastating. She had written me to say that in her present condition she had to smoke her medication through a pipe. The disease was rapidly eating away at her. On May 31, a week and a day before she died, I was able to place a call to her from confinement—a privilege accorded to runarounds. She told me not to call again until her birthday, June 19.

June 8, 1996, was the saddest day of my life. For the very first time I felt truly alone in the world. With my mom gone, I had no one I could depend on unconditionally. I was scared in a way that shook me. My grief was bottomless. In a stupor, I was led back to my cell. Terry wanted to know what was going on. I didn't answer. I resented his presence; I didn't want anyone around. In the darkness, I curled up in bed and sobbed.

I later learned that Aunt Kathy, my mother's dear friend, and my brother, Sean, had gone to Debbie Baigrie's home to tell her the news. Debbie wrote to express her condolences; she observed how much my brother resembled me even though he was much bigger. For the next three years, she and I fell completely out of touch, our friendship in tatters.

Or so it felt. Six months after my mom died, Aunt Kathy and Sean visited me to fulfill a deathbed promise to my mother. It was the first time in six years of incarceration that I had visitors who were either family or family friends. According to Aunt Kathy, my mom could never bring herself to visit me in prison because she felt the thought of leaving without me unbearable. I didn't know what to make of that.

IN 1997, AGE TWENTY, I WAS TRANSFERRED BACK TO Union Correctional Institution, even though the facility still offered no educational opportunity—the reason for my having been transferred from it years earlier. I wrote to the Tallahassee Central Office of the Department of Corrections to say that I was eager to improve myself through schooling. For reasons I knew nothing about, Florida's secretary of education and a colleague visited and assured me that if I stayed out of trouble for six months, I would be sent to a correctional facility where I could attend school. Having complied, I was sent to Columbia Correctional Institution nearby and assigned to less restrictive CM 2.

The deal I had made with the Central Office was that I could study and learn at Columbia only as long as I avoided disciplinary charges. But Columbia turned out to be a far more brutal and oppressive place than Union; it was an entirely different kind of prison. At Columbia, lights were kept on 24/7 as a way to disorient prisoners and keep them in check—a form of torture. There, guards were dousing prisoners with chemical agents, gassing them, for even minor infractions. I couldn't stand it—even though I myself was not victimized. I had to get out of there, I had to get back to Union. So I purposefully caught three charges. But

I hadn't banked on Columbia's recommendation that I be put on CM I upon returning to UCI.

I appealed to Union's close management board by telling the unvarnished truth; the board couldn't dispute anything I said. "Listen, I want y'all to check my record. I came to UCI January 1993, check my record. I've never gotten a disciplinary report here. I caught those disciplinary reports at Columbia strictly to get back to UCI. I'm home now. You don't have to worry about me getting in any trouble. Check my record." They did.

"Why is it that you can stay out of trouble here and nowhere else?"

"'Cause UCI's home. I growed up here. I'm comfortable with the surroundings. You don't gotta worry about me here."

ON NEW YEAR'S EVE THAT YEAR THE OFFICER ON DUTY opens all the food flaps on the confinement wing, as an act of generosity. Though he wasn't cool, he was trying to be friendly, to create a festive mood. He lets us shout out to each other, pass cookies around, fill our shampoo bottles for water gun fights through the flaps. Officer Thomson was a big ol' country boy, black and about six foot seven, 290 pounds. When I spot him on the wing I squirt him. He says: "See now, Jim-Jim, I got something for you." He gets a mop bucket full of water and proceeds to douse me and whatever is in my cell, including my sheets—cupful by cupful. Quickly he closes the flap and locks it so I can't get back at him. As my cell door faces the officers' station wing, I shout through its crack: "Jeff, man, come on back, lemme go out there and change my sheets." "All right, Jim-

Jim," he says, but forty-five minutes or so go by and he's not back.

Peering through the crack, I see a red-haired officer trying to open the door to the booth. "Hey, Officer," I call, and he walks over to my cell instead. No sooner do I start to explain what I need to do—change my wet sheets—than another officer in the station hurriedly beckons him back. A few minutes later, Officer Thomson arrives and lets me out of my cell.

"Jeff, man, it's New Year's Eve, let me call my people as long as I'm out here."

"All right, you can use the phone."

I call Aunt Kathy collect to let everybody know I'm OK and need a little money. I tell her to tell everybody to come visit me. Everything's copacetic. At the time I'm on CM 2—and because Union Correctional has no CM 3, I expect at last to be released from solitary confinement and join the general population, having completed six months of good behavior. When I hang up, CM 2 runarounds ask Officer Thomson for permission to use the phone. He lets them. I go back to my cell and fall asleep. I wake up; it's New Year's Day; everything's good: it's my month to get off solitary. You usually get your recommendation papers the first week of the month. Something goes awry: I hear I've gotten a disciplinary report—and start hearing rumors that so did the runarounds—presumably for unauthorized use of the phone. But how could this be? Inmates can't just walk out of their cells to make phone calls whenever they want. There must be some mistake or misunderstanding.

The red-haired officer who had come over to my cell on New Year's Eve, a trainee, was not supposed to be on the wing by himself. The officer who had called him back to the

station had instructed him on how to justify his unexcused presence on the wing and how to falsify a DR. The trainee now claimed that I had threatened him, that I had said: "Hey, man, my cell is wet. If you don't let me out this cell to get a mop, I'm a kill you the first chance I get." Spoken or written threats, especially against officers, are among the most serious infractions in prison, so serious that they can put you on CM 2 or even 1 as punishment. Initially, to my distress, the disciplinary board recommended CM 1—no possibility of joining open population any time soon for me. I appealed to the board's inspector; I told him the truth, about the actions of the white corrections officers that night, about the phone calls—but I pointedly left Officer Thomson out of it. After his investigation, the board rescinded the false DR but not in the way I had hoped.

"Manuel, you never threatened that man. So we're not gonna put you on CM 1. We're gonna keep you on CM 2 with a ninety-day review to see if you'll be eligible for CM 3, which we're initiating. In only ninety days you'll be on CM 3 if you behave yourself. Congratulations!"

I looked at them as if they were insane. Before the false DR I was headed for open population because no CM 3 existed and I had completed the required six months of good behavior to move up to a freer level of incarceration. A trainee had lied about me, which the board acknowledged. And my reward was what? The prolongation of my solitary confinement?

This is a system elaborately constructed of rules and regulations, a bureaucracy trudging along under the cumbersome weight of its own intricate and painstakingly defined terminologies and distinctions. The consequences for failing to comply with this dehumanizing array of mandates

were excessive. But, for me, the worst part was the way in which they were so arbitrarily enforced, the way they didn't seem to reward "good behavior" but instead seemed to only encourage an alternation between outrage and hopelessness at the bizarreness of it all.

ONE DAY IN 1998 I GOT A LETTER IN THE MAIL; THE ENVE-lope was slipped through the crack of my cell door. It was from Jimmy Reese, my father. If a letter included money, the amount was stamped on the envelope, standard practice, and this one said "$50." I knew that, like Grandma Linda, Jimmy Reese couldn't read or write, so someone must have written the letter for him. It said in part: "Baby, I know your momma gone and I just want to make up for all the years I wasn't there for you and to do anything I can to help you. Here's 50 dollars. Tell me what you need." I had not seen, heard from, or thought about my father in nearly a decade. He had been absent from my trial and sentencing. His letter came out of the blue. I was elated, grateful, but puzzled. What or who had moved him to reach out to me now, nearly two years after my mom's death? I didn't dwell too much on all this, though, because I was most eager to tell him what I wanted. I wrote back saying: "I don't hold it against you for not being there all these years. What matters is that you're here now." I included a list of newspapers and magazines allowed by the prison; I asked for subscriptions to USA Today; Florida Sentinel Bulletin, an African-American publication; People; and Sports Illustrated. I also begged him for books of stamps—trading currency behind bars. He gave me an allowance of ten books per month, the equivalent of a hundred dollars. And he kept it up until late 2000, the year of the millennium.

It turned out that Jimmy Reese, now more than likely in his late sixties, was an old drug dealer. Crack. One day police tried to ram into his home, and he fired shots at them through the door, missing. Firing at police was tantamount to an immediate death sentence; it was a wonder he didn't die at the scene. I learned from his letters to me, written by strangers, that he was tackled and handcuffed, dragged off to jail, and later charged with attempted murder. The charge for some reason was reduced and he ended up receiving two and a half years house arrest and six and a half years probation. By now he was very sick; I know he went to the hospital with fluid in his lungs. Communication with him soon became a thing of the past. In 2004 a chaplain informed me that Jimmy Reese's probation officer had called to say that my father had died out of state. I surmised in Georgia, where he had relatives.

THE LAST TIME I SAW MY FATHER WAS THE NEXT TIME I saw Debbie Baigrie. I was twenty-three. I had not seen Jimmy Reese since I was a child; I barely recognized the elderly black man sitting in the courtroom. Debbie and I had not seen each other since 1991 at my sentencing; we had not heard each other's voice since 1992; and we had not communicated since 1997. Both Jimmy Reese and Debbie Baigrie were at my resentencing hearing on June 29, 2000.

The year before I had bought a tattered and torn copy of the 1989 edition of Florida Rules of Criminal Procedure; I think it cost me about five packs of cookies. I read it carefully and came across an item plainly stating that life in prison is a maximal sentence. You cannot sentence an individual to life in prison without the possibility of parole and add life probation. In addition to such a sentence being absurd,

it is illegal. So in 1999, through Tampa public defender Mark Reinhold, I filed a motion to have my sentence corrected. Eight months later I was remanded to Tampa for resentencing.

Aunt Kathy gave me Debbie's telephone number and I called her. When she answered, there was a chill in her voice; she sounded understandably as if she had moved on. I told her that I had a court appearance and wanted to know if she could be there to support me. I had planned to present the *McCall's* article as evidence of her forgiveness. She said she knew all about it—the prosecutor had called—but, no, she was unable to come; she was going to be out of town that day. She wished me good luck.

At the resentencing hearing,[6] I turned to look at the audience before taking my seat. There was Aunt Kathy and a black man I supposed was Jimmy Reese, my father. There also was a white woman I imagined to be Debbie with a girl I took to be her daughter. At one point during the proceedings the prosecutor Donna Hanes told the judge that she expected both victims of my crime to be present but that only one wanted to be heard. The man who accompanied Debbie to her car that night, the man who my friends and I had victimized, spoke against any change in my sentence. Debbie did not speak against a sentence change and allowed my public defender to present the *McCall's* interview as evidence of her forgiveness and willingness to allow me to have a second chance at life. Aunt Kathy vouched for me, and then my father moved me with his powerful brevity: "I just say, Judge, have mercy on my son. I figure he done did enough time for the crime he had committed. I beg your honor please let my baby come home." The Honorable William Fuente agreed my sentence of life without plus

life probation was unlawful and wrong. He vacated the life probation ruling. "I will adjudge you guilty and I'll sentence you to forty years Florida State Prison to be served concurrently with the sentence served in counts one, two, and three. Giving you credit for all the time previously served on those three counts to be given to you on count four . . . I wish you well."

Though Judge Fuente's ruling did not immediately change my life in any way, it had important ramifications down the road.

IN JULY 1999, FRANK VALDEZ, AN INMATE ON DEATH ROW at Florida State Prison for killing a corrections officer during an escape attempt, was killed by nine prison guards. Armed with stun guns, they bum-rushed his cell and stomped him to death (the autopsy would show boot prints on Valdez's skin, in addition to broken ribs). According to inmates who witnessed the crime, the corrections officers first dumped Valdez's body in the hallway, cleaned his cell with bleach, dragged his body to another cell, and then placed an emergency call. The Department of Corrections' first story was this: Valdez had committed suicide by plunging headlong from his bunk to the concrete floor. Prosecutors, on the other hand, claimed Valdez had been murdered to prevent him from divulging facts about inmate abuse to the press. All nine officers were either acquitted at trial or had their charges—second-degree murder, aggravated battery, battery on an inmate, and official corruption—dropped. The Department of Corrections, however, dismissed them for falsifying reports and using excessive or unnecessary force.

At the time of Frank Valdez's murder, death row inmates were warehoused in cages measuring nine feet by six, twenty-four hours a day, seven days a week. No air-conditioning or fans abated sweltering summer humidity

and heat that often reached the nineties. This, in addition to the savagery of the prison guards, would spark a failed hunger strike five years later. The relief sought by the prisoners evoked not only their plight but also long-standing conditions promoting misery and suffering allowed by the Florida Department of Corrections. The prisoners' demands ranged from the mundane (the ability to purchase eight-inch plastic fans to withstand summers) to the righteous (security cameras to document the use of chemical agents against prisoners and polygraph tests for both the corrections officer and the inmate following any officer-on-inmate physical assault).

WHEN I ARRIVED IN MARCH 2000, THE ATMOSPHERE AT Florida State Prison, "the Green Monster," was tense, dangerous. Instead of physically brutalizing inmates for infractions serious or petty, real or not, corrections officers were gassing them with impunity from a distance. I was transferred to FSP.

After I was kept on CM 2 in the wake of the investigation that had vindicated me, I simply could no longer tolerate the shit. Everything that I had been holding back gushed out. I started verbally abusing these corrections officers with a sense of purpose. Gone was whatever willingness I had left to conform to such rules as making my bed military style. Gone was whatever inclination I may have had to heed orders barked at me as if I were subhuman. I was unable to bite my tongue when addressed without respect, which pretty much meant all the time. They would stare maniacally at me as if I'd slapped them in the face, so accustomed were they to brokenhearted obedience by their charges. To make matters worse, Officer Thomson was

busy lying about me to my fellow inmates, suggesting that during the investigation I had ratted on him and them. He went around falsely claiming that I had told the investigator that he had let me out of my cell and allowed the orderlies to use the phone. "Jim-Jim in there tellin' them everything, how the cigarettes get in, how y'all used the phone. He all up in your shit."

Officer Thomson was calling me a snitch—not an insult I could take lightly. Such an accusation could be deadly behind bars, putting me at risk of attack from any number of inmates and guards. In my mind Thomson and I were now mortal enemies. But before anything further developed, I was transferred from Union Correctional to Florida State Prison.

IT'S ONLY A FIVE-MINUTE DRIVE ACROSS A SHORT BRIDGE from Union Correctional Institution to Florida State Prison—home of the state's electric chair and lethal injection bed—where you can smell evil in the air. My Haitian friend—a big black man named David "Duplex" Jerome—Albert "Q" Quinn, a couple of other inmates, and I arrived in a white van that made its way through the back gate of the prison to the fabled long black steel ramp that leads to a doorway of FSP's second floor. Over the years I'd heard stories of how it was customary for a posse of guards at the back ramp to welcome chained and handcuffed prisoners with a reputation for unruliness at other institutions by beating and kicking them all the way up to the doorway. Luckily, we avoided this fate. Inside, we were registered and hustled to the medical bay for quick exams, then down a long hallway to our assigned wings.

There are thirteen wings at FSP: B, C, D, E, F, G, H, I, J, K,

L, M, and Q. Every wing has three tiers. Every cell is a single. Locked in a cell as hot as lava in summer and cold as ice in winter, you are left to your corrosive thoughts and imagination. Back then, no female officers worked the hallway; no female staff were permitted to walk it without a male escort. Access to a wing was through a big steel door with a double lock—one inside and one outside. Two or three Officers worked as turnkeys every shift. I was placed on K Wing, where there are approximately ninety cells, thirty per floor, cells facing each other. I was on the first floor in the middle of the left-hand side of the wing. Each cell had a bunk, small shelf, vent, toilet, sink, and a long, deep metal footlocker. Each cell also had a back window with a wire screen that could easily be ripped, enabling an inmate to fish through the bars for contraband or to engage in other illegal activities. Through the window you could also see the green grass below and the adjacent wing. Prisoners would often communicate with each other through their windows; they would engage in one-upmanship, trying to "shoot" (silence) their opponents with witty insults, playing their own version of the dozens.

IN MY EARLY TWENTIES, WHEN I WAS AT FSP, MY LEARN-ing expanded, thanks largely to some convicts I befriended who had been in prison for twenty-five years or more. The books they recommended sometimes spoke more to their condition than to mine. As men who had been incarcerated in the 1970s, they regarded themselves, no matter their crimes, as political prisoners of racist America to one degree or another. So books such as *Soledad Brother: The Prison Letters of George Jackson,* by the Black Power revolutionary, and his memoir *Blood in My Eye*—completed only days before

he was killed in 1971 by San Quentin prison guards while allegedly trying to escape—were akin to their Bible. I had never politicized my confinement; I always took it personally. Their conversations about books of egocentric, unconventional morality, such as Robert Greene's *The 48 Laws of Power,* and Ayn Rand's *Atlas Shrugged* and *The Fountainhead,* were heady stuff, supposedly with vague implications for my plight—though I found some of the reading difficult to plow through. My taste ran from the mammoth postapocalyptic novel *Swan Song* by Robert McCammon—the longest book I had ever read cover to cover—and the first two books of the Harry Potter series, *Harry Potter and the Sorcerer's Stone* and *Harry Potter and the Chamber of Secrets.* I was drawn to fantasies that gave my imagination flight, fantasies about a final struggle between good and evil to determine the fate of the world. Since those days a line, often quoted by one convict I knew, has stayed with me: "To live is to suffer; to survive is to find some meaning in the suffering."

IN 2002 OFFICER THOMSON, HAVING BEEN TRANSFERRED from Union Correctional Institution to Florida State Prison, found himself working on the wing that I was on. One day I was in my boxers sitting in my cell waiting for the nurse to bring me medication. Late at night my mind would race; I needed medication to grab and relax it so I could hit deep sleep. Instead I heard the clinking of the gas chain somewhere outside my door. This infernal device is like a fire extinguisher with an extended hose, and it has a distinctive sound that lets you know when the gas is coming. I didn't know what was going on until Officer Thomson and Sergeant Dougal got to my cell's flap. I heard Officer Thomson laughing, letting me know outright that he hadn't forgotten

the bad blood between us. He sprayed me with a chemical agent through the flap. The kind of gas they used on me was clear; the heat it generated on my shirtless body was intense, fiery. It was as if I were standing in front of an oven blasting, its door open. I couldn't get away from the pain for hours. I had to move constantly to lessen the hurt however slightly.

When my body cooled, the heat of my rage took over. Looking back even now, I'm still not sure how I was supposed to go anything but crazy in that moment. Brutally terrorized at the hand of state employees, with no possibility of recourse, no one to come to my aid. I was reduced to my most basic elements, fighting for my very existence, my most basic sense of dignity. I lost myself. I lost any hope I would ever go home, ever leave this prison. In my fiery rage and despair, I would immolate myself—literally. I wrapped myself in newspaper and set myself on fire. Thomson was forced to come to my cell, to witness what he had done, the lengths he had pushed me to. In my deepest of hopes and despairs, I would tackle him, take him down with me. But the officers only put the fire out and restrained me. They cuffed and chained me up, and hauled me off to the showers where I was forced to stand under the running water for hours. I was eventually dragged to the medical bay to have my wounds dressed and then to disciplinary confinement—administered by, among others, Officer Thomson.

It was at this juncture that the toll of long-term solitary confinement would begin to be felt most acutely and self-destructively. My life had shrunk to the size of an eight-by-ten cell. And my preoccupation became defending that cell and the shadow of the life remaining to me. Within that space—both physical and mental—I turned on my own

body and began cutting myself, as I saw numerous others in confinement do.

BLOOD, IT SEEMED TO ME, WAS THE ONLY THING RE-spected in Florida State Prison. Inmates commanded attention by spilling blood, either their own or others'. Cutting was prevalent among them; cell walls were scrawled with blood denouncing this or that. I had learned that prison guards would let you bleed to death in your cell unless you forced blood under the door, where a camera would see it—so I learned to do this.

"BLOODY MIRROR"

Imagine someone trying to kill you
but you don't know who they are.
But every time they touch you—
you see another scar.

You try to run away—
but they always run you down.
And leave you with your blood—
falling on the ground.

You hate whoever does it
with an overflowing passion.
Put gauze on top of wounds
under tape and plastic.
Before you even heal
he returns slashing.
Using stainless steel
pouring salt into your gashes.

You can't see who it is—
even with your glasses.
You can't see through the tears—
surrounded by the blackness.
If you could ever catch him
you'd question all his madness.
Why must he cut you open
and use you as his canvas.
Why does he draw your blood—

and use it as his paint.
Is it from a lack of love—
or just the way he thinks.
One day he returned—
when he thought he was unexpected.
That's when he was tackled
and you both begin to wrestle.
During the struggle—
you started losing blood.
Using his brush—
putting cuts up and down your arm.
Sometime during the struggle
your blood begin to puddle.
Until it was clear like a mirror
and you saw why you suffered.
When you looked into the blood
the image took your breath.
Because the person trying to kill you—
was nobody but yourself.

. . .

BEGINNING IN 2002, I KEPT A FRAGMENT OF RAZOR encased in a salt packet in my mouth everywhere I went, as a protective measure. I convinced myself that prison guards would never be able to put me in a situation from which I could not extricate myself. If they forced me into a freezing strip cell, for example, all I had to do was cut myself and they'd give me a blanket. When I was a child I once was wrestling with a friend in the backyard when suddenly he let go of me and my head hit a wall, injuring an area right above one of my eyes. I was rushed to the hospital, where my wound was sewn up. Time and again I cut precisely along that scar to bleed.

ONE DAY, HAVING BEEN PLACED ON SUICIDE WATCH, I was standing on the sink in my cell talking to another prisoner through the vent when an officer walked by, tapped the door, and told me to get off the sink. Usually what they did was gas you when they caught you talking. But because I was on suicide watch, their rules didn't allow this. The officers had their own way of handling this, usually by denying food. But I refused to beg, to plead for nourishment. They had taken all they were going to take from me.

When mealtime came and nothing was slid through my flap, I destroyed the sprinkler in my cell. It poured in my cell, drenching me, water rushing through the crack at the bottom of the door. The officer demanded that I cuff up or he would call the cell extraction team. Things always get extremely ugly with the cell extraction team. By now I am mentally exhausted and emotionally numb. Five prison guards arrive, dressed in riot gear. They lined up one behind the other, their hands on each other's shoulders. The lead

man holds the shield in front of him—I remember hoping it would be the plastic and not the electric one. I counter with the wet mattress from my bunk to protect myself against the inevitable onslaught and to cushion my fall when they would pummel and wrestle me to the floor. They drag me to medical, where they put me in four-point restraint. All the holding cells were full; so they swap one inmate out for me and tie me down.

ONE DAY A RAY OF SUNSHINE SHONE THROUGH THE DARKness of my life. I was led from my cell to take a legal call. Because of the motion to correct a legal sentence that I had filed in 2000, I had been appointed an appellate public defender named John C. Fisher. He was now calling to say that he had filed a writ of certiorari that had made its way to the U.S. Supreme Court, arguing that a fourteen-year-old should not have been sentenced to life without the possibility of parole because it was cruel and unusual punishment. Certiorari is a judicial process seeking review of a decision by a lower court. The Supreme Court had ordered the state of Florida to reply.

He was excited, joyful. "Ian, I've filed these petitions before and the court has never asked the state to respond. I think we got something here, man. Keep the faith."

A few weeks later he informed me that Florida had responded to the petition and the Supreme Court had dismissed the writ. He said he was sorry; he had done all he could do. He hoped that I would file for clemency and he wished me good luck.

"DON'T NEVER LET THEM TAKE YOUR MIND," MY MOM HAD told me when I was a boy, and that became my mantra for

survival. But this required staunch discipline: both unconscious and conscious repression of all manner of pain. The death of my grandmother, the death of my mother, the death of my father: the accumulation of loss weighed on me every time I was beaten, every time I was gassed, every time I lost an appeal. As a young man growing up, you learn that real men don't cry. This is reinforced exponentially in prison. You can't show signs of weakness; you can't cry. Otherwise they'll know what they can do to harm you. If you acknowledge the damage they are doing to you, they'll keep it up. So you push things down so as not to feel the pain. But beware the repressed: its return always comes at a cost. In T dorm Crisis Stabilization Unit, I was given short-term care, during which acute psychiatric syndromes, as expressed by mood and anxiety disorders, were diagnosed and treated. I refused medication, resulting in yet another disciplinary report against me.

BY 2005 I WAS A TWENTY-EIGHT-YEAR-OLD WHO HAD spent roughly half his life in prison—and most of that in solitary confinement. I was living an absurdity, serving a forty-year sentence concurrently with a life sentence without the possibility of parole. My anger had so deepened that I was no longer trying to get off CM. The intensity of my fury scared even me. I was back at Union Correctional Institution, in U dormitory, and one day I was led to medical for a call out. When I returned to my cell I saw that all of my property had been tossed. Prison guards had searched it for I don't know what: painkillers, ibuprofen? So I tore my mattress open and set it on fire, oblivious to the consequences. Officers rushed to put the fire out and pillaged my cell. I had kept my personal effects—pictures of my mother; letters

from her, Debbie, and my brother; and other irreplaceable objects of sentimental value—in my locker. They raided it and threw all its contents out, as if to erase whatever past I may have been clinging to as a human being. They lied; they said the fire had consumed it all. For the next thirty days, they tried to break me. Every time I was let out of my cell—to visit the nurse, to talk to a counselor—I was forced to wear a spit shield and some kind of black box strapped to my back; my feet were shackled. A chain, a leash, was attached to the handcuffs slicing into my wrists behind me, as I was commanded to walk.

Time expanded infinitely in my cell. Somehow I had managed to secure pen, paper, envelopes, and stamps. I attacked the formal grievance process; I spent whole days firing off grievance after grievance to functionaries at the Department of Corrections and others in the legal profession about how the prison was treating me.

IN 1999—THE YEAR FRANK VALDEZ WAS KILLED—MARK E. Osterback, a prisoner at Walton Correctional Institution in Florida and fourteen other inmates who had been subjected to close management (CM) filed a class action complaint against Michael E. Moore, Secretary, Florida Department of Corrections, and wardens throughout the state's prison system.

Its preliminary statement powerfully denounced the degradations of close management:[1]

1. This is a class action for declaratory and injunctive relief alleging that the Defendants house inmates assigned to Close Management under conditions so harsh, atypical and punitive as

to amount to Cruel and Unusual Punishment in violation of the Eighth Amendment to the United States Constitution.

2. The conditions under which Close Management inmates are housed result in serious mental and physical deterioration.

3. The conditions under which Close Management inmates are housed pose a danger to the public since a large, although unknown number of inmates complete their sentence while on Close Management and are released directly from Close Management to the street.

Among the suit's major allegations were these:

204. The effects of Close Management on the plaintiffs, and the Class they represent, are profound. Placement of prisoners with serious mental disorders on Close Management exacerbates their underlying mental disorders, induces psychosis, and increases the risk of suicide or other self-inflicted harm. Even mentally healthy prisoners are likely to develop mental illness after placement on Close Management.

205. Due to their mental disorders, some Class members never leave their cells, even to shower.

206. The restrictions imposed on inmates in Close Management are so punitive, atypical and harsh that they violate the Cruel and Unusual Punishments Clause of the Eighth Amendment, made applicable to the states by the Fourteenth Amendment.

Responding to the complaint, in an offer of judgment, the Florida Department of Corrections agreed in 2001, "without liability," to implement certain remedies:

> In order to minimize potential harmful effects of close management housing, Defendants have developed a Close Management Consolidation Plan, the key components of which include the following:
> 1. Reduce the number of institutions that house CM inmates from ten to four (one for females and three for males), to consolidate security, program, and mental health staff resources; and to facilitate more uniformity of program operation;
> 2. Conduct staff training on mental health issues relevant to the CM population;
> 3. Perform mental health screening before and after CM placement to help ensure timely access to necessary mental health services;
> 4. Assess behavioral risk for each CM inmate, in order to provide more objective information that will be useful for mental health and other service planning, as well as for administrative decision-making (e.g., modification of CM level or termination of CM status);
> 5. Provide full range of outpatient mental health services (e.g., group/individual counseling; case management; psychiatric consultation; psychotropic medications; and timely referral to inpatient care), commensurate with clinical need, as determined by the Defendant's mental health staff;
> 6. Provide self-betterment/stimulation programming to CM inmates.

Only two years later, the Department of Corrections sought to terminate the Order of Judgment, claiming its remedial goals had all been achieved to everyone's satisfaction. This brazen attempt to avoid responsibility for a disgraceful state of affairs resulted in the reopening of the discovery phase of the trial and the scheduling of an evidentiary hearing in September 2006. I was one of thirty-one prisoners and experts who testified. Attorneys for Osterback et. al. (the plaintiff) had searched Florida's penal system for witnesses to the horrors of close management. I, regarded as "a poster boy" for having served more time on CM than anyone else, and other prisoners—from FSP, Charlotte, Santa Rosa, and Lowell—were invited to Union Correctional Institution to testify via satellite. The video was transmitted to open court in Jacksonville, where Federal District Court Judge Henry Adams was presiding. I told the judge I had been in solitary confinement since I was age fifteen. I told him about the first time I cut myself. I pulled bandages off my arms and legs to show the fresh wounds currently on my body. In late August, I had slit my wrist and the nurse closed the wound with superglue before sending me back to my cell. I spoke of how solitary confinement had led to my "decompensation" ("a breakdown in an individual's defense mechanisms resulting in progressive loss of normal functioning or worsening of psychiatric symptoms," according to the dictionary of the American Psychology Association). I explained that, before solitary confinement, I had never hurt myself intentionally, but now I did so once a week with any sharp object ready to hand—a piece of metallic toothpaste tube, a tiny shard of glass.

· · ·

"DOES SEPARATION EQUAL SUFFERING: SOME STATE IN-
mates spend years in solitary. Critics say that is cruel and unusual." [2] This was the headline of an article by Meg Laughlin
that appeared in *The St. Petersburg Times*. It centered on my
testimony and was altogether empathetic. The Department
of Corrections would have none of it. Assistant State Attorney Jason Vail told the newspaper: "These prisoners don't
practice civilized behavior. They don't follow rules. They
don't deserve civilized treatment. It's a different world." A
few days later he called the paper to clarify his remarks:
"What I meant to say was that these inmates don't conform
and are there because they don't follow the rules. It's that
simple."

"FREEDOM'S JUST ANOTHER WORD FOR NOTHIN' LEFT TO lose," the song says. From around 2003 to 2010, I was free in solitary confinement. I was inured to it; I had adapted to the hellishness of my environment. As Guitar says to Milkman in *Song of Solomon*: "You wanna fly, you got to give up the shit that weighs you down." I did.

The prison system, as I saw it, was engaged in nothing but an all-out assault on my soul. It wanted me to cower before its rules and regulations, holding out rubbish as enticement. It said to me: "We're going to treat you like shit, lower than a human being, and you're going to take it gleefully for the privilege of our releasing you from close management to open population. We're going to burden you with unfairness: you must put up with eighteen months of insane rules. You can behave yourself for five months and twenty-nine days, trying to get out from one CM level to a more lenient one, but if on the thirtieth we write up a disciplinary report against you, justifiably or not, you'll have to repeat six months." Many inmates were willing to make that deal—to get back to their lovers, to be able to play basketball or watch TV. I grew to see these concessions as tools of mind control. I refused to succumb to the savagery

of the prison system's official violence. So fuck the recreation yard; fuck basketball; fuck TV.

IN THOSE DAYS, ARM-BREAKING BY CORRECTIONS officers—authorized by the chief of security—became common practice. Whenever a prisoner had a problem or a dispute—he wasn't fed or had a medical emergency—he would more often than not take the cell door flap hostage by placing his arm on it, preventing its closure, until the officer on duty spoke to someone in charge or the matter was resolved. Colonel Whitehurst judged this act to be a wanton violation of prison protocols, tantamount to an assault, and gave permission to any officer in such a situation to grab the inmate's arm, hold it aloft, and slam the flap down on it. Prisoners unaware of the rule and commandeering the flap—"I need to see the captain"; "I need to see the nurse"; "I've got a medical emergency"; "I wasn't fed last night"; "I need to go to group therapy"—were fodder, their screams chilling as they realized what was happening.

During these years I cherished my aloneness in solitary confinement. I was rarely bored. Boredom in addition to the intensity of the incarceration would have made me lose my mind, might have driven me to suicide. I spent hours on end imagining, practicing magical thinking. Suppose the ocean is a fantastical realm. Posit two aquatic animals: on the one hand, a swordfish whose large gills pull more oxygen out of water than those of most fish, allowing it to spend its entire life beneath the surface of the sea; on the other hand, a dolphin or a whale, with its diving reflex, which however long it stays submerged must periodically rise to the surface to breathe air through its blowhole because like humans it has no gills. In prison, an inmate who never emerges

from fantasy and delusion may be said to have slipped into schizophrenia, having completely withdrawn from reality. An inmate who dives deep into his imagination but is compelled for his survival now and then to rise from fantasy and delusion retains a firm grip on things as they are. I have always believed that I was of the latter party.

Most of my time I spent swimming in my imagination. I had a constant vision of my mother, at the feet of God seated in His throne in heaven, imploring Him: "Please let my baby go home." I wrote rap lyrics to express my ever-shifting feelings; read poets like Langston Hughes, Maya Angelou, and Eminem, imagining myself in competition with, and trying to outdo them; longed for visitations from the nurse just so I could see a female form on the wing. I dwelled on what life would be like outside prison, what I would do once I was out. I harbored childhood fantasies of becoming a rich and famous rap star. I would give back to those I had left behind in prison. Powerless as I was, I dreamt of wielding it. I would hire lawyers—they like money—to represent the interests of prison inmates and to abolish close management.

"MANUEL!" THE OFFICER KICKED MY CELL DOOR, ROUSING me from a reverie, sometime toward the end of October 2006. "Get up, you got legal mail. Come sign for it." I got up from my bunk and walked the three steps it took to get to the cell door. The officer opened the food flap and placed a piece of paper on it. I signed for the mail and he gave me the envelope and walked off. I studied the envelope; the letter was from an organization in Alabama. What could they possibly want with me? I didn't know anybody in Alabama. I tore the envelope open; God had sent me a gift, I thought.

Equal Justice Initiative
Of Alabama
Mr. Ian Manuel
DC # 518907
Union Correctional Institution
7819 N.W. 228th Street
Raiford, Florida 32026-4000

Dear Mr. Manuel:

I'm the director of a non-profit law firm called the Equal Justice Initiative in Montgomery, Alabama. We have a staff of attorneys who provide legal representation to people in prison. We have primarily handled death penalty cases for the last twenty years. However, we recently began a project providing legal assistance to individuals who have been sentenced to life imprisonment without parole as juveniles. After the U.S. Supreme Court's decision in *Roper v. Simmons* (2005) banning the death penalty for juveniles, we started working on the cases of prisoners who were sentenced to LWOP at a young age.

In identifying young people sentenced to life imprisonment without parole for offenses committed at age 14 or younger, we spotted your case. We believe that there may be a chance to reverse a sentence of life imprisonment without parole under an analysis that flows from the *Roper* decision and wanted to know if you were interested in meeting with us to discuss this possibility.

As you know, post-conviction litigation is very time-sensitive with lots of procedural defaults and

statutes of limitation that can bar review of claims. We are also limited in how many cases we can take on. However, a distant review of your case suggests that we might be able to offer you some legal assistance if you're interested and will get in touch with us quickly. We are a non-profit organization and do not charge anyone we represent a fee for the legal assistance we provide.

If you do not currently have legal representation and would like to discuss obtaining assistance, I'd like you to please call my office at 334-269-1803 as soon as possible. In addition to practicing law, I am also a law professor at the New York University School of Law and am frequently out of the office. If I'm not available, please speak with Aaryn Urell or Rebecca Kiley, who are attorneys working on this project. If you are not able to call our office because of restrictions placed on you by your prison, please write us immediately and we will make arrangements to try and meet with you at your prison. We look forward to hearing from you soon.

I enclose some additional information about our project with this letter and a return envelope in the event you cannot call us and need to write in response to this letter.

All the best to you.

Sincerely,
Bryan A. Stevenson
Executive Director

After reading Bryan Stevenson's letter, I was at once elated and skeptical. Two years earlier, I had written to Al

Sharpton's National Action Network, the ACLU, and Jesse Jackson after learning of their interest and involvement in the case of Lionel Tate. (I had requested their addresses from the prison law library.) In 2001, Tate was sentenced to life imprisonment without the possibility of parole for severely injuring Tiffany Eunick. The twelve-year-old boy said that he had been imitating wrestling moves he had seen on TV on the six-year-old girl, who died from her injuries. In 2003 an appeals court overturned Tate's conviction and paroled him. Given that the victim of my crime had survived and now supported my eventual release, I thought Sharpton, the ACLU, and Jackson might advocate to overturn my sentence. If memory serves me correctly, only the ACLU responded, and it was more concerned with mounting a class action suit than challenging my sentence. One year later, in 2005, a Florida State University law professor contacted me offering to come to my aid, only to dash my hopes and dreams by deciding not to take my case. Something about Bryan Stevenson's letter seemed different, genuine, more intimate. It asked me to call or write; I decided to do both. I persuaded the dorm lieutenant that I needed to make a legal call. My hands were cuffed in front of me and I was taken to the nurses' station supply room. Handcuffs jangling, I dialed the numbers on the letter. I closed my eyes and silently prayed that Bryan would be there. "EJI," a woman answered. I told her who I was and that I was calling to speak to Bryan Stevenson. "I'm sorry, Mr. Stevenson is busy right now; may I take a message?" I looked down at the letter and thought quickly to ask: "Are Rebecca Kiley or Aaryn Urell in? Bryan told me to ask for them if he wasn't available." The secretary put me through to Aaryn.

"Aaryn speaking."

"Ms. Urell, this is Ian Manuel calling from a prison in Florida. I received a letter from your organization telling me to call, and you'd send some lawyers down to see me."

"Excuse me? Sorry, Mr. Manuel, but we're a small law firm in Alabama. And we mostly deal with death row cases in Alabama. Are you on death row?"

"No, but I received a letter from your executive director. And he promised to send lawyers down to see me if I called."

"What's the name on the letter?"

"Bryan Stevenson."

"Hold on."

As I waited, smooth jazz wafted through the receiver; the song was "Like a Star" by a young British R&B singer being celebrated everywhere, it seemed. The lyrics were all too appropriate: "Just like a star across my sky/Just like an angel off the page/You have appeared to my life." I looked over my shoulder and saw the lieutenant, his face pressed against the window. He was losing patience and mouthed: "Hurry up, Manuel." I shouted angrily: "Man, they got me on hold." The officer stared at his watch and signaled with his hand that I had five minutes. My response to him was cut short by words issuing from the receiver.

"Hello, is this Ian?"

"Yes."

I was moved by the calm friendliness of the voice: "This is Bryan Stevenson, how are you?"

The first words out of my mouth weren't about his letter, the law, or lawyers, but about the song I had just heard.

"I'm fine. Was that Corrine Rae Bailey I was listening to while on hold?" Mr. Stevenson corrected me in a sweet,

fatherly way: "Ahh, Corinne Bailey Rae. She's quite a talented artist. How do you know of her?"

"I read about her in a magazine recently," I replied. I wanted a connection with this man beyond the fickle attorney-client relationships I was used to. I asked him about the letter he had sent. Was he serious about assigning attorneys to my case? He assured me that he was. He asked me a few questions: How old was I when I committed the crime? Did I currently have an attorney? By now the lieutenant was banging on the window and yelling: "Time's up, Manuel. Time's up."

"The officer is saying I have to go."

"Don't worry. EJI attorneys will visit you in the next couple weeks."

"You promise?"

I was so used to being disappointed and lied to by lawyers I was desperate for confirmation before hanging up.

"I promise."

ONE THING ABOUT BRYAN STEVENSON: HE IS A MAN OF his word; when he tells you he is going to do something, he follows through. A couple of weeks after I spoke to him on the phone, two young lawyers, Rachel Germany and Irene Joe, flew down from Alabama to see me. Rachel, a light-skinned black graduate of NYU Law School, hailed from Brooklyn. Darker-skinned Irene was from Houston by way of Nigeria. Both were committed warriors against racial injustice. They told me they couldn't make me any promises. They sought to get the measure of me by verifying my age when I committed my offense and inquiring about its circumstances. Equal Justice Initiative, it appeared, was interested in representing me because I was so young when

I was sentenced to life without the possibility of parole and because the crime I had committed was nonhomicidal. Rachel and Irene would report to Bryan, and if EJI decided to take on my case, they would be back with a retainer for me to sign.

They returned with a photographer in tow. You have to understand that for years I had not seen myself; mirrors were not a luxury afforded me in prison. I was eager to see how I looked and wondered whether I would recognize myself in the photos. I asked EJI for copies to send to distant family and acquaintances as proof that I was still alive.

Equal Justice Initiative sought to base its case on the unconstitutionality of cruel, and unusual punishment, which it hoped to argue before the U.S. Supreme Court—success being a long shot, hinging on a Hail Mary pass, as I saw it. Jailhouse lawyer that I thought I was, I at first quibbled with their strategy. I had spent nearly a decade and a half dealing in Florida state courts. EJI seemed intent on creating new law, which I thought would fall on deaf ears in the state. I wanted them to engage Florida law already on the books and argue manifest injustice in my case. Manifest injustice refers to an unfairness shocking to conscience, an unfairness that is direct, obvious, and observable. I wanted EJI to argue that my original plea of guilty was not knowingly and voluntarily given, that there had never been a competency hearing. On February 22, 1991, my lawyer had told the judge that there were aspects of my background that called my competency to stand trial into question. According to the law, if a defendant's competency is questioned before the court, the judge must order an evaluation, which he did in my case. But the judge did not hold a hearing to determine my competency as required. Two psychiatrists did in fact

examine me and said I was fit, even as they called me a sociopath—but not in an open hearing with a declaration by the judge.

The suitability of adult sanctions imposed on me was also questionable. There is to this day a Florida law that says a child of any age indicted for a life-or-death felony shall be treated in every respect as if he were an adult. There are criteria that a juvenile must meet to be sanctioned as an adult; the judge cannot simply serve up conclusionary language, offering no specific evidence related to the criteria for transferring a juvenile to adult dominion. The judge in my case did precisely that. It should be noted that Florida tries more children as adults than any other state. As an "issue commentary" of the James Madison Institute states: "Florida prosecutors have virtually unfettered discretion to decide which children to try as adults. While Florida law authorizes 'judicial waiver' [a court hearing to determine whether a child should be tried as an adult], more than 98 percent of children tried as adults are 'direct filed' in adult court by prosecutors—with no hearing, due process, oversight, or input from a judge."[1]

THE MIDDLE-AGED BLACK MAN SITTING ON THE OTHER side of the Plexiglas barrier was there to save my life. He wore a gray suit and reddish tie. He was serene and soft-spoken. His manner was professorial. On my side I sat hand-cuffed, shackled, waist-chained. My blue prison uniform hung loosely from my body. Years of malnutrition and blood loss from cutting gave me the look of a concentration camp survivor. Bryan Stevenson was visiting to connect with me human to human and explain how his legal strategy applied to my case, gently disabusing me of my legal presumptuous-

ness. In 2005 the U.S. Supreme Court had acknowledged the fundamental differences between children and adults, and had determined that children could not be subjected to the death penalty because of the Eighth Amendment, which forbids cruel and unusual punishment. As Bryan would write in *Just Mercy,* "My staff and I discussed how we might use the constitutional reasoning that banned the execution of children as a legal basis for challenging juvenile life-without-parole sentences."[2] He would file cases in Alabama, Arkansas, California, Delaware, Florida (mine), Iowa, Michigan, Mississippi, Missouri, Nebraska, North Carolina, Pennsylvania, South Dakota, and Wisconsin. Were any of these cases to reach the Supreme Court, resulting in a favorable ruling, juvenile life-without-parole sentences would be overturned. Bryan promised to stay in touch and send me copies of the amicus briefs filed in support of Equal Justice Initiative—prominent individuals and organizations felt what had been done to us as kids was wrong and should be corrected.

During the visit I told Bryan how in 2007 I had fallen in love with poetry and how it sustained me. Writing poetry had become a routine for me; I would spend four to five hours a day at it. Sometimes words to etch a situation would come swiftly; at other times I would struggle to find the right ones. No matter, for in either case I lived in my imagination, at once far away from and deep within the brutal realities of my condition. I found the practice healing, therapeutic—and profitable. Fellow inmates paid me to write poems for them to send to their families and lovers. As our visit ended, I asked Bryan if he would accept a gift of poetry. He said sure. I flipped through the stack of handwritten poems I had before me, searching for four I regarded as my best at the

time: "Genie in a Bottle," "Pound Puppy," "Yes We Did," and "Uncried Tears." Bryan honored me by including the last of these in his book *Just Mercy*:

Imagine teardrops left uncried
From pain trapped inside
Waiting to escape
Through the windows of your eyes

"Why won't you let us out?"
The tears question the conscience
"Relinquish your fears and doubts
And heal yourself in the process."

The conscience told the tears
"I know you really want me to cry
But if I release you from bondage,
In gaining your freedom you die."

The tears gave it some thought
Before giving the conscience an answer
"If crying brings you to triumph
Then dying's not such a disaster."

THERE IS AN MSNBC DOCUMENTARY CALLED *LOCKUP: Inside Florida and Santa Rosa Correctional Institution.*[3] At the beginning a deep voiceover intones: "There are more than 102,000 men and women doing time in the Florida State Prison system. Of the fifty-six state prisons for men, one is considered the end of the line, the place male inmates go when other prisons can't handle them. The Santa Rosa Correctional Institution, located on Florida's panhandle."

Inmates there are considered "the worst of the worst." If you engaged in cutting, seeking attention or special treatment, for instance, corrections officers simply ignored you. As one guard put it, Santa Rosa inmates are there because of "their repeated disciplinary reports in the department, their disruption of institutions throughout the state, their disobeying orders from staff, their non-receptiveness to the correctional process as a whole." I was transferred from Union Correctional Institution to Santa Rosa in the fall of 2007, when I was thirty years old.

SOMETIME IN 2008 MY BROTHER SEAN CALLED SANTA Rosa prison from the hospital in Tampa. At first the prison refused to allow me to accept the call, but Colonel Barnes, whom I had known at Union, relented. Sean announced that he was dying; he didn't have long to live. I implored him to be strong. He said he was trying, but he was too far gone. His heart was a disaster. I asked whether he had inherited his disease, fearing that I myself might one day succumb to it: "Man, you dyin' kinda early; do I have to worry about this?" He said no; he had quickened his demise by abusing alcohol and drugs. I would be fine, he insisted, because I was in prison and didn't suffer from his addictions. Before he died I talked to him twice. I wrote a poem for him called "While There's Still Time," which I read over the phone. I forgave him for not supporting me during my incarceration. I vaguely alluded to what he had done to me as a child, and I forgave him that as well. While there was still time, I wanted to assure him I harbored no ill will. I wanted him to die in peace. Aunt Kathy would later read my poem at his funeral.

9

I REMAINED AT UNION FROM SEPTEMBER TO DECEMBER 2008, before being sent back to Santa Rosa. The psychiatric team at Union in charge of evaluating me—including my therapist and counselor during my previous stint there—came to the conclusion that I was fine, far from insane. "You ain't crazy. Your ass is going back to Santa Rosa," they said, even though it was not until November that they removed my spit shield—a contraption that looks like a cross between a surgical mask and a beekeeper's hat without the crown—which I had been wearing when I stepped off the van from Santa Rosa. I had never spat at anyone in my life; the spit shield was meant simply to debase and humiliate me into subservience.

THE EQUAL JUSTICE INITIATIVE HAD INTELLIGENCE THAT I was struggling, that things were not right with me. So—in addition to sending me canteen money for necessities—Bryan Stevenson assigned a social worker to assess my needs and provide constant support. On October 22, 2008, Maria Morrison entered my life; she came to Union Correctional Institution to visit me (she had recently joined EJI to manage clinical and therapeutic services for incarcerated clients as well as for formerly incarcerated people and their

families). Her sister Charlotte was a Rhodes Scholar and had been at EJI since 2000; she was now a senior attorney there. Maria is herself brilliant and well read, and at the time had already earned three academic degrees. When we first met at Union we were allotted the customary two hours to talk, but I barely lasted one and a half, even though I was struck by Maria's uncanny attentiveness. I was in severe physical distress: through the spit shield my breathing was laborious; my hands were cuffed behind my back instead of in front of me, common practice allowing an inmate to take notes or sign documents during a legal visit; the chains constricting my body were so tight they cut into my kidneys. I was constantly shifting from one uncomfortable position to another. Empathizing with my anguish—appalled by my condition—Maria at one point tried to snatch the spit shield from my head, but instinctually I leaned back, preventing what would have been deemed a breach of security, possibly barring her from ever visiting me again. I excused myself by saying I had to go to the bathroom, but not before imploring her to promise that she would visit me again.

Maria returned to Union at least once a month, and we wrote to each other often. My decades-long ordeal had led me to construct nearly impenetrable defenses against the abuses of prison life, but, more important, against the notion of vulnerability. It had become impossible for me to trust anyone. Maria from the start seemed able to navigate around some of those defenses. She encouraged me, through building a connection with her to care about myself and others. In Maria I found the reliable compassion that I had been missing all my life.

Maria's dedication to me was unswerving, even though it sometimes invited snarky, sexist comments from prison staff.

This occasional unpleasantness did not deter her. She was always clear and insistent about two things: she accepted me just as I was; and she would be there consistently for me, as long as I needed her. To be clear, her acceptance did not mean we didn't argue. Maria regularly reminded me I did have something to lose now—I had a legal team who cared about me and were working to overturn my sentence. And she encouraged me to "always keep your long-term goals at the front of your mind, Ian." Over the next five years, she dutifully copied by hand sections of a GED prep book and mailed them to me to study. Of the four sections of the exam—social studies, mathematical reasoning, science, and reasoning through language arts—mathematical reasoning was my weakest subject. She sent me sample exams to study and was relentless in her instruction. Together we read and discussed books that a high school student might read, such as George Orwell's *Animal Farm* and Harper Lee's *To Kill a Mockingbird*.

Orwell's allegory about the rebellion of farm animals seeking equality against a totalitarian farmer spoke to me, especially the betrayal of the rebellion leading to the authoritarianism of the pig Napoleon. *To Kill a Mockingbird*—supposedly about racial injustice and the corruption of innocence—left me cold. I found it interminable. Atticus Finch was no hero to me; he was the paragon of a lawyer out for himself, a man of dubious integrity. I found the whole white-man-as-savior-of-black-man story objectionable in the extreme. Atticus to my mind was full of shit, like many of the lawyers I had tussled with. Maria's exposing me to a wide range of ideas, some of them conflicting, encouraged me to trust her, at first cautiously, then wholeheartedly.

I once begged Maria, while I was beginning to feel a need for spirituality in my life, a need for exploring the possibility of a larger meaning, to send me a popular psychology best-seller I had heard about (with forewords by Oprah Winfrey and Maya Angelou, no less), *The Seat of the Soul* by Gary Zukav; Jay-Z claimed it had made a difference in his life while improving his relationship with Oprah. I was a convert, or so I wanted to think, to its philosophy of the proper alignment of personality and the soul. The book became my Bible; time and again I repeated this passage whenever I confronted an especially onerous vicissitude of my condition: "Say to the universe, 'Find me and take me where you know I need to be.' Let go and trust that the universe will provide, and so it shall."

THREE YEARS EARLIER, IN 2005, IN RESPONSE TO *ROPER V. Simmons,*[1] the U.S. Supreme Court ruled that the Eighth and Fourteenth Amendments to the Constitution prohibited the death penalty for offenders who were younger than eighteen years of age when their crime was committed. Reaffirming the need to be informed by "the evolving standards of decency that mark the progress of a maturing society," Justice Anthony Kennedy, writing for the majority (Kennedy, Stephen Breyer, Ruth Bader Ginsburg, David Souter, and John Paul Stevens), stated: "When a juvenile offender commits a heinous crime, the State can exact forfeiture of some of the most basic liberties, but the State cannot extinguish his life and his potential to attain a mature understanding of his own humanity." The opinion added that "retribution is not proportional if the law's most severe penalty is imposed on one whose culpability or blameworthiness is diminished,

to a substantial degree, by reason of youth and immaturity." Chief Justice William Rehnquist and Justices Antonin Scalia, Clarence Thomas, and Sandra Day O'Connor dissented.

It was the *Roper v. Simmons* ruling that encouraged and emboldened Bryan Stevenson and the Equal Justice Initiative to embark on a nationwide litigation project against the cruel and unusual punishment of juveniles sentenced to life without the possibility of parole—a righteous campaign against their death in prison, which was tantamount to the imposition of the death penalty. According to EJI, at the time there were only eight people in the world serving life without parole for crimes committed when they were thirteen, and all eight were in the United States. Only two had committed nonhomicide offenses, and both were inmates in Florida. Both had already spent more than half their lives behind bars: Joe Sullivan and me.

IN 1989 JOE, A SERIOUSLY MENTALLY DISABLED THIRTEEN-year-old boy, had been lured by two older teenagers to join them in the burglary of a home in Pensacola. Later that day, someone raped a seventy-two-year-old woman there. Lena Bruner, the victim, who was blindfolded and beaten, testified that her assailant was "a colored boy"[2] who "had kinky hair and he was quite black and he was small." Joe admitted to the burglary but strongly denied the rape. DNA evidence that might have exonerated him was destroyed before his trial and was not even requested by his public defender. One of Joe's accomplices, the likely culprit, however, implicated him in the sexual battery in exchange for a light sentence in juvenile detention. In court proceedings that lasted less than a business day, Joe was tried and convicted by a six-person jury on five counts: two each for burglary and sexual bat-

tery, and one for grand theft. Having exhibited remarkable indifference and incompetence (he barely addressed the court), Joe's public defender was later barred from practicing law in Florida. Treated as an adult when he was thirteen because he had a criminal record, and sentenced to life in prison without the possibility of parole, Joe—now a thirty-three-year-old man wheelchair bound because of multiple sclerosis—was about to get his proper day in court after nearly a score of years of prison misery—as was I.

The Equal Justice Initiative's representation of me began in 2007 with the filing of a postconviction relief motion in the Thirteenth Judicial Circuit of Tampa—a so-called 3.850 pursuant to Florida's Rules of Criminal Procedure—which seeks to vacate, set aside, or correct a sentence through a "collateral attack." A collateral attack is an attempt to impeach or overturn a judgment with factors that are not in the court record of the original action—the court record itself being the basis of an appeal. A judgment may be challenged on these grounds: it violated the Constitution or laws of the United States or the state of Florida; the court lacked jurisdiction to impose the sentence; the sentence was above and beyond that which was authorized by law; and the plea was involuntary. A 3.850 had been filed on my behalf by my public defender in 1993, but it went nowhere, and the statute of limitations for doing so was two years, so we held out little hope for this EJI filing. The Thirteenth Circuit denied the motion and we appealed for a review of its decision to the Second District Court of Appeal. As my case languished there, two developments unfolded that would have a profound impact on my life.

The First District Court of Appeal in Florida dismissed EJI's appeal on Joe Sullivan's behalf with prejudice on

procedural grounds and argued that the *Roper* decision "established only one new constitutional right, the right for a juvenile not to be given the death penalty."[3] The court offered no opinion on the appeal, disallowing recourse to Florida's Supreme Court. Its decision dramatized a legal fact: it's easier to get a death penalty reviewed at all levels of the judiciary than it is a life sentence. In December 2008—around the time I was returned to Santa Rosa Correctional Institution—EJI filed a petition with the United States Supreme Court asking it to find Joe's sentence of death in prison for committing a nonhomicide crime when he was thirteen cruel and unusual. Florida's attorney general at the time, Bill McCollum, waived his right to respond to the petition, perhaps because he deemed it without merit. But on May 4, 2009, the U.S. Supreme Court miraculously (because such decisions are so rare) agreed to hear not only *Sullivan v. Florida* but also *Graham v. Florida,* a case filed by Bryan S. Gowdy, an attorney unaffiliated with EJI.

Terrance Graham, who suffered from attention-deficit/hyperactivity disorder, was the son of crack-addicted parents in Jacksonville and had led a troubled life. In 2003, when he was sixteen, he was charged as an accomplice in an armed burglary and attempted armed robbery of a barbecue restaurant. Terrance pled guilty and, because he had neither participated in the violence nor stolen money, he was sentenced to one year of detention in a juvenile facility and three years' probation. In 2004 Graham was accused as a codefendant in a home invasion and of having held the robbery victim at gunpoint. Two years later, when he was nineteen, he was convicted of violating the terms of probation and was punished with Florida's maximum statutory penalty for the violation, life without parole. The First Dis-

trict Court of Appeal rejected Graham's challenge of his sentence's constitutionality under the Eighth Amendment, even as Florida's Supreme Court refused to review the case. So the stage was set for a historic day, May 4, 2009, when the United States Supreme Court would hear oral arguments for not only *Graham v. Florida* but *Sullivan v. Florida,* regarding the constitutionality of sentence at issue. Meantime, EJI filed and was granted a motion in the Second District Court of Appeal to stay the proceedings of my case until there was a ruling in either of the two relevant cases before the highest court in the land.

DISCIPLINE CONFINEMENT TIME STOPS WHEN YOU ARE IN a mental health dorm. You become, in effect, frozen in time, remaining in a solitary cell while never making progress toward being released back to open population, unless, of course, you reach the end of your sentence and are released directly to the street. Conditions in the mental health dorm at Santa Rosa had devolved from bad to worse in ways that defeated imagination, courting not only the absurd but the unconscionable.

An edict was issued for this dorm that directed officers to refrain from intervening in response to any form of self-injury. What ensued was horrible. Men in the dorm, suffering a range of mental health conditions in the worst possible settings, caused untold harm to themselves—and were left to bleed and suffer alone in their cells. The medical staff were directed to offer no anesthesia when stitching self-inflicted wounds.

"You didn't care about anesthesia when you were cutting yourself; the pain was good to you, wasn't it? So why now? Man up!" With consummate officiousness, the doctor who

barred me from Q dorm said: "Manuel, you're just an inmate like everybody else. You're not going to get any special treatment; you're going to have to work your way through CM, through level 1, level 2, and level 3." Did she know that I had been in solitary longer than anyone in the state? Did she know it began when I was fifteen? Did she know I had lost my entire family in that time? Did she know someone out there still loved me? That I was someone? I was someone.

I HAD HEARD THROUGH THE PRISON GRAPEVINE WHO would write back to you if you sent them a letter and who wouldn't. I had written to Florida's U.S. Senator Bill Nelson a couple of years before about my criminal case. He had responded that as a federal agent he could not involve himself in a state judicial matter. In February 2010 I learned that a Cuban dissident had died in prison after a long hunger strike protesting the government's violation of human rights. I decided to approach Senator Nelson anew from this angle. As I am not in possession of the letter I wrote, I'll paraphrase its contents. "Listen, I've been in solitary confinement since I was fifteen years old. I'm now thirty-three. I've been in here seventeen and a half years, and I'm starting to decompensate. The staff are allowing me to hurt myself and not doing anything about it. All I want is the opportunity to get treatment and be released from solitary confinement, man. This is unjust. I wrote you before, and you told me that you couldn't get involved in my criminal case. But what I'm writing about here is cruel and unusual punishment, a violation of the Eighth Amendment of the Constitution. I hope you can intervene in this matter."

Senator Nelson sent my correspondence to the head of Florida's Department of Corrections, who in turn contacted

the warden of Santa Rosa. The same doctor appeared outside my cell one day. She slid a document under my door—a
form authorizing release of medical and psychiatric information to Senator Nelson. She wanted me to check and initial only one box specifying something or other and sign at
the bottom. I refused. I was determined to check all boxes;
I wanted the senator to know everything about me—my
medical record, my psychiatric record, my dental record,
my HIV status. When I said as much to her, she demanded
the document back and walked away. Minutes later, the
warden, the assistant warden, the colonel, and the woman
approached my cell.

"Manuel, what's wrong with you, what's wrong with
you, man?" the warden asked and then continued: "I do
everything in my power, everything in my power to help
you, and this is what I get?"

"You do everything in your power to help me? What are
you talking about?"

"What are you writing to Senator Nelson for, telling him
all this shit about how nobody wants to help you? Huh?
Didn't you know you were about to be assigned to CM 3?"

"No. Since when?"

"You know, I wonder about you sometimes. And is there
a reason you told the doctor you weren't going to sign the
release?"

"I said I would if she allowed me to initial whatever I
wanted to initial and sign."

"Initial whatever, sign wherever, let's just get this over
with," the doctor chimed in, defeated.

The upshot was this: in a meeting room near Q dorm,
there was a huddle including the warden, the assistant warden, the prison's head of mental health, the Department of

Corrections's head of mental health (by phone), and me to chart my future. The powers that be intimated that they had done everything to break me, to make me conform, unsuccessfully, and were ready to try a different tack. They made me an offer I didn't refuse. In exchange for assuring doctors associated with the Department of Corrections at the state level that being in close management did not cause me to decompensate—in essence to say that I had lied to Senator Nelson—I would be discharged from the mental health unit, and if I breezed through CM 1, 2, and 3 in ninety days with good behavior, I would be placed in open population. Everything proceeded as planned, but after ninety days, the warden came to me to say that Tallahassee had had a change of mind.

"Ian, Tallahassee is not going for it. You've been raising hell for seventeen and a half years; ninety days of being clean is not going to do it. But here's what they're offering instead: a transfer to Suwannee. It's a brand-new prison and you'll get a fresh start there. Go there, be clean for ninety days, and they'll transfer you anywhere in the state you want to go."

In confidence, he went on, "Ian, in my twenty-five years of being an officer I have never seen an inmate write one letter and motherfuckers start jumping through hoops to please him. I don't know what you put in that letter or what you got goin' on, but you good!"

The prospect of being in open population after eighteen years of solitary confinement gave me a sliver of hope that I was closer than ever to going home, that one day I would walk out of my cell—no handcuffs, no shackles—and feel sunshine on my face.

. . .

THREE MONTHS AFTER MY LETTER TO SENATOR NELSON, and one week after the U.S. Supreme Court agreed to hear *Graham v. Florida* and *Sullivan v. Florida,* the following appeared in the *Tampa Bay Times*: "When he was 13 years old Ian Manuel shot a woman in the face in a botched robbery in Tampa. She lived and he got life. Manuel, now 33, has spent nearly all of his time in prison in solitary confinement, caught in an endless cycle of misbehavior and punishment. As Florida's longest-serving inmate in solitary, he has no work skills, no formal education and so much psychological damage that he once set himself on fire. People always assumed—whether he killed himself or died of old age—that Ian Manuel's death would happen behind bars. Not anymore. He may walk out of prison in the next year. The U.S. Supreme Court is considering two Florida cases that deal with the constitutionality of locking away children for life when they haven't killed someone. A favorable ruling in either case could result in Manuel's sentence being thrown out. Confronted with the possibility of his release, prison officials, who had kept Manuel as far away from civilization as they could, are scrambling to prepare him for life outside. And his attorneys are laying out a plan that will attempt to protect Manuel from a world he fears will present him with more choices than he can handle. 'The uncertainty out there makes me nervous,' he says, 'but I'm determined to succeed.'"[4]

In the run-up to oral arguments for *Sullivan v. Florida* and *Graham v. Florida* before the Supreme Court in the fall, members of the press started reaching out to me for local color and commentary. Among them was Meg Laughlin, the reporter from *The St. Petersburg Times* who had followed my case with determination and empathy since first

interviewing me in 2006, and had now ferociously braved prison bureaucracy to visit me. In 2010, even as tougher punishment for youth who had committed serious crimes was increasing, while mass incarceration was in full swing, there was intense focus nationwide on the pros and cons of sentencing youth whose offenses were nonhomicidal to life in prison without the possibility of parole. An editorial in *The New York Times,* published on the very day of oral arguments, November 9, staked out a progressive position. With respect to Joe Sullivan and Terrance Graham, the *Times* concluded: "These were two very troubled children in need of adult supervision and perhaps even time behind bars. But it is insupportable to conclude, as the courts did, that children who committed crimes when they were so young were beyond rehabilitation. The laws under which they were convicted violate current human rights standards and the Constitution."[5] I wondered whether victory for either Joe or Terrance would be a victory for the child I had been—and what precisely that would mean.

WHEN THE SUPREME COURT HAS MORE THAN ONE CASE concerned with the same matter, it will often choose only one to adjudicate or will conjoin them for a single ruling. Regarding *Sullivan v. Florida* and *Graham v. Florida,* the court decided to rule on each case separately—perhaps a concession to its ideological factions—giving rise to the possibility of different outcomes with different consequences for inmates like me. On May 17, 2010, it handed down its judgments. With respect to *Sullivan,* it took a decision that was no decision, affirming the conclusion of the First District Court of Appeal of Florida: "The writ of a certiorari is dismissed as improvidently granted."[6] Translation: having

agreed to hear the case, the court declined to rule on it—largely because, as Justice Ginsburg had intimated during oral arguments, the challenge to the Eighth Amendment had come too late, after the statute of limitation in Florida had expired, and because there seemed to have been a disagreement about *Roper v. Simmons*: was the death penalty "different" from "life without the possibility of parole," as Justice Scalia maintained?

The disposition of *Graham* was an altogether different matter. The court was clear, voting 6 to 3 for Terrance Graham; Justices Antonin Scalia, Samuel Alito, and Clarence Thomas dissented. Justice Kennedy announced the opinion of the majority: "The limited culpability of juvenile non-homicide offenders and the severity of life without parole sentences all lead to the conclusion that the sentencing practice under consideration is cruel and unusual. This court now holds that for a juvenile offender who did not commit homicide the Eighth Amendment forbids the sentence of life without parole. . . . The state need not guarantee eventual freedom to juveniles convicted of nonhomicide crimes, but it must give them some meaningful opportunity to obtain release based on demonstrated maturity and rehabilitation."[7] In his dissent Justice Thomas upbraided the majority for, as he saw it, substituting its own moral judgment for that of the American people. The man who had replaced Thurgood Marshall on the Supreme Court deemed this ruling "a mistake" that he hoped would one day be struck down.

The ruling in *Graham v. Florida* held out hope of remedy for 129 inmates across the country who, as juveniles, had been sentenced to life without parole for nonhomicide crimes—77 of whom were imprisoned in Florida, like Joe

Sullivan and myself. But not only did the Supreme Court not guarantee freedom but the ruling stated: "It is for the states in the first instance to explore the means and mechanisms for compliance [with its decision]."[8] Who would determine what "meaningful opportunity to obtain release" meant? Who would assess whether "maturity and rehabilitation" had been achieved? My fate was far from certain.

"IT'S OVER! IT'S OVER! I'M OUTTA HERE," I KEPT SHOUTING with giddy excitement as I paced back and forth in my cell on the day of the Supreme Court's decision regarding Terrance Graham and Joe Sullivan. I was in confinement in, I believe, dorm C at Santa Rosa. I owned a radio that I had somehow bought and managed to smuggle into my cell. I was an avid fan of National Public Radio then—the guards being none the wiser because I would listen stealthily through headphones.

At around one o'clock on May 17, 2010, on whatever NPR show was coming on, there was an announcement of the top stories that day and out of the blue I thought I heard "in a six to three decision, the U.S. Supreme Court overturned life sentences for juveniles"—or something like that. My mind raced. Jesus Christ! Could I really have heard that? The fleetingness of the announcement was frustrating beyond belief. I had to wait half an hour—the longest thirty minutes of my life—for an update. Now here it was: in a 5–4 decision, the U.S. Supreme Court has agreed to overturn all life sentences for juveniles who committed nonhomicide crimes. Still, only at five o'clock did a journalist analyze the decision and what it meant. The discrepancy between 6–3 and 5–4 apparently had to do with Chief Justice Roberts:

even though he had written an opinion concurring with the majority—he deemed Graham's punishment to be disproportionate to his crime—he thought the court's categorical ban of life without parole for nonhomicide crimes committed by juveniles overly broad and argued that such cases should be adjudicated individually.

About a week later I got a call from EJI. Maria and Alicia D'Addario, a lawyer assigned to Joe Sullivan's case, were ecstatic to assure me that the *Graham* decision applied to me and that I should expect to be resentenced soon. They congratulated me richly. The Equal Justice Initiative appealed to the Second District Court of Appeal to have the *Graham* ruling control my case.

By September 2010, I had not been charged with a single disciplinary report since February; I was determined to stay on the straight and narrow to comply with the Santa Rosa warden's stipulation that if I kept my nose clean I would be transferred to Suwannee, the new prison, where, if I continued to conform to expectations, I would earn the right to be sent to a prison of my choice. Suwannee was at first all I imagined it would be; it was a good camp where abuse of power was not a constant theme. The warden there was getting ready to retire the following year and wanted to keep things on an even keel. His attitude was "Let's run this place exactly how it's supposed to be run, so we won't have no problems."

DURING THOSE THREE MONTHS, AS I FOCUSED INTENSELY on making sure I remained disciplinary-report-free, something happened that nearly derailed my hopes. It concerned, of all things, poetry. When I arrived at Suwannee, I was given a job as an orderly. I passed out food trays, cleaned

the dormitory—chores like that. I was on the least restrictive level of control management. I was assigned to meet with a therapist monthly while at Suwannee. Therapy relationships in prison are not what they are in the free world. You are asked to share your deepest feelings and thoughts with someone who reports to the administration tasked with imprisoning you. Letting your guard down can lead to punishment, as I was reminded during this time of change and hope in my life. Beginning to imagine my life ahead of me, my hopes for all the things we all hope for—a home, fulfilling work, security, love—I was writing a lot of poetry. Lulled into a sense of comfort with my therapist, I shared one of my poems with her. Moved by the poem, she asked if she could have a copy of the poem, and I gave her my clean draft. My therapist shared the poem with her supervisor, who came by herself to see me a few days later.

"Ian, what are you doing? You're about to get off CM; you can't be writing poems to my staff."

"What? What are you talking about?"

"The poem you wrote can be considered an attempt to establish a personal relationship with a staff member. You know what that means—sixty days in confinement—don't you? If I write you up, you won't be getting off CM anytime soon. Tell me why you did this."

I didn't think I had done anything wrong; in my mind the poem was just one of many I had written. I do find it curious that, as strong as my memory is, I don't remember the title of the poem nor do I know it by heart as I do so much of my writing. Perhaps I was too distracted by the trouble the poem stirred up to take the time to memorize it. The hoopla over the poem—the warden was apprised of it—happened in late October or early November, ten days or so before I

was to appear before the CM review board. I was haunted by my past: every time I had been on the verge of getting off CM, something would happen that would prevent me from getting off. Oh shit, I thought. Not again?

Sitting before the CM review board, I heard for the first time in eighteen years, "Ian, we're releasing you to open population." My therapist and her supervisor had declined to make a ruckus about what I had written. I couldn't believe the words I had just heard. Was I dreaming? Had my mind finally yielded to a fantasy? Do you know what it's like to wait on something for so long you think it will never happen—and then it does all of a sudden? I grew increasingly nervous; I was desperate to get to the compound to prove to myself that life in open population was indeed my new reality. But procedures had to be followed before I got there.

After the CM review board hands down its decision, you are visited by a state classification officer, who has the power to approve, modify, or deny the board's decision. So if the CM board had, for instance, decided to send me back to CM 2, the state classification officer could have said no, let's keep him on CM 3. He is the final arbiter 95 percent of the time. The officer eventually made his rounds, stopping by the cell door of each inmate who had appeared before the CM board during the past week. Getting off CM means that you have the right to be transferred to a prison of your choice for good adjustment. When the official reached my cell door, he inquired where I wanted to go. He ran down a list of institutions; I chose Everglades CI, near Miami, because I didn't like the sound of some of the other available prisons.

. . .

A COUPLE DAYS LATER, SOMETIME BETWEEN EIGHT AND nine o'clock in the morning, there was a knock on my door. It was the dorm's lieutenant.

"Hey, Manuel, get up and get dressed; somebody wants to talk to you."

I do as I'm told and walk out of my cell—because I'm on CM 3, I'm allowed to leave my cell unshackled as long as I remain in the dormitory. But the lieutenant escorts me downstairs leading to the quad's front door (you are not supposed to go beyond the front door without being hand-cuffed and shackled if you are a CM inmate). I recall the walk to the chapel in 1996—nearly fifteen years earlier—when I was told that my mom had died. I have no one else to lose now: not only my mother but both my grandmothers, my brother, and my father are all dead.

"Where are we going?"

"Somebody wants to talk to you."

I find myself in the warden's office. He is there and so is the assistant warden.

"Ian, congratulations! You did it, you got off CM. The classification officer has signed your papers. But we had to stop your transfer to Everglades CI. We're gonna keep you here with us on the compound."

"Whoa, hold up, hold up! That ain't the deal I was prom-ised. I appreciate everything y'all done for me. Thanks very much and all that, but I was told that if I did three months on CM 3 at Santa Rosa clean, I would be transferred here; if I did three more months clean at Suwannee, I'd get to pick whatever prison I wanted to go to. I was gonna choose someplace close to home. The classification officer didn't seem to know anything about that deal, so I chose the best option from the prisons he listed."

"You're from Tampa and that ain't nowhere close to Miami. We're gonna keep you here, which is closer to Tampa, and if you do three more months here clean in open population we'll transfer you to wherever you wanna go."

"All right, man."

I now understand the bait and switch to be a Department of Corrections modus operandi, but what choice do I have? They order me back to CM dorm to pack my stuff. They release me after lunch when count clears.

MY VERY FIRST REACTION TO BEING IN OPEN POPULATION was nothing I could have anticipated. As soon as my ID was activated, I bum-rushed the canteen, intending to eat in a single day all kinds of foodstuff I had been denied for twenty years, from honey buns to little microwavable chicken sandwiches. My canteen account had grown: most of my money—in addition to the money Maria sent every month—was from strangers who had read Meg Laughlin's article about me, sympathized with my plight, and wanted to keep in touch. You weren't allowed to spend more than sixty-five dollars per week in the canteen, but with the holiday season approaching another ten dollars was added to the limit. I was overwhelmed by the kaleidoscope of provisions. I wanted everything.

"How much are those Ritz crackers?"

"That's expensive shit, man, two dollars and twenty-five cents. Nobody buys them."

"Well, I'm going to."

At the dorm assigned to me—half of which was reserved for inmates in open population and half for inmates in confinement—I met Detroit, an old-school player, a sharp inmate with a seriously messed-up eye who had just come

back from court, where he was suing the Department of Corrections for what had happened to him at Florida State Prison. Power had gone out; the place had gone dark. In the belief that the prison's cameras were disabled, guards had jumped Detroit and beaten him to a pulp. But it turned out that the cameras were working fine; the prison had a backup generator. Detroit promised to look out for me and show me the ropes in open population—a blessing, for the scene had to have changed in the twenty years since I was last in it. At first blush my early days in open population were a blur of gambling, dreadful poker player that I was. I got back into Georgia skin, while betting on football and baseball. Directly, Detroit taught me something about spending money that I still remember to this day: everything going out and nothing coming in equals zero.

One day he and I were coming back from chow, and as we passed the captain's office near our dormitory, someone in it who had been trying to start a basketball league for inmates asked Detroit if he wanted to be the compound's "basketball commissioner." Detroit said no, leaving an opening for me brashly to volunteer. "Shit, I'll do it." I had no idea what I had signed up for, even what the first steps should be. Detroit helped me to build the league and organize a tournament; he was my bracket man. We went from dorm to dorm to let everybody know that teams needed to be formed and named. The Miami Heat—of K or L dorm—proved to be the best. I assigned a time and a scorekeeper—and even someone to sweep the basketball court.

What I appreciated most about my job was the freedom of movement it allowed. I remember shouting a Lil Wayne lyric as I strolled the compound: "I'm so official all I need is a whistle." Some inmates would tease me: "You

already have a whistle, commissioner," referring to the one that proudly hung from my neck. Sometimes even officers would get in on the act: "Ain't no game today, so why you walkin' around with that whistle?" The whistle became my talisman; it made me feel important, more consequential than ever before.

IN LATE NOVEMBER, I WAS TOLD TO PACK UP MY BELONG-ings; I would be going to Tampa. I was immediately elated, imagining that I might be headed home at last. But then I was informed that, because the Second District Court of Appeal had handed down its opinion that the *Graham* ruling applied to my case, and assuming I was still represented by a public defender, a judge in Tampa had taken it upon himself to act on the opinion and had summoned me for resentencing. The county sheriff came to Suwannee to pick me up for the two- to three-hour drive. As the van entered my city and I stared out the window, I grew misty-eyed, recalling my early years and the disappointment of my resentencing hearing in 2000. I was placed in solitary confinement again, albeit temporarily, first in Orient Road Jail, then in Falken-burg Road—Tampa had a policy that any inmate with more than a twenty-year sentence had to be so housed. These fast-breaking developments came as a surprise to me and EJI. I was allowed to call Maria and my auntie to let them know where I was. Mark Shapiro, my EJI attorney, flew down to represent me.

At the resentencing hearing Florida's attorney general dropped a bombshell: he would appeal to the state's Supreme Court to review the Second District Court of Appeal's rul-ing, which, he argued, should have had nothing to do with me. The attorney general maintained that the *Graham* case

concerned only juveniles who had committed nonhomicide offenses. I, he insisted nonsensically, had been charged with attempted murder, which falls under the homicide statute. To put it kindly, his position was a stretch, lacking legal basis. Everyone in the courtroom was shocked by his brazen bullshit for the sake of vindictiveness, his foolish wrangling with a decision handed down by the U.S. Supreme Court as the law of the land. I was in solitary confinement again from late November to right after Christmas—peak holiday season—which darkened my mood. I grew bitter, resentful of the state's petty vendetta against me. I was hauled back to Suwannee to await the Florida Supreme Court's ruling.

IN MAY 2011 THE FLORIDA SUPREME COURT REFUSED TO hear the case; in October the U.S. Supreme Court followed suit. But by then Suwannee had changed. A new warden was in charge—a short, bald-headed man who looked like a poster boy for Ku Klux Klan membership, and whose clear mission was to make the lives of inmates as miserable as possible. He instituted the infamous 5:00 a.m. to 5:00 p.m. rule: you had to be up and dressed by 5:00 a.m., your bed made with strict precision; you could lie down only after 5:00 p.m.; if you were caught awake or asleep in bed during those twelve hours, you would be gassed and stripped for seventy-two hours. He shut the basketball league down, depriving inmates of something to do and me of whatever sense of personal power I had cultivated in open population. A terrifying pall fell over the place. Guys with nothing to do took to drugs, especially K2, a dangerous synthetic cannabinoid, which induced, among other side effects, paranoia, psychosis, and hallucinations. Corrections officers would seize the slimmest justification to search your cell, flinging

your belongings about like so much refuse to emphasize your worthlessness. You could smell fear in Suwannee now, as violence against prisoners ramped up.

One incident captures the sickening atmosphere of the place. A hulking officer—about six four and 250 pounds—was walking a little white inmate—about five three and 125 pounds—to the shower for having gotten into a heated argument with his black cellmate. Because the officer's charge was rotating his wrists as if he were trying to get out of his handcuffs, the officer lifted him up and threw him facedown into concrete, splitting his skull. Blood shot out of the inmate's head, his nose, and his mouth. I saw this with my own eyes. Black inmates nearby started laughing, which pissed me off. I went to my cell door and screamed:

"What the fuck are y'all laughing at? Because he white? What he do to him he'll do to y'all. He turned blue just like y'all will." If I had been introduced to prison life then and there, I don't know what would have become of me.

"WHICH ONE OF YOU IS MANUEL?" THE MUSCULAR BLACK deputy in white shirt and green slacks with a black stripe running down the leg asked as he looked into the holding cell. There were only two of us in it: Cedric from Tampa Park and me. Even two decades later I recognized Cedric from my childhood days in Central Park. Back then he was tall for his age, slim, light-skinned, a pretty boy with deep waves who was popular with girls. Now he was in a holding cell awaiting an evidentiary hearing seeking DNA testing for an offense he swore he didn't commit. I, a thirty-four-year-old man who had spent twenty-one years in prison, was about to witness a courtroom battle between EJI and the state of Florida to determine whether I was a redeemable human

being (deserving of a future) who had made amends for a nonhomicide crime he had committed as a thirteen-year-old child. In short, on December 9, 2011, I was in Tampa yet again for a resentencing hearing during Christmas season, this time to learn how the *Graham* case affected my own.

"Good luck, boy," Cedric said.

"'Preciate it." I nodded.

The deputy escorted me to the courtroom. I shuffled in my shackles past a window to the right offering a view of downtown Tampa, where I had committed my offense, and a fire department where, as an excited and frightened six-year-old, I had slid down the pole on a school visit. A vision snapped me out of my reverie: I recognized the judge who had presided at my failed hearing in 2000, William Fuente, darting out of one room and into another. As I entered the courtroom, I saw—in addition to my EJI attorneys, Tatiana Bertsch and Ben Schaefer—Aunt Kathy and Lynn, my mother's closest friends, and "Cousin" Anthony there to lend support. There, too, was Debbie Baigrie, with whom I had been out of touch for more than a decade. Tatiana and Ben had reached out to her, and she had agreed to be present. As Tatiana would later put it to the judge: "[Debbie] did want us to relay to you that she is in support of Mr. Manuel's immediate release with the understanding that his immediate release isn't possible today because he is serving the forty-year sentence and that will remain after today."

"All rise,"[1] the bailiff shouted, as Judge William Fuente emerged from his chamber. Tatiana made a valiant case on my behalf, accounting for my troubled childhood and tumultuous decades of imprisonment and, most important, the progress I had made (how I welcome structure and consistency): "Mr. Manuel sort of defies what the prediction

might be for someone who has been in isolation for that long because he has responded so well. And he is—in terms of a window of how he would do transitioning into the free world, his transition into open population has been tremendously positive. He has also received some recognition for his writing. He writes poetry, and he's gotten two certificates at the prison for his writing and was also asked to read a poem. Recently, he received a certificate for organizing a basketball league at the prison—sort of a league; but yes, organizing the team activities. He is very, very interested in pursuing his education upon release, and we are in a position to support that."

I spoke up for myself by reading from a prepared statement: "Your Honor, I sit before you today as a grown man and respectfully request my release. I served twenty-one consecutive years for crimes that I wish were never committed. It is my hope that you reach the conclusion that retribution has been served not just in years of incarceration but in losses incurred during this painful experience, the loss of my mother, brother, father, grandmothers, and every immediate family member I had. But through it all I never lost the audacity of hope or the ability to dream and continue to cling to faith as microscopic as a mustard seed that I must one day be free. My sitting before you today under these miraculous circumstances is fruition of that faith. It's not too late for me to be what I might have been, Your Honor. I ask for the opportunity to become it."

For his part, representing Florida, Assistant State Attorney Thomas Dickerhoof sought to paint me as a hopeless sociopath who at thirteen had been diagnosed with antisocial personality disorder, a diagnosis that still obtained, as he would have it: "According to the DSM-IV, the symptoms

of antisocial personality disorder include long-standing pattern of disregard for the rights of others. There is a failure to conform to society's norms and expectations that often results in numerous arrests for legal involvement as well as a history of deceitfulness where the individual attempts to con people or use trickery for personal property. Impulsiveness is often present, including angry outbursts, failure to consider consequences of behavior, irritability, and/or physical assault, all of which he's demonstrated while he's been incarcerated in prison." Dickerhoof argued for a seventy-five-year sentence to run consecutively with the forty years I was already serving, which meant that with full credit for "gain time" I had already earned and would continue to earn, I would be released in thirteen years. Tatiana argued for twenty-seven to forty years to run concurrently with the sentence I was serving, which with "gain time" would have resulted in a much earlier release date.

After listening to Tatiana's declaration that my "remorse is also part of healthy maturation," Judge Fuente looked down at her and said something that led me to believe I would not be going home anytime soon: "You all know even back in 1990 pursuant to Chapter 921 the Legislature told Courts that the primary purpose of sentencing is to punish, not to rehabilitate." With that he disappeared into his chamber. While he was gone Tatiana, Ben, and I talked legal strategy. I wanted to know whether EJI would appeal any sentence that was excessive. I told Tatiana and Ben I didn't think Judge Fuente would announce a consecutive sentence because I thought I heard him cite a precedent. They advised me not to be so sure. There was a lull among us. I turned to look at Debbie. I saw compassion in her eyes.

After a half hour or so, Judge Fuente emerged from his

chamber and got right down to business: "I've taken all these matters [comments of counsel, comments of Mr. Manuel, the Defense Counsel's social worker report, the State's Sentencing Memorandum, the 1991 Presentence Investigation, his psychological assessment before sentencing, etc.] into consideration. So the sentence will be as follows. Mr. Manuel, I'll sentence you to sixty-five years in Florida State Prison. Each count to be served concurrently with the other. Each sentence to be followed by two years of community control. Each sentence to be followed by ten years of probation. All standard conditions apply. The one special condition is you participate in the PREP program suggested by Defense Counsel. Since the crime happened in 1990 I'll give you twenty-two years credit against these new sentences. He is entitled to an appeal. He has thirty days to do so."

The bailiff grabbed my arm and led me back to the holding cell, where my mind, addled by crushed expectations, dwelled on what had just happened.

A FEW HOURS LATER I WAS DRIVEN BACK TO FALKENBURG Road Jail and led directly to my confinement cell in housing unit 1. I grabbed my Walkman and tuned it to Q105 FM. I was half-expecting to hear my current favorite song, "Someone Like You" by Adele—it was in heavy rotation at the time. I sat on my bunk and started frantically jotting down notes to discuss with my legal team, who had promised to stop by that evening before heading back to Alabama.

"Manuel!" I heard my name called from the intercom in the cell.

"Yeah."

"Get dressed, you got a pro visit."

A pro visit simply meant a legal visit. As I stood up the

first chords of the song I had been waiting for came on. "I heard that you're settled down." I scribbled the lyrics of "Someone Like You" on my legal pad and waited for my escort. Falkenburg Road Jail is huge. It's larger than any prison I've been held in. At no other prison did you need a golf cart to get around. The deputy soon arrived to chain and shackle me up. Once we exited the quad he loaded me onto the back of a caged golf cart and drove toward the legal visiting area at the front of the jail. Tatiana, Ben, and Maria had already assembled in a tiny room. Tatiana, whom I now called Ta-Ta, told me that, according to her calculations, my sixty-five-year sentence with credit for gain time for good behavior meant that I would be out in seven or eight years. I was not good at math, but I knew she was being wildly optimistic. All the same, I appreciated her trying to keep my spirits up. I went through my list of issues to raise, possible grounds for appeal.

"The judge sentenced me to sixty-five years for both the robbery and attempted murder. The max he could give me for the attempted murder was forty years. So is my new sentence illegal?"

"Are you sure, Ian?" Tatiana asked. "I thought I heard him say forty."

"Yes, I'm sure. He was so anxious to railroad me he messed up again."

"We'll take a look when we get the transcripts. But if that's accurate that's definitely grounds for a reversal."

We had talked for about an hour when Tatiana reached across the table and pointed to an item on my list I had not discussed and had crossed out, the lyrics of "Someone Like You."

"Ian, are you a fan?" I couldn't quite make out her tone.

I glanced at Maria and asked if she had remembered to bring Adele's *21* CD, which I had begged her for, and the pair of Nike Air Max shoes that Mrs. Cooper, an old Christian lady, had sent after reading about me in the newspaper and that I had never gotten to wear. I must have assumed when I made my request that after the hearing I would be leaving with everyone for Alabama.

"Yes, it and the shoes."

The seemingly ordinary exchange slammed me to the core. I felt the full impact of the demolition of my dream of early release. And I did something I don't do. I cried. Full of compassion, Maria wrapped her arms around me as I sobbed. She whispered:

"It's different this time, Ian."

She was reassuring me I was not alone as I had been in 2000, when I was fighting for my freedom on my own. I now had a team of dedicated EJI lawyers standing by me—and a social worker who loved and cared for me unconditionally.

"Yes, but it hurts more this time, Maria."

I cried on her shoulder for several minutes. Then we separated and sat back down. I wiped my eyes and regained my composure. I could see pain in Tatiana's and Ben's eyes but no tears. They were being strong for me. We said our good-byes; they all promised to be in touch before Christmas.

A week later I was chained and loaded into a van in the early morning hours. I was returning to Suwannee to start my sixty-five-year sentence. Once the garage door opened we drove quickly away from the jail and were on the highway in no time. I lowered my head and squinted through the small oval openings of an iron panel. I stared at the Tampa skyline and landscape as they receded. I was entranced: I imagined Judge Fuente's face as these "Someone Like You"

lyrics popped into my head: "I hate to turn up out of the blue, uninvited/But I couldn't stay away, I couldn't fight it/I had hoped you'd see my face/And that you'd be reminded that for me, it isn't over . . . /'Don't forget me,' I beg . . . / 'Sometimes it lasts in love but sometimes it hurts instead.'"

"I'll be back," I muttered.

My sadness turned to anger and determination as we drove beyond the city limits. I didn't know how and I didn't know when I would return, but I was certain in my soul that Tampa had not seen the last of me.

RIGHT BEFORE CHRISTMAS 2011, WHEN I RETURNED TO Suwannee crushed by not having been set free at my resentencing hearing, as I had all too unreasonably expected, my anger was tempered by the festive aura of the holiday season. I was beginning to come to terms with how arduous the legal fight for my freedom would be, and was looking forward to Ben and Maria's visit. Things were going fine—as fine as they can be in open population. I had money in my account, sent to me by strangers while I was in Tampa's county jail, and had amassed even more right after I returned to Suwannee when I won a football pool. I was feeling lucky. One day I was sitting in P dorm playing poker with a few of the guys, even though I am as terrible a poker player as they come because I can't hide my emotions. Over the intercom I heard my name. You receive a "call out" when you must report to a medical, dental, or mental health appointment or when you have classification issues or business in the property room. When I got up to cash in my chips I realized that I didn't have any.

I walked out the dormitory door toward the gate, and standing there was Sergeant O'Shea, the gang sergeant, a short—five foot four or so—blond woman with a reputation for planting knives on inmates and locking them up

for nothing. If you knew what was good for you, you'd stay clear of her. I knew as much, and yet . . .

"You seen me coming, why'd you close the gate?"

"What? Who are you talking to?"

"I'm talking to you." My instinctual response was crazy; I should have gone out of my way not to mess with this lady, but I couldn't help it—and I should have been able to, given the stakes. Did I have it in me to comport myself so as to avoid ever being on close management again? The gate was remotely popped and as I walked through she addressed me.

"You keep mouthing off like that, Manuel, and you're gonna have to report to my office."

"Well, shit, let's head there right now." This was all on me, and it was not going to end well.

"Turn around," she ordered.

"Turn around? For what?"

"You goin' to jail, you just threatened me."

She puts a hand on her Mace canister. If I say or do anything that might result in her gassing me, she will justify it by saying I assaulted her—and that will send me immediately back to CM. We're standing near the gun tower and, of course, cameras are trained on us. I turn around; she handcuffs me. She will still have to fabricate an excuse for forcing me once again into confinement, but now I am solely responsible for the predicament in which I find myself.

She escorts me to the back door of medical and stops. I had stared at her with all of the pent-up anger that had been simmering in me for more than a week, since my resentencing. She is clearly terrified by the look on my face, and she presses the panic button on her walkie-talkie. Officers come running from all over the compound to assist her.

"You were gonna jump me when I opened the door, weren't you?"

"What's wrong with you, lady? I'm handcuffed."

Her boyfriend, another sergeant, grabs me and drags me to a holding cell. After they uncuff me, I slice my arm with the razor I keep in my possession everywhere I go. While I'm in medical, the sergeant and her beau visit my cell and rifle through my things, flinging them around. They find letters from Maria on EJI stationery with her standard sign-off, "Love, Maria." They accuse Maria of conducting an unprofessional relationship with me and ban her from visiting me for more than a year and a half.

My cutting myself triggers routine procedures. I am at once bored and transfixed by their sameness. I am hauled off to Suwannee's crisis stabilization unit (CSU) for a spell, and something unexpected changes my life. It is early morning one weekend. Officers like to come through raging at the crack of dawn while inmates are asleep, but I'm an early bird and already up. To make life easy for themselves, they try to dissuade you from going to the dayroom, which is your right, by putting you in chains and shackling you before leading you there. Sometimes, to add to your anxiety, they search your cell while you're away, and you never know what they might find or plant. They want you to be as miserable as possible, and that is why the dayroom television set features only PBS programming, as opposed to the sports and entertainment shows that inmates love to watch.

The hour-long documentary playing that day—intended as a form of correctional punishment—enthralled me. It was called *To Be Heard* and had won a bunch of awards. It was about three teenagers from the South Bronx struggling to change their lives through devotion to writing and

reciting poetry as self-expression—poetry of frustration and hope, love and friendship, among other vicissitudes of life. A powerful bond formed among them as they strove to address the circumstances of their lives through language. These teens—Anthony, a slim, thick-lipped young man full of energy who reminded me of Jay-Z; Pearl, a stout, strong, soulful black girl; and Karina, passionate and good-hearted and of mixed racial heritage—rocked me deeply. I had been writing poetry as a means to cope, a form of therapy, but I had never been exposed to the sheer force of power poetry, slam poetry.

I was so inspired by what I had seen and heard that I couldn't wait to get back to my cell to try this new medium out. I put pen to paper, and the result was a poem I called "Every Time I Breathe," about valuing and enjoying life. The next week I shared my efforts at a group therapy session with other inmates. Their response was highly encouraging. I recall our counselor saying that the poem should be read in every crisis stabilization and transition care unit in the state of Florida.

EVERY TIME I BREATHE

Every time I breathe I feel the need to justify my
existence
To take this moment that I'm living and enjoy every
millisecond in it
My life and my struggles not many can comprehend it.
My desire for freedom burns like a sausage in a skillet
Tomorrow isn't promised so I'm thankful for this
minute.
Though imprisoned merely existing it's like my life has
been suspended.
But that means it's temporary because I haven't been
expelled.
And I still got a chance as long as I can in and exhale.
Every time I breathe.
Every time I breathe I'm thankful for the oxygen from
the trees.
And little things like little bees that get overlooked
until they sting.
Everyday I'm faced with obstacles that block the
progress to my dreams.
But the blockades are only masquerades like costumes
on halloween.
I've been through enough pain to make a sane man
just scream.
But instead I take a deep breath and just breathe.
Every time I breathe the cosmos come out of my
nostrils.
Like particles of Prada coming out of your console.

My soul is like a chihuahua you didn't include in your carpool
My lungs relax and collapse like a bottom sitting on a bar stool.
Every time I breathe.
Every time I breathe I become an intergalactic being.
Stepping out of character like a chiropractor snapping peas.
I've prayed so many times it's like I've got arthritis in my knees.
But I still get down and bow my head because I continue to believe.
That as long as I can breathe God's going to make a change.
And my circumstances are only chances for me to glorify his name.
You don't know me homie. But there's odds I've already overcame.
So if praying works. But hurts. Then I can stand a little pain.
I want to end this part by thanking God for bringing me to these heights.
And I make a promise to always honor and cherish this breath of life.
Every time I breathe. Every time I breathe. Every time I breathe!

. . .

BECAUSE SUWANNEE LACKED A TRANSITIONAL CARE UNIT, I was shipped off again to Lake Correctional Institution. There my worst fears were realized: I was confronted with disciplinary reports that Sergeant O'Shea had made up, requiring time in confinement—perhaps even CM—on my return to Suwannee. I was ashamed that I had put myself in this position. If I had only . . . Maria called to embolden me: "Ian, you can't run from this. You have to face it." While at Lake, I received a visit out of the blue from the former warden at Santa Rosa who had arranged for me to be transferred to Suwannee. He was now a regional director in the Department of Corrections.

"Manuel, God damn you. I got you off CM and now I hear you're trying to get back."

"No, sir, I ain't. I'll be honest with you. When I first got to Suwannee, things were fine. I was doing good. I was in the rec department; I was the basketball commissioner. I learned how to lead—how as a leader you have to delegate authority to people who are better than you at certain things for your team to succeed. But then that new warden came in and turned that place upside down. He turned it into a hellhole."

"So what now? What you want?"

"Man, I wanna go to one of them private institutions. Graceville or South Bay."

"No, I don't think that will be happening. I'm keeping you right here in Region Three with me."

"In that case, you remember when we had that conversation at Santa Rosa and you told me I wouldn't like Charlotte and you sent me to Suwannee instead? Well, how 'bout Charlotte?"

"Wherever I send you, the warden will come talk to you. Just be patient."

IT WAS TIME TO RETURN TO SUWANNEE TO FACE THE music—to deal with the lies Sergeant O'Shea had told about me in her disciplinary reports, lies about how I had threatened or even attacked her. Given my conversation with the regional director, however, I was not expecting to remain at the institution for long, much less to be placed on close management. All the same, you never know. It would be untrue to say I wasn't worried. At the time, all forms of confinement at Suwannee—administrative, disciplinary, or CM—were savage, the difference being only a matter of degree. On the most basic level, the cells were freezing, sometimes in the fifties; your food tray was flung into your cell, splattering the walls; and then, of course, there was the infamous 5:00 a.m. to 5:00 p.m. rule. When I met with the warden and Sergeant O'Shea, one of them said (I don't remember which):

"Manuel, if I wanted to, I could fuck you up, send you back to CM, starve you to death, but I don't want none of that. I want my confinement time. I want my ninety days."

I was placed not in CM but in open population confinement for disciplinary reasons. In open population, you leave your cell for breakfast, lunch, and dinner; in open population confinement, you eat all meals in your cell. In open population, you can go to call outs without being handcuffed or shackled; in open population confinement, you cannot. In two weeks during those ninety days, I furiously wrote down my life story to age fifteen and called it *Inside/Out*. The other nineteen years were too painful to contemplate.

The transactional nature of life behind bars—between the Department of Corrections and correctional facilities, wardens and guards, guards and inmates, and among inmates themselves—informs this demand. Why did authorities of a facility renowned for its brutishness all of a sudden want "none of that"? What was in it for them? What transaction—about which I was in the dark—had taken place between them and perhaps the regional director? I was released to open population in June 2012.

A sergeant working L dorm remembered me from when she was an officer at Union Correctional Institution and shared a perception of me as a troublemaker. One night when she was doing count, I violated procedure. I think she caught me talking and called me out. She called for help and yet again I was put in confinement, where I proceeded yet again to cut myself. I spent the night in a suicide observation cell. The next day the captain who ran the ship was making his rounds and stopped by.

"Listen, man, a couple things—don't be giving my officers no problem. I need you to stay calm. I've got two inmates in here for assault on officers and I'm getting ready to gas 'em. I need you to stay out of my business. Don't be hollering and carrying on as you always do when we do what we gotta do."

"OK, but I'm gonna need something from you. When I get out from this cage I'll need a move."

"A move? That's it? No problem."

The captain walked away. That night, as I tried to sleep, I heard screams and smelled the gas. It smelled of oranges; I knew it burned skin like hot peppers in your mouth.

IN L DORM THERE WAS A MAN NAMED JOSHUA; HIS BOY-friend slept in O dorm. They often met furtively at the medi-

cation window at noon to spend a little time together. Joshua was permitted to be there but not his partner, and so they sometimes were written up for "corrective consultation"—less than a disciplinary report. Joshua became frustrated and said to me:

"Ian, I'm tired of this shit. I wish I could get a move on."

"I can get that done; but you're gonna have to pay."

"How much?"

"Fifty dollars."

A formal request to move from one dorm to another involved filling out a slip that was never answered or was denied. I stood to make good money if I could move Joshua's partner to his dorm. I approached the captain who, when I was in confinement, had promised me a move.

"Look, I'll do this move for you," he told me. "I know who you're talking about; he a gang member. If I move him to L dorm and he starts any bullshit, I'm gonna gas you and do you worse than you've ever been done."

"Cool."

The captain moved Joshua's boyfriend; Joshua couldn't believe it.

Neither could I. I had gone from being unable to move, stuck inside a box and denied any human interaction, to being able to move others. I had become a businessman, and I was stunned to find myself in a position to help others while supporting myself. The more transactions I made, the more resentment grew among some inmates. Gangbangers threatened to snitch if I didn't give them a piece of the action. Others claimed that I myself was doing the snitching—why else would the nastiest captain on the compound be favoring me? What they didn't know was that, in essence, the captain was moving people for me in exchange for me keep-

ing things calm and hassle-free for his officers. I had become a part of the DOC's corrupt system of management.

The captain was a good ol' boy. Even though he was under scrutiny, there was no tangible proof against him. I wasn't about to provide that proof, even though when he was not helping me out he was gassing and beating inmates. Prison is complicated, transactional. I don't know what eventually happened to him. Me? In the dead of night I was transferred to Charlotte Correctional Institution.

FOR YEARS I HAD BELIEVED THAT INCARCERATION AT Charlotte was more desirable than elsewhere—I had heard it on the grapevine. On the bright side, Maria was allowed to visit me for the first time in a year and a half. She came with Ben and Tatiana for a legal and social visit, at the end of which Maria asked whether I had noticed anything different about her.

"Did you gain a little weight?"

"Ian, I'm pregnant."

I had never given much thought to Maria's life outside of our friendship and her devotion to my case, yet this development somehow made me feel insecure, vulnerable to abandonment. All the same, I was struck by how happy she looked and congratulated her. On the dark side of Charlotte in 2013, I was remanded to close management for the first time since 2010 and, because Charlotte did not have a CM program, I was sent back to Santa Rosa to satisfy the order. Whatever hope of freedom I may have been harboring collapsed.

I did the ninety days of good behavior at Santa Rosa and, as has happened time and again, the rug was pulled from under my feet.

"Ian, you've done so well; we can tell you're a different man now. We're going to put you on CM 3 with a ninety-day review. Behave yourself for ninety days more, and you're back in open population. It don't get no sweeter than that."

I shudder when I hear this; I worry that in those three months something within or beyond my control will happen, resulting in a DR that will put me back on the CM treadmill—and sure enough, something does. I don't like going to the dayroom here to watch TV because they strip you naked before they take you, but one day I ask to go. Officers come to my cell, shout bullshit that I have not made my bed correctly, and deny me my privilege. I am beside myself with fury; they gas me with their canisters. An inmate in such a circumstance must be gassed only if he is trying to hurt himself. I am not. The punishment I receive is gratuitous, and that is why I am not charged with a disciplinary report. I remain on CM 3. I confide to a mental health counselor that I have been gassed for no reason, that I will ask my lawyers to investigate the incident and shut this kind of shit down. She advises me not to be so threatening.

In December I am issued a falsified disciplinary report for having threatened correctional officers. It says officers came to my cell to take me to shower and I stated: "If you open that door, I'm going to kick Officer such-and-such's ass." Make up whatever name you wish, because it was a lie. One month before I am to be released to open population— and based on a lie—I am forced to regress from CM 3 to CM 2. I am subjected to heightened security. Whenever I must leave my cell for whatever reason, I must back out and kneel immediately to be handcuffed and shackled.

In the wake of my 2011 resentencing hearing, this was one of the grimmest periods of my life, among the hardest

for me to reckon with, when time just seemed like an abyss in which I was falling endlessly, even as I clung to the tenuous belief that there had to be a divine rationale for my suffering and pain, and that someday I would walk out of prison a free man.

HERE, IN THE FULL GLORY OF ITS PERVERSITY, IS THE legal madness pertaining to time that I had been dealing with. On April 11, 1991, when I was fourteen years old I was sentenced to "natural life" on count one (attempted armed robbery); fifteen years in prison on count two (attempted robbery); life without parole on count three (attempted murder in the first degree with a firearm); and life probation on count four (attempted murder with a firearm). The sentences for counts one, two, and three were to run concurrently, while the sentence for count four was to obtain, in effect, after "natural life."

On April 17, 2000, the court partly denied and partly granted my motion to correct this sentence. It found that my initial sentence of two terms of life followed by life probation was beyond guidelines. On June 29, 2000, the court resentenced me, on count four only, to forty years to run concurrently with the sentences for counts one, two, and three—ensuring that my debt to society would be settled at the expiration of my life without parole sentence, meaning at the expiration of my life.

In the wake of the U.S. Supreme Court's ruling on *Graham v. Florida* in 2010—stipulating that "for a juvenile offender who did not commit homicide the Eighth Amendment forbids the sentence of life without parole"—the court, on December 9, 2011, resentenced me, for counts one and three, to sixty-five years in prison, plus two years of com-

munity control and eight years of probation, to run concurrently with the sentences for counts two and four. Directly after this hearing, in early 2012, my EJI lawyers filed on my behalf a motion to correct the sentence on counts one and three—based on the *Graham* decision and because the maximum allowable sentence for a life felony, according to Florida statutes, is either forty years in prison or a life sentence. The court denied me relief for count one (sixty-five years for robbery) but resentenced me for count three to forty years instead of the previous sixty-five. This minor victory was a cosmic joke.

FOR FORTY DAYS AND FORTY NIGHTS I WAS ON DEATH row—actually, underneath death row—and it helped me to understand how sacred life is, and that there were conditions even worse than mine. I had been transferred to Florida State Prison in September 2014 to serve the rest of my CM 3 time in a confinement wing below death row. I was looking forward to being released yet again to open population; inmates on death row were anticipating, whether imminent or not, their inevitable annihilation by the state. Their hopelessness had a pure authenticity about it. Yet you learn that death row inmates are granted privileges that you are not; they can, for example, order tobacco products—and in prison tobacco as a commodity is king. One day, together with other inmates, I was taken to the exercise cage in the yard. While doing pull-ups on a bar, I realized I was exercising next to the death chamber, where they strap you down and kill you. There was a window draped with white; I couldn't see through it. But being in such close proximity to the killing room does something to you; it alters you in an unexpected way; it compels you to appreciate life in

full. And my association with death row inmates made me understand deep in my bones something that I was unable to articulate at the time but that is captured in Bryan Stevenson's *Just Mercy*: "Each of us is more than the worst thing we've ever done."

Dontae Morris, father of a seven-year-old, shot and killed five human beings, including two police officers in Tampa between May and July 2010. For his crimes he was at first sentenced to life imprisonment but subsequently was sentenced to death three times. This notorious cold-blooded murderer, a reputed member of the Bloods gang, was supposedly a man without a conscience. But when I arrived at Florida State, he showed me empathy, even though by then prison had made him crazier than he probably was otherwise. One of the prison runarounds told me that Dontae was right above me. I got on the vent and yelled upstairs:

"Hey, Dontae, Dontae: check this out, this here's Jim-Jim from Central Park. I know you might not know me, man, but I just got here from Santa Rosa and I ain't got a lot of property. Soon as I get my property I'll be straight. I need you to let me borrow some stamps, envelopes, writing paper, and something to eat, until I get my property."

"All right I got you, man, what cell you in?"

Dontae arranged for his minions to provide for me without expecting anything in return. I learned a lot from his kindness: even Dontae Morris—deemed most contemptible and irredeemable among us—was capable of a simple act of decency.

ON NOVEMBER 19, 2014, EJI FILED ANOTHER MOTION TO correct sentence—sixty-five years for count one (robbery)— based on the resolution of a case that seems in retrospect to

have been a serendipitous godsend. Who knows what my fate might have been without it? I felt that *Peters v. State*[1] represented some kind of cosmic realignment in my life. As Maria had said, this time it was different. Now I was convinced—I had substantive legal reason to believe—that, finally, my time would come, and the state of Florida would have no grounds for appeal. Roughly a year earlier, Florida's Fourth District Court of Appeal had published a ruling that was especially germane to my situation.

The *Peters* court was obliged to take the U.S. Supreme Court's *Graham* decision—which held that the Eighth Amendment's cruel and unusual punishment clause prohibits juveniles from being sentenced to life in prison without parole for a nonhomicide offense—into consideration when it reviewed a juvenile sentence for a first-degree felony punishable by life. It found that a sentence of more than forty years in prison for a first-degree felony was unconstitutionally disproportionate because a similarly situated juvenile convicted of a life felony could receive a sentence of no more than forty years in accordance with statutory language between October 1, 1983, and July 1, 1995. Thus *Peters v. State* determined that a more severe sentence for a less serious offense is an affront to the Constitution. As a result of this "statutory anomaly," it concluded that "juvenile defendants convicted of aggravated first degree felonies committed between October 1, 1983, and July 1, 1995, may not be sentenced beyond forty years imprisonment." This meant that if the court reviewing EJI's "motion to correct sentence" were to rule in my favor, I would have to be released from prison imminently, because of time I had already served plus "gain time."[2]

In August 2015, a judge in the Thirteenth Judicial Circuit

Court could not hide his displeasure at having to rule by the book in my favor:[3]

> After reviewing defendant's motion, the state's response, defendant's reply, the court file, and the record, the court vehemently disagrees with reasoning of the *Peters* court in reaching its specific holding regarding limitations on sentencing juveniles for first degree felonies punishable by life. Yet, consistent with its oath, this court finds that it is bound to follow the existing and binding case law from the Fourth District Court of Appeal . . . The court notes its belief that the Second District Court of Appeal would likely decide this issue differently and thus the issue is ripe for the Second District Court of Appeal to rule upon any appeal of this ruling and certify conflict to the Florida Supreme Court.

Here was the state of Florida—and a judge to boot—suggesting, a quarter century after my nonhomicide crime and imprisonment, that a law its own judicial system had handed down, a law that would set me free, should be proscribed. Confidently optimistic though I may have been, I was not entirely out of the woods yet. In August 2016 the Second District Court handed down its decision: "We agree with *Peters* that it requires Manuel to be resentenced to no more than forty years in prison on the 1990 offense of robbery with a firearm in count one due to the statutory anomaly. Thus we affirm the trial court's order." Coming when it did, the ruling meant that I had been given an extra year of prison time on the house.

. . .

ON NOVEMBER 10, 2016—TWO DAYS AFTER DONALD J. Trump was elected president of the United States—I was back in Tampa to be resentenced as the Second District Court had stipulated. That morning in Hillsborough Circuit Court Annex, my EJI family, Ben Schaefer and Maria Morrison, and members of my extended family—my mother's friends Aunt Kathy and Aunt Lynn—were there to support me. So too, with grace, was Debbie Baigrie, a victim of the crime I had committed twenty-six years earlier. I had not seen Debbie since 2011 and had not communicated with her in more than a decade, but she had been in frequent contact with my legal team and had agreed to attend the hearing in support of my release. Now thirty-nine years old and having spent two-thirds of my life in prison, I stood before a man I had regarded as my nemesis for sixteen years, the Honorable William Fuente, who on two previous occasions, in 2000 and 2011, had frustrated my motions to correct sentence. His tone, however, was different this time, warmer, sympathetic:

"Well, as you know, the law has changed dramatically since the early nineties, when you were before the court originally, and today the law requires a much more different attitude and view toward juveniles. Be that as it may, the crimes can still be serious. In any event, in keeping with the—in accordance with I guess the mandate from the Second DCA . . . I'll vacate the most recently imposed sentence in count one, which I think this court imposed, which was sixty-five years FSP followed by two years community control, followed by eight years of probation. And at this time I'll resentence Mr. Manuel to forty years Florida State Prison to be served concurrently with all other counts with credit for all time served, including any earned gain time that he

may have gained with the Department of Corrections . . . And that essentially—that probably puts him in fairly close to release, doesn't it?"⁴

"Thank you, Jesus, thank you, Jesus," Aunt Kathy screamed, piercing the fleeting silence in the courtroom. As raucous jubilation broke out around me, I was stunned, for a moment not knowing what to think. Was my ordeal finally over? The world was all before me now, but what exactly did that mean?

That night at around 9:30, as I walked out of Hillsborough County Jail in prison garb, carrying the barest of possessions in a bag, Maria rushed past Ben, Aunt Lynn, and Lynn's grown son, who were there as well to greet me. She embraced me and spun me around and gave me clothes—a red shirt and jeans—and the pair of unworn Air Maxes she and I had agreed I would wear when I was released. After I had changed and thanked Aunt Lynn and her son before bidding them goodbye, Maria, Ben, and I proceeded to a gas station just down the street from the jail. It had been agreed that Debbie would meet us there. She and I stared at each other and grinned before hugging. Ben was busy trying to figure out where we would eat; we were all starving. He settled on a pizza joint downtown, not realizing that it was ever so close to where I had shot Debbie a quarter century before. When I got out of the car, I grabbed Debbie and kissed her on both cheeks to acknowledge the disaster that brought us into each other's life. I ate pizza greedily, devouring my own and sampling everybody's. The wall behind us featured a framed picture of the Brooklyn Bridge.

That night, Ben, Maria, and I drove out of Tampa on the first leg of our trek to Alabama, where I would enroll in EJI's reentry program to reacquaint myself with the rudiments of

life in society. Dozing on and off in the backseat of the car, I reflected on the statement I had read before Judge Fuente in court:

"I stand before you today, Your Honor, against all judicial odds. It is rare and improbable for someone with my particular set of circumstances to be standing before you again to be resentenced for the fourth time for a sentence determined to be illegal and unconstitutional. Initially, I was a child sentenced to die in prison, an adolescent full of aspirations, cast into this vast ocean filled with adult sharks and predators and told to swim, survive, find my way back to shore the best way I could. Well, here I am, but I'm not unscathed by my journey. My heart bears the pain of my punishment. Look around this courtroom, it is different. The faces have changed from the original cast members. The Judge, the State, the Defense, my mom, dad, brother, et cetera, everybody except Debbie and me, two people with one common interest waiting on the justice system to catch up with my remorse and her forgiveness. Hopefully, today is the day we can stand together as an example, in a country deeply divided by so many racial dimensions, that justice does prevail, that wrongs will be made right [and that as] English Lit teaches us, all sentences have a period that brings them to an end."

Acknowledgments

First and foremost, I'd like to thank God for making all of this possible.

To my editor, Erroll McDonald. To my agents Peter and Amy Bernstein.

To Maria Morrison, Tom and Andi Bernstein, Charlotte Morrison, Ben Schaefer, Meg Laughlin, Martha Elliot, Lynn Creal, Kathy Miller, Anthony Baker, Lili Lynton, Jason Flom, Bob Gilbertson, and to a host of others responsible for the man I am today.

Notes

CHAPTER 3

1. Debbie Baigrie, as told to Roul Tunley, "I Forgave the Guy Who Shot Me," *McCall's,* September 1996, 54.
2. *The Tampa Tribune,* Wednesday, August 22, 1990, 14.
3. Baigrie, Debbie, as told to Tunley, Roul, "I Forgave the Guy Who Shot Me," *McCall's,* September 1996, 56.
4. The following re-creation comes from the transcript of: State of Florida v. Ian Manuel, 90-12780, RPR-CP (13th Cir. 1991).
5. Hillary Clinton, "superpredators" (speech, Keene State College, NH, January 28, 1996), https://www.youtube.com/watch?v=j0uCrA7ePno.
6. State of Florida v. Ian Manuel.
7. Ibid.

CHAPTER 4

1. Bryan A. Stevenson, "Cruel and Unusual: Sentencing 13- and 14-Year-Old Children to Die in Prison" *Current Issues in Criminal Justice* 20, no. 1 (2008): 135–140. https://doi.org/10.1080/10345329.2008.12056193.
2. Proverbs 30: 24–28 (New International Version).

CHAPTER 5

1. Amy Roe, "Solitary Confinement Is Especially Harmful to Juveniles and Should Not Be Used to Punish Them," *ACLU Washington,* November 17, 2017, https://www.aclu-wa.org/story

/solitary-confinement-especially-harmful-juveniles-and-should
-not-be-used-punish-them.

CHAPTER 6

1. Mary Hawthorne, "Charles Dickens on Solitary Confinement," *New Yorker,* March 23, 2009, https://www.newyorker.com /books/page-turner/dept-of-amplification-charles-dickens-on -solitary-confinement.
2. Ibid.
3. Fla. Admin. Code R. 8H-3.02, 33-601.800 Close Management.
4. John J. Dilulio, *Body Count* (New York: Simon & Schuster, 1996), 27.
5. Debbie Baigrie, as told to Roul Tunley, "I Forgave the Guy Who Shot Me," *McCall's,* September 1996.
6. Following quotes come from State of Florida v. Ian Manuel, 90-12780, (13th Cir. 2000).

CHAPTER 7

1. Osterback v. McDonough, 549 F. Supp. 2d 1337 (M.D. Fla. 2008).
2. Meg Laughlin, "Does Separation Equal Suffering?" *Tampa Bay Times,* August 25, 2007.

CHAPTER 8

1. Deborah Brodsky and Cyrus O'Brien, "No Place for a Child: Direct File of Juveniles Comes at a High Cost; Time to Fix Statutes," James Madison Institute, February 2016.
2. Bryan A. Stevenson, *Just Mercy* (New York: One World, 2014).
3. *LockUp,* "Inside Florida and Santa Rosa Prison," MSNBC.

CHAPTER 9

1. Roper v. Simmons, 543 U.S. 551 (2005).
2. Adam Liptak, "Defining 'Cruel and Unusual' When Offender Is 13," *New York Times,* February 2, 2009.
3. Sullivan v. Florida 560 U.S. 181 (2010).
4. Meg Laughlin, "In Ian's World," *Tampa Bay Times,* May 17, 2010.

5. "Imprisoning a Child for Life," *New York Times,* November 9, 2009, 22.
6. Sullivan v. Florida 560 U.S. 181 (2010).
7. Graham v. Florida 560 U.S. 48 (2010).
8. Ibid.

CHAPTER 10

1. State of Florida v. Ian Manuel, 90-CF-12780, TD-2 (13th Cir. 2011).

CHAPTER 11

1. Peters v. State, 919 So.2d 624, 628 (Fla. 1st DCA 2006).
2. Florida state law also allows inmates to accumulate "gain time," by which they can shave ten days off their sentences per month. Inmates can earn gain time by things including good behavior, education, and educational achievement.
3. State of Florida v. Ian Manuel, 90-CF-12780, TD-2 (13th Cir. 2015).
4. State of Florida v. Ian Manuel, 90-CF-12780, TD-2 (13th Cir. 2016).